STEVENS AND SIMILE

A THEORY OF LANGUAGE

STEVENS AND SIMILE

A THEORY OF LANGUAGE

JACQUELINE VAUGHT BROGAN

PRINCETON UNIVERSITY PRESS

Copyright © 1986 by Princeton University Press
Published by Princeton University Press, 41 William Street
Princeton, New Jersey 08540
In the United Kingdom: Princeton University Press, Guildford, Surrey

All Rights Reserved

Library of Congress Cataloging in Publication Data will be
found on the last printed page of this book

ISBN 0-691-06689-2

Publication of this book has been aided by a grant from
the Whitney Darrow Fund of Princeton University Press

This book has been composed in Linotron Caledonia

Clothbound editions of Princeton University Press books
are printed on acid-free paper, and binding materials are
chosen for strength and durability

Printed in the United States of America by Princeton University Press
Princeton, New Jersey

DESIGNED BY LAURY A. EGAN

FOR TERRY

CONTENTS

PREFACE	ix
ACKNOWLEDGMENTS	xi
ABBREVIATIONS	xii
CHAPTER ONE: *Introduction*	3
CHAPTER TWO: *Metaphor*	27
The Necessity	37
The Possibility	46
The Extension	55
The Restraint	65
CHAPTER THREE: *Fragmentation*	72
The Necessity	78
The Possibility	94
The Extension	106
The Restraint	111
CHAPTER FOUR: *Simile*	117
The Relation	119
The "As If"	127
Simile	139
The Resemblance	166
CHAPTER FIVE: *Conclusion*	178
BIBLIOGRAPHY	193
INDEX	205

PREFACE

THE FIVE CHAPTERS that follow have as their collective purpose four goals, explicit and implicit in varying degrees. This is a natural consequence of a text focused on the self-consciousness of such a highly self-conscious *corpus* as that of Wallace Stevens' poetry.

The first explicit goal is to describe the poles of the competing theories of language inscribed throughout Stevens' work—essentially a unitive/realist/or logocentric conception of language, in which the work is regarded as naming at the source of being, and a disjunctive/nominalist/even deconstructive conception of language, in which the word is regarded as a deferral of being and even of meaning. Although the parameters of this conflict are summarized in the first chapter, these two poles, with their philosophical and theological extensions, are treated separately in Chapters Two and Three under the rubrics of *metaphor* and *fragmentation*.

The second and more important of the goals is to stress the degree to which Stevens refuses to accept or to articulate either of these linguistic theories absolutely and to expose how, through the often-ignored device of *simile*, he found a way of sustaining the interaction of these competing poles simultaneously. The fourth chapter traces the poet's increasingly sophisticated use of similes in order to demonstrate how Stevens found in *simile* both a form and a mode of expression that "satisfies" both his own intellectual needs and those of "modern poetry." The final chapter suggests why this mode of speech allows Stevens' late poetry to be both human and humane.

The remaining two goals, although implicit, are extensions of the argument presented in these chapters. As intimated by allusions to earlier texts (especially those of medieval French realists and nominalists), the battle between competing theories of language is by no means limited to Stevens' poetry or to the critical debates of the twentieth century. The controversy between those who regard the *logos* as having an intimate connection to being and those who see in language a rupture of being has, historically, been a central concern of the best writers and thinkers of Western civilization. The implicit extension is that what is suggested here about language itself in terms of Stevens' use of similes has bearing on many other texts as well, especially other texts so relentlessly aware of the unavoidable conflict between linguistic mutability and the desire for meaning. This extension is borne out by the writings of such different authors as Hans Vaihinger and St. Thomas Aquinas, whose analysis of the phrase "as if" and conception of the *analogy of being*, respectively, are themselves analogous to Stevens' use of similes.

The final goal, which follows from the preceding one, is to offer a certain perspective from which to regard the recent conflict among those who presently study and work in the humanities. From this perspective the recent developments in post-structuralist criticism and theory must be seen as far less radical than they are often judged to be. More important, the divisiveness that has occurred between those who accept the most avant-garde critical tenets and those who adhere to a more traditional understanding of language and literature can be regarded as inevitable and fruitful, rather than as destructive or debilitating. As Stevens' poetry attests, such conflict is a compelling and continuing source of intellectual and artistic creativity.

J. V. B.

ACKNOWLEDGMENTS

I AM INDEBTED to the University of Texas and to the University of Hawaii for granting me financial assistance that enabled me to complete this book. I would like to express my deep appreciation to several colleagues and friends for their invaluable time, support, and suggestions—among them Louis Mackey, Thomas Cable, Charles Sherry, and Roy Harvey Pearce. And I would like to give special thanks to Marjorie Sherwood, Miriam Brokaw, and Gretchen Oberfranc, who guided this book through the various stages of production with great energy and care.

Finally, I cannot begin to express adequately my gratitude to Imogene and Ned Pilcher for their unwearying editing and to my husband, Terry Vance Brogan, for all the minute particulars of his help.

Portions of some of the chapters that follow have also appeared, in different forms, in *TSLL, The Wallace Stevens Journal, American Poetry,* and *American N & Q.* The prose and poetry of Wallace Stevens are reprinted here by permission of Alfred A. Knopf, Inc.

ABBREVIATIONS

CP *The Collected Poems of Wallace Stevens* (New York: Alfred A. Knopf, 1954; rpt. 1975)

L   *Letters of Wallace Stevens,* selected and edited by Holly Stevens (New York: Alfred A. Knopf, 1966)

NA Wallace Stevens, *The Necessary Angel: Essays on Reality and the Imagination* (New York: Alfred A. Knopf, 1951)

OP Wallace Stevens, *Opus Posthumous,* ed. Samuel French Morse (New York: Alfred A. Knopf, 1957)

PM *The Palm at the End of the Mind: Selected Poems and a Play,* ed. Holly Stevens (New York: Vintage Books, 1967, 1972)

STEVENS AND SIMILE

A THEORY OF LANGUAGE

variously merging and dividing like language itself
—Kenneth Burke

Men think in terms of models.
—K. Deutsch

A. A violent order is disorder; and
B. A great disorder is an order. These
Two things are one. (Pages of illustrations.)
—Wallace Stevens

CHAPTER ONE

INTRODUCTION

> To say more than human things with human voice,
> That cannot be; to say human things with more
> Than human voice, that, also, cannot be;
> To speak humanly from the height or from the depth
> Of human things, that is acutest speech. (*CP*, 300)

THROUGHOUT his poetry and his prose, Wallace Stevens is concerned with the relation of the imagination and reality, at times favoring one or the other,[1] but most often asserting their equality and interdependence:

> [T]o come to a decision regarding the imagination and reality . . . [is to] find that it is not a choice of one over the other and not a decision that divides them, but something subtler, a recognition that here, too, as between these poles, the universal interdependence exists, and . . . that they are equal and inseparable. (*NA*, 24)

As Stevens further explains in "The Noble Rider and the Sound of Words," he is "interested in the nature of poetry": and by defining the "interdependence of the imagination and reality," he is describing "one of the many points of view from which it is possible to state . . . the nature of poetry" (*NA*, 27). The purpose of this study is to examine another way in which Stevens defines the nature of poetry, which is to explore the interdependence of what may be called the

---

[1] As J. Hillis Miller says, "At times he [Stevens] is unequivocally committed to bare reality. At other times he repudiates reality and sings the praises of imagination" ("Wallace Stevens' Poetry of Being," *ELH*, 31 [1964], 89).

unitive and disjunctive tendencies in language. Though discussed to some degree in his prose, this second way of defining the nature of poetry is principally elaborated in the poetry itself. As an analysis of his poetry reveals, and as shall be demonstrated in this study, in that commonly disparaged figure of speech, simile, Stevens finds a powerful way of sustaining both the unitive and disjunctive tendencies of language simultaneously.

It is not surprising that Stevens' poetry would consider certain tendencies of language and that, in doing so, it explores certain aspects of the nature of language: his poetry is "metalanguage or . . . metapoetry—speech about speech."[2] J. Hillis Miller takes this idea one step further, saying that "Stevens' poetry is . . . not merely poetry about poetry. It is a poetry that is the battleground among conflicting theories of poetry. . . ."[3] And conflicting theories of poetry necessarily involve conflicting theories of language. For the purposes of this study, the conflicting theories of language that Stevens explores in his poetry will be divided between language as metaphor (which will serve as a model for the unitive tendency in language) and language as fragmentation (which will serve as a model for the disjunctive tendency). This division not only corresponds to the "poles" of language that Stevens considers in his poetry, but also bears a resemblance to that found in other discussions of language.

Metaphor, for example, has continued to be one of the most prominent topics of literary and philosophical discussions throughout Western civilization, having "probably attracted more critical attention than any other figure of

[2] Mac Hammond, "On the Grammar of Wallace Stevens," in *The Act of the Mind: Essays on the Poetry of Wallace Stevens*, ed. Roy Harvey Pearce and J. Hillis Miller (Baltimore: Johns Hopkins University Press, 1965), p. 184.

[3] J. Hillis Miller, "Theoretical and Atheoretical in Stevens," in *Wallace Stevens: A Celebration*, ed. Frank Doggett and Robert Buttel (Princeton: Princeton University Press, 1980), p. 275.

CHAPTER ONE

speech."⁴ Metaphor continues to excite critical comment because the "subject [of metaphor] . . . is infinite."⁵ Despite at least one tradition that views metaphor negatively as being false, as deviating from proper or common-sense language, the high status afforded metaphor by Aristotle has hardly diminished in the subsequent centuries. Calling it "the mark of genius," Aristotle declared that the "greatest thing by far is to be a master of metaphor," that it "is the one thing that cannot be learned from others."⁶ And, although interest in the subject waned in favor of symbols under Coleridge's influence during the nineteenth century, it has certainly been rejuvenated during the recent decades of the twentieth century. In 1978, for instance, *Critical Inquiry* devoted an entire issue to metaphor; in 1971, Warren A. Shibles' *Metaphor: An Annotated Bibliography and History* required 414 pages for the annotation of articles, essays, and books on the subject.⁷ Certainly many twentieth-century poets—especially Wallace Stevens—have contributed to the recent widespread interest in metaphor. As Cleanth Brooks, Jr., said in 1952, when Stevens was writing the poems of his last book, *The Rock*, "[T]he most fruitful modern criticism" is "a rediscovery and recovery of the importance of metaphor."⁸

One of the reasons that metaphor has been so favorably

---

⁴ George Dickie, *Aesthetics: An Introduction* (Indianapolis: Pegasus, 1971), p. 131.

⁵ Michel Bréal, *Semantics: Studies in the Science of Meaning*, tr. Mrs. Henry Cust (New York: Dover, 1964), p. 131.

⁶ Aristotle, *Poetics* (tr. Butcher), ch. 22, sect. 9.

⁷ *Critical Inquiry*, 5 (1978). Warren A. Shibles, *Metaphor. An Annotated Bibliography* (Whitewater, Wis.: Language Press, 1971). For further references to recent discussions of metaphor (as well as for another discussion of metaphor), see Stephen Owen and Walter L. Reed, "A Motive for Metaphor," *Criticism*, 21 (1979), 288 n. 2.

⁸ Cleanth Brooks, Jr., "Metaphor and the Function of Criticism," in *Spiritual Problems in Contemporary Literature*, ed. Stanley R. Hopper (New York: Harper, 1952), p. 133.

INTRODUCTION

regarded is that there is at least an impulse in metaphor toward identification—an Adamic naming and/or creating. Although most definitions of metaphor manage to account for the fact that two *different* things are joined in a metaphor, the emphasis is often on the *joining*, the fusion, or the identity of the two. "Most non-analytical" predications made with " 'to be' could be fruitfully considered as metaphor," says R. J. Kaufmann,[9] since "is" implies "equals" or identification. And, although Philip Wheelwright calls this view of metaphor (also held by Martin Foss) "trivial,"[10] it is one that Wallace Stevens' discussion of metaphor supports. Having divided metaphors into three categories, Stevens cites "God is good" (an expression which Wheelwright might not readily call a metaphor) as an example of the third category of metaphor; that is, the one in which "two imagined things" are compared (NA, 72). Ernst Cassirer, too, emphasizes the identification implied in metaphor: "there is much more in metaphor than a bare 'substitution,' a mere rhetorical figure of speech; . . . what seems to our subsequent reflection as a sheer transcription [of one thing or idea in terms of another] is mythically conceived as genuine and direct identification."[11]

What these various excerpts, wide-ranging as they are, have in common is the assumption that metaphor illustrates, or is itself a metaphor for, the original creative act. This is, to some extent, the view of metaphor to which Stevens subscribes: "A poetic metaphor—that is to say, a metaphor poetic in a sense more specific than the sense in which poetry and metaphor are one—appears to be poetry at its source. It

[9] R. J. Kaufmann, "Metaphorical Thinking and the Scope of Literature," *College English*, 30 (1968), 37.

[10] Philip Wheelwright, *The Burning Fountain. A Study in the Language of Symbolism*, rev. ed. (Bloomington: Indiana University Press, 1968), p. 121.

[11] Ernst Cassirer, *Language and Myth*, tr. Susanne K. Langer (New York: Harper, 1946; rpt. Dover, 1953), p. 94.

CHAPTER ONE

is" (*NA*, 81). The resulting domination of the word "metaphor" in his poetry and his prose has encouraged both critical attention to his use of metaphors and critical prejudice in favor of his use of metaphors. For example, Roy Harvey Pearce says in reference to "Notes toward a Supreme Fiction," that "the essence of the poetry is a 'testing' of metaphor, an inquiry into its grasp of 'reality.' For the questions Stevens asks are: What, and how valid, is our Supreme Metaphor? How may we know it? Why must we know it?"[12] At least until fairly recently, the serious attention given to Stevens' metaphors, excluding the early deprecation of his metaphors as indulgent dandyism,[13] has tended to focus upon

---

[12] Roy Harvey Pearce, *The Continuity of American Poetry* (Princeton: Princeton University Press, 1961), p. 395.

[13] Probably the most famous of these is Yvor Winters, "Wallace Stevens, or the Hedonist's Progress," *The Anatomy of Nonsense* (Norfolk, Conn.: New Directions, 1943), pp. 88-119; or Randall Jarrell, "Reflections on Wallace Stevens," *Partisan Review*, 18 (1951), 335-44, reprinted in *Poetry and the Age* (New York: Vintage Books, 1955), pp. 121-34. However, such condemnations of Stevens had wide currency in the early years of Stevens criticism. For example, see Edmund Wilson, "Wallace Stevens and E. E. Cummings," *The New Republic*, 38 (19 March 1924), 102-3; and Mark Van Doren, "Poets and Wits," *The Nation*, 117 (10 October 1923), 400-402. By 1940, Cleanth Brooks was saying that "probably none [of the poets] . . . in our time has had to face so continually the charge that his work was precious—obvious ivory-tower ware" (*The Harvard Advocate*, 127, 3 [December 1940], 29). In 1954 Samuel French Morse still finds himself having to defend Stevens' poetry: "[A] good deal of the criticism, favorable and otherwise, lavished upon the poems has been written from a point of view which seems to imply that for all their deftness they are either trivial or morally suspect" ("A Poet Who Speaks the Poem as It Is," *New York Times Book Review*, 3 October 1954, p. 3). As Joseph N. Riddel summarizes it, Stevens once "was thought the dandy among a select group of coterie 'romantics' " ("The Contours of Stevens Criticism," *ELH*, 31 [1964], 106-38, reprinted in Pearce and Miller, eds., *The Act of the Mind*, p. 243). An interesting aside: the only article on Stevens that I know of which uses the word "Dandyism" in its title does so with pos-

their creative power of uniting or reconciling reality and the imagination:

> The primary function of metaphor in the poetry of Wallace Stevens is to effect a relation between the abstract and concrete elements of language that is indicative of the existing situation in human experience. All of Stevens' speculations about the nature of man and of the world revolve around the complexity of the relation between imagination and reality. . . .[14]

Recently, however, the topic of signification—or, rather, lack of signification—has received equal, if not more, critical and philosophical attention than his metaphor. Beginning with such seminal works as Jacques Derrida's "White Mythology: Metaphor in the Text of Philosophy" and *Of Grammatology*, the intent has been to "deconstruct" the "apparently innocent proposition" of "the metaphysics of the logos, of presence and consciousness," and to illustrate that the "signified is originarily and essentially . . . *always already in the position of the signifier.*"[15] What Derrida convincingly

---

itive connotations; see Gorham B. Munson, "The Dandyism of Wallace Stevens," *The Dial*, 79 (1925), 413-17.

[14] Suzanne Juhasz, *Metaphor and the Poetry of Williams, Pound, and Stevens* (Lewisburg: Bucknell University Press, 1974), p. 16. To some extent this notion fills James Baird's *The Dome and the Rock: Structure in the Poetry of Wallace Stevens* (Baltimore: Johns Hopkins University Press, 1968). See also Northrop Frye, "The Realistic Oriole: A Study of Wallace Stevens," *Hudson Review*, 10 (1957), 353-70, reprinted in *Wallace Stevens: A Collection of Critical Essays*, ed. Marie Borroff (Englewood Cliffs, N.J.: Prentice-Hall, 1963), p. 169: "The normal unit of poetic expression is the metaphor, and Stevens was well aware of the importance of metaphor, as is evident from the many poems which use the word in title or text." For earlier references to Stevens' metaphors, see Marianne Moore, "Well Moused, Lion," *The Dial*, 76 (1924), 88; Harry Levin's statement in the Stevens issue of *The Harvard Advocate*, 127, 3 (1940), 30; and Hayden Carruth, "Without the Inventions of Sorrow," *Poetry*, 85 (1955), 290.

[15] The quotation is taken from Jacques Derrida, *Of Grammatology*,

CHAPTER ONE

demonstrates is that a "signifier is from the very beginning the possibility of its own repetition, of its own image or resemblance. . . . From the moment that the sign appears, that is to say from the very beginning, there is no chance of encountering anywhere the purity of 'reality,' 'unicity,' 'singularity' "—qualities that at least some writers would attribute to metaphor.[16] There is no question about the fact that Derrida and the Tel Quel School have led to (and are continuing to lead to) major reevaluations of literary works, including those of Wallace Stevens.

For example, recent discussions of Stevens' poetry have tended to focus upon that which "we do not speak" (CP, 311) upon the deconstructive elements of his work. Discussions of the "romantic" aspect of what Miller calls the "second theory of poetry" (i.e., that the "*logos* as being comes into the open by way of the *logos* as words . . . as metaphor") are more and more replaced in Stevens studies by its "deconstructive" corollary—that "the *logos* captured in language, is the annihilation of the *logos* as the hidden one."[17] Whereas we used to talk of Stevens' poetry in terms of the relationship between the dome and the rock or the interdependence of the imagination and reality, we now talk of the lack of relationship or the "unbridgeable gap" that "yawns between experience and the articulation of experience."[18] Similarly, in contrast to his earlier assessment that Stevens'

---

tr. Gayatri Chakravorty Spivak (Baltimore: Johns Hopkins University Press, 1974, 1976), p. 73. "White Mythology: Metaphor in the Text of Philosophy," tr. F.C.T. Moore, is published in *New Literary History*, 6 (1975), 5-74.

[16] *Of Grammatology*, p. 91. See I. A. Richards, *The Philosophy of Rhetoric* (New York: Oxford University Press, 1936; rpt. 1976), or Philip Wheelwright, *The Burning Fountain*, in which he discusses the "identification" of narrative and significance in myth in terms of the vehicle and tenor of metaphor (pp. 148-53).

[17] Miller, "Theoretical and Atheoretical," pp. 276-77.

[18] Isabel G. MacCaffrey, "The Ways of Truth in 'Le Monocle de Mon Oncle,' " in Doggett and Buttel, eds., *Celebration*, p. 207.

INTRODUCTION

poetry is a "poetry of flittering metamorphosis" that is "simultaneously true to both imagination and reality" and, consequently, the "only poetry which will catch being," Miller now concludes that Stevens' "authentic voice" is a "principle of discontinuity"—a conclusion that bears a certain affinity to Helen Vendler's judgment that "the poetry of disconnection is Stevens' most adequate form."[19] Likewise, Joseph N. Riddel emphasizes not the flamboyant ease that early critics (however slightingly) found in Stevens' work, but rather the "dis-ease that is marked by the exile of writing."[20]

Although the "deconstructive" discussions of Stevens' poetry vary as greatly as the more traditional ones, what they have in common is the desire to explore seriously a possibility that Stevens obviously recognizes, the possibility that "metaphor . . . murders metaphor"—even if Stevens urges us in that particular instance to "defy" that possibility (*NA*, 84). With these more recent explorations we have gained insights into the disjunctive elements in Stevens' work and the corresponding characteristics of his style, such as the use of

[19] Miller, "Poetry of Being," p. 103; "Theoretical and Atheoretical," p. 283; Helen Vendler, *On Extended Wings: Wallace Stevens' Longer Poems* (Cambridge, Mass.: Harvard University Press, 1969), p. 65. Similarly, in contrast to the "conjunction of imagination and reality" that Miller discusses in the 1964 article, "Poetry of Being" (p. 97), in his later article, "Stevens' Rock and Criticism as Cure" (*Georgia Review*, 30 [1976], 5-31), Miller stresses the disjunction in Stevens' poetry. In this later discussion Miller is concerned almost entirely with "the abyss, the *Abgrund* or *Ungrund*, the chasm, the blank, the unapproachable, of which the poem ["The Rock"] . . . is a *mise en abyme*" (p. 29). From the vocabulary, the influence of Derrida on the later article should be obvious enough.

[20] Joseph N. Riddel, "Metaphoric Staging: Stevens' Beginning Again of the 'End of the Book,' " Doggett and Buttel, eds., *A Celebration*, p. 309. Riddel summarizes the shift in critical perspectives (as well as defending "deconstructionist" readings) in "The Climate of Our Poems" (*The Wallace Stevens Journal*, 7 [1983], 59-75).

CHAPTER ONE

the conditional "if," the subjunctive "may," and the indefinite "it."[21] We have seen that, despite the desire of some poems to achieve unity, "Every poem . . . is a metaphor of a metaphor, a remove of one plane from another"—something which "can never lead back to the 'irreducible X' of the unrepresented or the identical."[22]

In a more moderate fashion, Vendler analyzes the various elements of grammar, syntax, and diction that Stevens employs to maintain a "middle ground" or "accommodation" between "unqualified assertions" or doctrine. Among the various ways that Stevens maintains a hypothetical status in his poetry are the use of common modal auxiliaries (such as "may" and "might"), questions which "function as suggestions," infinitives that "imply a future . . . without reminding us that it is a future and not yet accomplished," and "aspectual 'seems.' " In addition, Stevens uses the "indispensable conjunction 'if,' which takes away with one hand what the poet has already given with the other," imperatives, and his "characteristic 'as if,' " which "forms a bridge between perception and reflection." Vendler also mentions "conjectural" terms, such as " 'would have been,' 'not X,' 'or,' 'like,' " as "signs of Stevens' mitigated assertion." What Vendler convincingly demonstrates is that stylistically, as well as thematically, Stevens rejects dogmatic statements "in favor of all the shifting moods of desire."[23]

Yet, despite such extensive examinations of his work, Stevens' characteristic use of similes is left largely unexplored. I find this curious since increasingly throughout his poetry and far more than most poets (especially those influenced by Imagism, which tended to delete even the "is" of metaphors), Stevens turned to similes. In fact, some of his poems, such as "The Load of Sugar-Cane" (*CP*, 12) and "Va-

[21] See MacCaffrey, "Ways of Truth," especially pp. 212-17.
[22] Riddel, "Metaphoric Staging," p. 329.
[23] Vendler, "The Qualified Assertions of Wallace Stevens," in Pearce and Miller, eds., *The Act of the Mind*, pp. 163-78.

11

INTRODUCTION

cancy in the Park" (*CP*, 511)—to take a very early and a very late example—are constructed almost exclusively around and by similes. This particular characteristic of Stevens' poetry has, however, been largely ignored, even in critical discussions of the characteristic elements of his style. Frank Doggett, for instance, focuses upon the predicate nominatives and appositives in Stevens' late work, but does not include his similes at all. Moreover, Doggett says, "After tone, the poet's practice with metaphor is the element that contributes most to what is recognizable in his style."[24] In earlier assessments of Stevens' poetry, the prejudice in favor of metaphor (and against simile) has even led to such statements as that found in Northrop Frye's "The Realistic Oriole: A Study of Wallace Stevens":

> A world of total simile, where everything was like everything else, would be a world of total monotony; a world of total metaphor, where everything is identified as itself and with everything else, would be a world where subject and object, reality and mental organization of reality, are one. Such a world of total metaphor is the formal cause of poetry.[25]

The reason simile has largely been ignored is twofold: first, there is a traditional disparagement of simile; second, Stevens is particularly reticent about using the word.

Traditionally, simile has been considered an extended,

---

[24] Frank Doggett, *Wallace Stevens: The Making of the Poem* (Baltimore: Johns Hopkins University Press, 1980), pp. 150-51, 149. Doggett mentions similes only once, in passing, in reference to "The Curtains in the House of the Metaphysician" (p. 144).

[25] "The Realistic Oriole," p. 170. In a somewhat similar fashion, Hi Simons finds that Stevens' mature style is to be a "master of the rhetoric of implication," which Simons attributes to "the metaphor rather than the simile," specifically a "peculiar usage of metaphor" common to contemporary poetry ("The Genre of Wallace Stevens," *Sewanee Review*, 53 [1945], 566-79, reprinted in Borroff, ed., *Collection*, p. 52).

and therefore inferior, form of metaphor. Wheelwright rightly suggests that this tradition begins with Aristotle, who judges simile "inferior to metaphor on two counts: it is lengthier, therefore less pleasing; and 'since it does not affirm that this *is* that, the mind does not inquire into the matter.' "[26] As Derrida summarizes it, "there is no more classical theory of metaphor than treating it as an 'economical' way of avoiding 'extended explanations': and, in the first place, of avoiding simile."[27] The preference for metaphor has continued, since most people agree that, as opposed to simile, "What is expressed [in metaphor] is an extraordinary unity, a condensation approaching the simplicity of vision."[28] In a similar fashion, Michael Polanyi says with some qualification that "metaphor loses its force even when transposed into a simile."[29] Even Wheelwright, who wishes to rescue us from the "tyranny of grammarians" who have collapsed simile into metaphor from "syntactical, not semantic considerations," uses simile to illustrate the superiority of metaphor in " 'energy-tension' " and the ability to give a "sudden revelation."[30]

A notable exception to the lack of regard given to simile is the 1969 publication, *Ancient Rhetorical Theories of Simile and Comparison*.[31] In general, however, simile has been subsumed into what is considered its superior relative, met-

[26] Wheelwright, p. 103; citing Aristotle, *Rhetoric*, Bk. III, Chap. 4, 1406b, 20 ff.

[27] Derrida, "White Mythology," p. 20; for a more extended discussion of this subject, see also pp. 20-23.

[28] Louis Mackey, "On Terms and Terminations: The Dissolution of the Medieval Metaphor," *Texas Quarterly*, 21 (1978), 81. Mackey is summarizing Walter J. Ong's views in *The Barbarian Within* (New York, 1962), pp. 42-47.

[29] Michael Polanyi and Harry Prosch, *Meaning* (Chicago: University of Chicago Press, 1975), p. 79.

[30] Wheelwright, pp. 103-5.

[31] Marsh H. McCall, Jr., *Ancient Rhetorical Theories of Simile and Comparison* (Cambridge, Mass.: Harvard University Press, 1969).

INTRODUCTION

aphor. In contrast to the overwhelming number of entries for metaphor in Shibles' four-hundred-page book, those for simile cover half of one page. Similarly, to choose an example at random, Northrop Frye's *Anatomy of Criticism* lists, not atypically, sixteen entries for metaphor and none for simile.[32] Again, *A Handbook for Literature* concludes its discussion of simile by telling us to "See Metaphor"; but under "Metaphor" simile is not mentioned at all.[33] Clearly, then, metaphor has generally been more highly regarded than simile. And yet, as we shall see, Wallace Stevens increasingly turned to similes to create that "energy-tension" most often attributed to metaphor.

Stevens is, however, particularly reticent about using the word "simile." I can find only one instance (in an early letter

[32] See the index to Northrop Frye's *Anatomy of Criticism: Four Essays* (Princeton: Princeton University Press, 1957; rpt. New York: Atheneum, 1967). Note, however, that Frye does discuss simile in his text, but only as a displaced form of metaphor. For example, he sees the "radical form" of metaphor ("A is B") reduced on the descriptive level to simile ("A is like B"): "Descriptively, then, all metaphors are similes" (p. 123). More important, in Frye's view there are various forms of increasingly displaced metaphors (such as simile and analogy) that have corresponding modes of literature. Thus, the "identification" implicit in the radical form of metaphor corresponds to the mythic mode in literature, and the *"displacement"* of identity implicit in simile corresponds to the "displacement" of mythic identity implicit in naturalism (pp. 136-37). In other words, in Frye's theory simile is reducible to a form of metaphor. I should clarify that the view of simile I present in this study is not reducible to a form of metaphor or to a form of something else, nor is it most appropriate for naturalism in literature. Rather, the view of simile elaborated here is that there are certain aspects of language in general (regardless of the mode of literature) that are most adequately revealed in simile and that are fully exploited by Stevens in his poetry. This view is discussed at length in the following chapters.

[33] C. Hugh Holman, *A Handbook to Literature*, 3rd ed. (New York: Odyssey Press, 1972), pp. 313-15, 498.

CHAPTER ONE

to his wife) when Stevens uses the term.[34] In fact, when discussing what Stevens calls "the creation of resemblance by the imagination" (NA, 72), Stevens invariably uses the word "metaphor," even when the word "simile" would be more accurate.[35] Proof of this assertion can be found in "Prologues to What Is Possible," a poem in which Stevens specifically calls the eighteen lines following an opening simile "The metaphor":

I
There was an ease of mind that was like being alone
    in a boat at sea,
A boat carried forward by waves resembling the
    bright backs of rowers,
Gripping their oars, as if they were sure of the
    way to their destination,
Bending over and pulling themselves erect on the
    wooden handles,
Wet with water and sparkling in the one-ness
    of their motion.

The boat was built of stones that had lost their
    weight and being no longer heavy
Had left in them only a brilliance, of
    unaccustomed origin,
So that he that stood up in the boat leaning
    and looking before him

---

[34] In the letter to Elsie Moll, dated 24 March 1907, Stevens writes: "But principally, I have been walking in the rain. I let it rain on my head and in my face. You know all my similes, yet once more it was like a spring in a desert" (L, 98).

[35] We should note at this point that just as the "word *imagination* is used in many senses in the essays and letters of Stevens" (Doggett, pp. 14-15), so too is the word *metaphor*. Other senses in which Stevens uses the word will be discussed more fully in later chapters.

INTRODUCTION

> Did not pass like someone voyaging out of and
>   beyond the familiar.
>
> He belonged to the far-foreign departure of his
>   vessel and was part of it,
> Part of the speculum of fire on its prow, its
>   symbol, whatever it was,
> Part of the glass-like sides on which it glided
>   over the salt-stained water,
> As he traveled alone, like a man lured on
>   by a syllable without any meaning,
> A syllable of which he felt, with an
>   appointed sureness,
> That it contained the meaning into which
>   he wanted to enter,
> A meaning which, as he entered it, would shatter
>   the boat and leave the oarsmen quiet
> As at a point of central arrival, an instant
>   moment, much or little,
> Removed from any shore, from any man
>   or woman, and needing none.
>
>   II
> The metaphor stirred his fear.
>   (*CP*, 515-16)

   This poem is particularly interesting because it explores what is often ignored in the discussions of metaphor—the frightening potential of the impulse toward unity: annihilation of individuality in the "one-ness." The "metaphor" is frightening because such unity or "one-ness" would be more than human speech, even more than human: as the poem says, if the "point of central arrival," the place where meaning and syllable could unite, were attained, the entrance into it must "shatter the boat and leave the oarsmen quiet." In other words, if the impulse toward unity were realized, we would no longer have that "differance" Derrida explains is requisite for the play of language: instead, we would have

CHAPTER ONE

only "quiet," the unspoken where being and essence are joined, that which is "more than human" and cannot be said "with human voice."[36] As a result, such unity or "one-ness" ironically means utter isolation, traveling "alone," "voyaging out of and beyond the familiar," "Removed from any man or woman, and needing none." It is essentially the isolated condition of God.

The genius of this poem is that it deliberately evokes the possibility of metaphor's "one-ness" and the frightening potential of that unity, while simultaneously undercutting that possibility. To use Derrida's vocabulary, the poem deconstructs its own potential of metaphorical unity, most obviously when the poem refers to itself ("The metaphor stirred his fear"). That line disrupts the pattern in the poem of increasing movement toward unity, "one-ness," "unac-

---

[36] Using the French verb *différer* (which "indicates difference as distinction, inequality, or discernibility" on the one hand, and "on the other . . . expresses the interposition of delay," i.e., to "differ" and to "defer"), Derrida coins the word "differance" to suggest both meanings at once. He then concludes that "Differance is what makes the movement of signification possible . . ." (Jacques Derrida, "Differance," *Speech and Phenomenon*, tr. David Allison [Evanston: Northwestern University Press, 1973], pp. 129, 142; first published in *Bulletin de la Société française de philosophie*, 62, 3 [July-September 1968], 73-101).

With regard to Stevens' poetry as it is discussed above, we should note that it is useful to consider his poetry against the background of that of both his British and American romantic precursors, such as Shelley and Emerson. Stevens' suggestion that metaphoric unity would be "more than human" implies a diminishing of the concept of human imagination. In Stevens the romantic possibility of the imagination's forging "real" unities exists, but without the courage of his precursors' convictions. For extensive considerations of Stevens in relation to his precursors, see Harold Bloom, *Wallace Stevens: The Poems of Our Climate* (Ithaca: Cornell University Press, 1976), and Roy Harvey Pearce, *Continuity*. In addition, see Helen Vendler, "Stevens and Keats' 'To Autumn,' " in Dogget and Buttel, eds., *A Celebration*, pp. 171-95.

customed origin," as the rowers, boat, and water are absorbed into the "ease of mind," so that "one-ness" is revealed to be aloneness.

Yet the "disruption" has been an intrinsic part of the poem from the opening simile of the first line, which deliberately withholds the "one-ness" that the poem posits: it never *is* the "ease of mind"; it is only "like" that. Other words and phrases, such as "resembling" and "as if," further frustrate identity and maintain what Stevens calls the "acutest speech" of speaking "humanly" by undercutting the very unity (or possibility of unity) that the poem raises. As I hope to show, such a movement as that illustrated by this poem is not simply a deconstructive displacement any more than it is simply a metaphoric union. It is an example of the interaction and interdependence of seemingly opposed tendencies in language that Stevens desires to create in his poetry. And the richness of the "human voice" that Stevens evokes through his complex use of language can be understood to a large degree by examining his use of similes.

With the particular advantage of the chronological arrangement that Holly Stevens has provided in *The Palm at the End of the Mind*, we are in a position to see the rise in frequency with which Stevens uses that supposedly inferior form. In addition, we can see the increase in frequency with which Stevens turns to a related form, the "as if" construction, which shares several important characteristics with the simile, despite the difference in grammatical status.[37] Specifically, by my count, in the earliest poems of *Harmonium*

---

[37] In "The Qualified Assertions of Wallace Stevens," Helen Vendler mentions Stevens' "characteristic 'as if' " and notes that Walsh's *Concordance* "lists over 100 uses of 'as if' in this conjectual sense"; she adds that its "frequency increases in the later poetry" (p. 173 n 5). Also, in reference to the eighth stanza of "Notes toward a Supreme Fiction," Doggett says "The exquisite poignancy" of the stanza "lies in the qualifying phrase, 'as if,' for the qualification implies that the wave is always broken and the thoughts of poetry, the things it says, are not easily achieved" (*Making of the Poem*, p. 99).

CHAPTER ONE

(1915-1919), Stevens uses "like" as a simile .69 times per page, the "as" form of a simile .35 times per page, and the construction "as if" only .02 times per page. In *The Rock* (1950-1955), however, Stevens uses "like" .92 times per page; "as," .56; and "as if," .40 times per page. Moreover, in certain periods of his writing, there are dramatic increases in his use of these words—periods that correspond to what may be called major poetic breakthroughs:[38]

	like	*as*	*as if*
1915-1919	.69	.35	.02
1921-1924	.72	.79	.14
1933-1937			
including "The Man with the Blue Guitar"	.65	1.75	.1
excluding it	.47	.34	.13
for an average of	.53	.82	.12
1938-1940	.50	.92	.17
1941-1942	.72	1.15	.28
1943-1946	.87	.91	.33
1947-1949	.58	1.53	.24
1950-1955	.92	.56	.40

[38] We should note at this point that similes are not the sole indicators of a certain quality in Stevens' poetry. There are many other recurrent words and phrases that are equally suggestive: for example, Stevens' use of the phrase "the way" and of the verb "seem," his complex use of the verb "like," his frequent employment of puns as well as convoluted negations, his tendency to use qualifying words such as "unless" or "or," as well as his habit of writing appositives, using ellipses, and even occasionally writing incomplete "if-" clauses. It is tempting to tabulate these various stylistic elements as well as Stevens' use of similes; however, since the treatment of the similes alone demands a lengthy discussion, I have chosen not to include these other aspects of his style. In addition, to include them would be to repeat to some degree the extensive work done by Vendler in "Qualified Assertions," pp. 163-78.

INTRODUCTION

In arriving at these statistics, I have attempted to count only those "like's" and "as's" used as similes and to discount those used as conjunctions or as elements of time. Often, however, Stevens' use of these words is (perhaps intentionally) quite ambiguous, as in the following excerpt from "Domination of Black":

> Was it a cry against the twilight
> Or against the leaves themselves
> Turning in the wind,
> Turning as the flames
> Turned in the fire,
> Turning as the tails of the peacocks
> Turned in the loud fire,
> Loud as the hemlocks
> Full of the cry of the peacocks?
> (CP, 9)

At least the first two "as's" of this excerpt would appear to have double function: both create an analogy, and both suggest temporal simultaneity. Thus, an adequate paraphrase of these lines must take both functions into account: the leaves turn in the wind, analogously to the way the flames turn in the fire, analogously to the way that the peacock tails turn in the loud fire; but the leaves also turn in the wind, while the flames are turning in the fire, while the peacock tails are turning in the loud fire. The ambiguity here allows the relationships posited by the comparisons to be made even more dynamic by their participation in time. Such ambiguity, occurring often in Stevens' poetry, is in keeping with his rejection of the permanent (or static) ideal—as in "Sunday Morning"—and with his embracing of the world of time and change.

The previous statistics indicate a major change in Stevens' style that suggests certain changes in how he used and thought about language. According to Riddel, few critics have "found it advantageous to approach the poetry chronologically" since there seems to be in Stevens' poetry a "con-

CHAPTER ONE

sistency of thought from first to last."[39] In essence, I agree, for the concerns that dominate his late poetry (such as the nature of poetry and the nature of the relationship of imagination and reality) are basically the same concerns found in his early poetry. I would say, however, that in terms of his use of similes, there is a chronological development that provides an indication of the way Stevens came to resolve the latent tension of language and that shows how Stevens managed to sustain both poles of language simultaneously. I would even say that what he learned from his use of similes led to a certain ease with language that allowed the simple grandeur of his great, last poems (which are without the strain of either pole and sometimes even without the presence of similes).

Despite certain vacillations, in general Stevens' poetry shows a consistent increase in his use of similes and the "as if" construction. We are thus able to chart a particular development in Stevens' craft that may help us to understand more fully his often enigmatic poetry. If it is true that style was for Stevens the integration of language and thought, then it follows that this particular development in his style reveals something of a development in his language and thought.[40] What we may learn from examining Stevens' sim-

---

[39] Riddel, "Contours," pp. 262-63. Riddel says that of the major critics on Wallace Stevens only Frank Kermode has found it useful to consider the poetry chronologically (*Wallace Stevens* [London: Oliver and Boyd, 1960]), although in his notes Riddel adds a disparaging review of John J. Enck's chronological study, *Wallace Stevens, Images and Judgments* (pp. 262, 276 n 20). We should add, however, that since the appearance of this article (1965), there has been at least one major work published that deals with Stevens' poetry chronologically: Michel Benamou's *Wallace Stevens and the Symbolist Imagination* (Princeton: Princeton University Press, 1972).

[40] See Doggett's discussion of style, *Making of the Poem*, p. 24. Note in addition that Hayden Carruth says, "As it happens, Stevens' delight in language is concomitant to his entire vision, his argument" (p. 293).

21

iles may also help to resolve at least part of the "warfare of current literary criticism"—that is, the war between the more traditional approaches to literature in general (and Stevens in particular) and the more recent deconstructive perspectives.[41]

Admittedly, throughout this study, I will oversimplify many subtle ideas about language. I. A. Richards' discussions of the "interinanimation" of metaphor, for example, are not as one-sided as I shall first present them: he not only says that a metaphor achieves "meaning" by the "interaction" of the things compared, but he also insists that "there are very few metaphors in which disparities between tenor and vehicle are not as much operative as the similarities."[42] Similarly, even for Derrida, the "sign" does not simply open up the great abyss. Although he says that language "*adds itself* to presence and supplants it, defers it within the indestructible desire to rejoin it," Derrida also says, more optimistically, that the "passage from one structure to another" might be considered "negatively as catastrophe, or affirmatively as play."[43] As Geoffrey Hartman summarizes, "Derrida agrees both that signs are indefinite (they defer absolute knowledge) and that they mean."[44] There is, always, the trace.

Nevertheless, I will initially consider certain views of language as antithetical to each other in order to posit what I hope is a useful and revealing model for understanding Ste-

---

[41] J. Hillis Miller, "Stevens' Rock and Criticism as Cure, II," *Georgia Review*, 30 (1976), 348. See also Riddel, "Climate of Our Poems," especially, pp. 59-68.

[42] Richards, pp. 93, 127.

[43] *Of Grammatology*, pp. 280, 294. In fact, Derrida makes the "play" of language the focus of an entire essay: "Structure, Sign, and Play in the Discourse of the Human Sciences," *The Structuralist Controversy: The Languages of Criticism and the Sciences of Man*, ed. Richard Macksey and Eugenio Donato (Baltimore: Johns Hopkins University Press, 1972), pp. 247-72.

[44] Geoffrey Hartman, *Criticism in the Wilderness: The Study of Literature Today* (New Haven: Yale University Press, 1980), p. 169.

CHAPTER ONE

vens' use of language (and perhaps language in general) and, therein, resurrect certain ideas about language from my own abyss of categories and generalizations. *Metaphor*, therefore, will include concepts ranging from recent ideas of interconnection and creation to the earliest exaltation of metaphor as the union of flesh and spirit (the ultimate form being the hypostatic union of the Incarnated Word);[45] *fragmentation* will include post-structuralist ideas about language as well as earlier, more classical ideas of nominalism.

It is perhaps not as far-fetched as it might seem to put together either contemporary ideas of deconstruction and older ideas of nominalism or modern senses of metaphor and, essentially, medieval ideas about realism.[46] From a certain perspective, the new developments of Derrida and his followers are less radical than they are currently judged to be. The fear of the "abyss" that we may now feel[47] is, in certain respects, similar to the twelfth-century French realists' fear of their contemporaries' nominalist ideas. The suggestion that nominalism would undermine universals and, therefore, the Trinity[48] is similar to the current anxiety

[45] In his discussion of the problems of "universals" and "singulars" in the twelfth century, Mackey offers what he calls the "Franciscan Perspective" as a resolution. At the end of that discussion, Mackey says, "The structure of the created order—in particular the relationship of singular and universal—is incarnational. The Incarnation is the supreme metaphor—the metaphor that came true, so to speak . . ." ("Singular and Universal: A Franciscan Perspective," *Franciscan Studies*, 39 [1979], 161).

[46] In this respect, consider Carruth's statement that in Stevens' poems we find "the many influences on the art of our time . . . French, pastoral, metaphysical, Homeric, etc." (p. 289).

[47] Throughout *Criticism in the Wilderness* Hartman refers to the problem of writing and understanding criticism today, precisely because "contemporary criticism aims at a hermeneutics of indeterminacy" (p. 41) since the "issue of language has now reached criticism itself" (p. 85). Or, as he says of Shakespeare, "the word takes its revenge on the Word" (p. 89).

[48] "When the controversy over universals first arose, it was only

INTRODUCTION

(which might be called the "anxiety of differance") of being abandoned in the great abyss of infinite regress should the campaign against "Logocentricity" prove successful. As M. H. Abrams has shown in *The Mirror and the Lamp*, similar conflicting notions about language go back at least as far as Aristotle and Plato[49]—an "old song" as Stevens says:

> Twenty men crossing a bridge,
> Into a village,
> Are twenty men crossing twenty bridges,
> Into twenty villages,
> Or one man
> Crossing a single bridge into a village.

technically a dispute about the proper interpretation (at third hand) of a point of Aristotle's logic. What gave the controversy its passionate, often bitter intensity was its theological implications. Nominalists like Abelard feared that realism would lead to pantheism. If every common noun names a substantial universal, why should not 'being' or 'substance' name a single reality univocally encompassing God and creature? Realists on the other hand feared that the divisive particularism of the nominalists would crumble such foundations of the faith as the doctrine of the triune God and the doctrine of original sin. Realist and nominalist alike took universal and singular to be contraries" (Mackey, "Franciscan Perspective," p. 159).

[49] See especially the "Introduction: Orientation of Critical Theories," in M. H. Abrams, *The Mirror and the Lamp: Romantic Theory and the Critical Tradition* (New York: Oxford University Press, 1953; rpt. 1980), pp. 3-29. See also Miller, "Theoretical and Atheoretical," p. 275: "The various theories of poetry that generate in their conflict the vitality of Stevens' poetic language are not, however, modern inventions. They are not tied to a particular time in history. Nor is it an accident that just those theories are present and that the poet cannot choose among them. The conflict among three theories of poetry is as old as our Western tradition. It goes back to Plato and Aristotle, and behind them to their precursors. It may be followed through all the languages and cultures that inherit the Greek tradition, the tradition, as it has been called, of Occidental metaphysics. Moreover, the conflict among these three theories of poetry is woven into the fabric of our language." I would add that such a conflict is not restricted to theories of poetry, but is present in theories of language as well.

CHAPTER ONE

> This is old song
> That will not declare itself. . .
> *(CP, 19)*

Stevens articulates this conflict, and its necessity, most clearly through the similes of his poetry. In fact, his subtle but consistent exploration of the nature of similitude suggests that *simile* rather than metaphor or fragmentation may provide the best model for understanding language. Essentially, what is clarified in Stevens' use of similes is that it is only a function of limited perspective which makes it appear as if language unites or fragments in some prediction. Just as it is necessary to have positive and negative poles in order to have a current of electricity (an analogy suggested by one of Stevens' letters),[50] the "poles" of language described through *metaphor* and *fragmentation* are necessary for the movement of language itself. Although the two poles are ultimately interdependent, their interaction demands a lack or resolution between the two rather than a total synthesis of the two. The corollaries that follow from this argument, and which are also exposed in Stevens' poetry, are that metaphor can be as divisive as fragmentation and that the fragmenting elements of language can be as uniting as metaphors.

I should clarify that for my purposes I will not be concerned with the negative attitudes toward metaphor which, from as early as Plato, have often included a distrust of all figurative language and of poetry in general, nor will I be interested in representing the resistance to such ideas as those propagated by the Tel Quel School and its followers. Both the distrust of figurative language and the discomfort with deconstruction would seem to stem from a desire to have a "real," literal, or univocal meaning in language. Yet to fulfill this desire, notions of the "interinanimation" of language are ultimately neither more helpful nor more harmful than notions of "differance." Absolute meaning remains beyond

[50] See L, 368.

INTRODUCTION

reach. As Derrida rightly notes, "Only infinite being can reduce the difference in presence. In that sense, the name of God, at least as it is pronounced within classical rationalism, is the name of indifference itself."[51]

I should also clarify that I will not be concerned with revising Stevens' place in modern poetics or with reconsidering his relationship to his contemporary poets,[52] though further investigation of Stevens' use of similes would probably clarify his resistance to Imagism as well as expose a deliberately subversive attack against the assumptions about language implicit in the "objective" poetry of his contemporaries, particularly that of William Carlos Williams.[53] I do hope, however, in the course of this discussion to suggest how the examination of Stevens' similes may explain why Stevens' last poetry may be not only his best but his most "human." For, although the nature of the interdependence of imagination and reality is also beyond the scope of this study, the question of language, and especially that of similitude, invariably involves the status of the human being in his complex, paradoxical relationship to thought and to the world.

[51] *Of Grammatology*, p. 71.

[52] For a recent discussion of Stevens' interaction with contemporary writers, see Glen G. MacLeod, *Wallace Stevens and Company: The* HARMONIUM *Years 1913-1923* (Ann Arbor: UMI Research Press, 1983). See also n. 38 above for discussions of the larger context of Stevens' work.

[53] Riddel discusses Stevens' relation to Imagism at several points in *The Clairvoyant Eye: The Poetry and Poetics of Wallace Stevens* (Baton Rouge: Louisiana State University Press, 1965). His particular insights into Stevens' relation to William Carlos Williams (see pp. 105-6, 154) might well be amplified by considering the use of similes in Stevens, as in "The Poems of Our Climate," as a theoretical attack against the possibility of descriptive or "objective" poetry typified by such poems as Williams' "Nantucket" (*Collected Poems: 1921-1931* [New York: Objectivist Press, 1934], p. 42).

CHAPTER TWO

METAPHOR

> Professor Eucalyptus said, "The search
> For reality is as momentous as
> The search for god." It is the philosopher's search
>
> For an interior made exterior
> And the poet's search for the same exterior made
> Interior. . . .
>
> <div style="text-align:right">(<i>CP</i>, 481)</div>
>
> In the yes of the realist spoken because he must.
> <div style="text-align:right">(<i>CP</i>, 320)</div>

IN THE CHAPTER "Metaphor" of *The Philosophy of Rhetoric*, I. A. Richards says,

> First, that not to see how a word *can* work is never by itself sufficient proof that it will not work. Second, conversely, that to see how it ought to work will not prove that it does. Any detailed examination of metaphor brings us into such risk of pedantry and self-persuasion, that these morals seem worth stress.[1]

Richards' statement speaks to the difficulty of speaking about language. It is difficult, if not impossible, to speak about language without turning to a representation of language taken from the natural world that is itself represented in language. But, according to Paul de Man, language is incapable of attaining the "absolute identity that exists in a natural object": "In everyday use . . . words are used as established signs to confirm that something is recognized as

[1] Richards, p. 106.

being the same as before; and re-cognition excludes pure origination."[2] De Man's conclusion sounds much like Stevens when he writes, "What is it he desires? / But this he cannot know, the man that thinks" (*CP*, 188).

Jacques Derrida, as we have seen, places this disjunction in language itself. It is interesting, then, to see Derrida's comments on the poet's relations to words: "[T]he poet has a relationship of truth and literalness with that which he expresses, he keeps himself as close as possible to his passion. Lacking the truth of the object, he speaks himself fully and reports authentically the origin of his speech."[3] Derrida's description of the poet's relation to language, the ability to report "authentically the origin of his speech," is similar to de Man's description of "poetic language," which for him implies the "pure origination" or "absolute identity" excluded for everyday language:

> But in poetic language words are not used as signs, not even as names, but in order to *name*. . . . [P]oets know the act of naming . . . as implying a return to the source, to the pure motion of experience at its beginning.[4]

A return to the source or any beginning is impossible, as Derrida has pointed out. Such a return would be an absolute identification of the signifier with the signified; such absolute identification would, however, obliterate the sign.[5]

---

[2] Paul de Man, "Intentional Structure of the Romantic Image," in *Romanticism and Consciousness*, ed. Harold Bloom (New York: W. W. Norton, 1970), pp. 66-67.

[3] Derrida, *Of Grammatology*, p. 277.

[4] De Man, "Intentional Structure," p. 67.

[5] This is the tenet of much of Derrida's discussions of language. He deals specifically with metaphors in this respect in "White Mythology: Metaphor in the Text of Philosophy." See in particular the section, "Metaphysics: The 'Sublation' and Elevation of Metaphor," pp. 60-74. Of the lines of "self-destruction" inherent in metaphor, Derrida says, "One of these is a line of resistance to the spreading of the metaphorical in a syntax which at some point and above all involves an irreduc-

CHAPTER TWO

Nevertheless, such a state of unity is precisely the possibility that Stevens insists upon when he says, "The word must be the thing it represents; otherwise, it is a symbol. It is a question of identity" (*OP*, 168) or "There was a myth before the myth began, / Venerable and articulate and complete" (*CP*, 383). We have already seen that Derrida shows that language cannot be articulate *and* complete: language precludes "unicity" and "singularity" and potentially leads to a consciousness of alienation.[6] As Harold Bloom says, "the painfully thought 'I am' of Adam is the muddy precedent to the sophistications of consciousness."[7] De Man, likewise, insists that ultimately even "poetic language" cannot "return to the source" and that such an idea is only the desire of the poet; he goes on to show that the temporal predicament of language precludes "origination."[8]

De Man's statements about "poetic language" as opposed to words in "everyday use" offer convenient points of departure for distinguishing between the two processes of language which we will be considering in this chapter and the next: i.e., the tendency of language to move toward union, in the manner often attributed to *metaphor*, and the tendency of language to divide, which we are calling *fragmentation*. However, instead of contrasting poetic language with non-poetic language, we will be contrasting one kind of poetic language with another, essentially a unitive poetics versus a disjunctive poetics.

As we have already seen, the assumption which either underlies or is overtly stated in many of the discussions of met-

---

ible loss of sense: this is the metaphysical 'sublation' of metaphor into the proper sense of *being*" (p. 71).

[6] See, for example, de Man's discussion of the "self-escalating act of consciousness" in "The Rhetoric of Temporality," *Interpretation: Theory and Practice* (Baltimore: Johns Hopkins University Press, 1969), p. 202.

[7] Harold Bloom, "Notes toward a Supreme Fiction: A Commentary," in Borroff, ed., *Collection*, p. 80.

[8] See especially p. 66-70 of Paul de Man's "Intentional Structure" and the entirety of "The Rhetoric of Temporality."

aphor is that in metaphor language is capable of attaining "absolute identity." For some theorists metaphor not only presents "an extraordinary unity," but it is also "mythically conceived as genuine and direct identification."[9] This conception of language is radically different from the sense of language we are calling *fragmentation*. De Man, for instance, argues that, rather than being immediate, language mediates, creating a "reflective disjunction," since language is "unable to give a foundation to what it posits except as an intent of consciousness."[10]

Stevens is clearly aware of both "theories" of language (although for him "theories" remain "possibilities"), and he explores and exploits them for the substance of much of his poetry—rather like the "Comedian": "Thus he conceived his voyaging to be / An up and down between two elements, / A fluctuating between sun and moon" (*CP*, 35). On the one hand, Stevens seems to agree with the unitive theory of metaphor, when he says that metaphor not only "appears to be poetry at its source," but that "It is" (*NA*, 81). On the other hand, he denies that metaphor can achieve the point of pure identity, the "predicate of bright origin" (*CP*, 481), by saying that "We are not dealing with identity. Both in nature and in metaphor identity is the vanishing-point of resemblance" (*NA*, 72). This dichotomy leads to the distinction Stevens makes between the "desire to believe in a metaphor" and the knowledge that such a belief "is not true":

> Yet to speak of the whole world as metaphor
> Is still to stick to the contents of the mind

---

[9] For a counter-argument to such ideas about metaphor, but one that is not necessarily "deconstructive," see James Guetti, *The Limits of Metaphor: A Study of Melville, Conrad, and Faulkner* (Ithaca: Cornell University Press, 1967).

[10] The phrase "reflective disjunction" is taken from de Man, "The Rhetoric of Temporality," p. 196; the following quotation in the text is from "Intentional Structure," p. 69.

CHAPTER TWO

> And the desire to believe in a metaphor.
> It is to stick to the nicer knowledge of
> Belief, that what it believes in is not true.
> (CP, 332)

This is, as the title says, "The Pure Good of Theory."[11]

Despite an awareness of both possibilities of language in Stevens' poetry, it is necessary to prescind discussions of the fragmenting elements of Stevens' work from the most part of this chapter in order to focus upon a possibility that he seriously explores in much of his poetry—that is, that language is unitive rather than disjunctive, immediate rather than mediating. Stevens accepts neither possibility absolutely. But, as Donald Sheehan says of the "subject" and "object" in "Stevens' Theory of Metaphor," "Stevens clearly does *imply* the existence of such absolutes—if only to establish where he does not wish to go. It is crucial, though, to see clearly what Stevens is *not* doing to see what poles he will approach but not embrace."[12] As I hope to clarify in Chapter Four, the opposing ideas of language presented in this chapter and the next depend upon each other and only appear to be in opposition. As Stevens says, "Two things of

---

[11] In relation to the lines cited above, consider Derrida's discussion of the "concept of metaphor" with regard to philosophical discourse in "White Mythology": "Only philosophy itself would seem to have any authority over its metaphorical productions. But on the other hand, and for the same reason, philosophy deprives itself of what it gives. Since its instruments belong to its field of study, it is powerless to exercise control over its general tropology and metaphorics. Indeed, they can only be perceived around a blind spot or a deaf point. The concept of metaphor would describe this outline but it is not even sure that in doing so it is circumscribing an organizing center; and this strict law holds for any element of philosophy" (p. 28). It is an interesting idea that this "strict law" holds true for poetry as well.

[12] Donald Sheehan, "Stevens' Theory of Metaphor," in *Critics on Wallace Stevens*, ed. Peter L. McNamara (Miami: University of Miami Press, 1972), p. 32.

opposite natures seem to depend / On one another" (*CP*, 392).

In "The Sail of Ulysses," Stevens writes, "We shall have gone behind the symbols / To that which they symbolized" (*PM*, 391). To join the "symbols" and the "symbolized" is essentially to reach the "point of central arrival" spoken of in "Prologues to What is Possible." The desire for such a center is the desire to transcend the disjunction inherent in the sign, and as such raises the possibility of a unitive poetics, one in which words are immediate, capable of touching, even creating, reality, and ultimately capable of being joined in the Word. For example, in "An Ordinary Evening in New Haven" Stevens announces the desire for

> The poem of pure reality, untouched
> By trope or deviation, straight to the word,
> Straight to the transfixing object, to the object
>
> At the exactest point at which it is itself. . . .
> (CP, 471)

Although this excerpt may seem to disparage language as a "deviation" from reality, it still asks for the *poem* of reality, for an intimate connection between the world and words,[13] such as is found "In the yes of the realist spoken because he must" (*CP*, 320). "Realist" is used here in the sense of philosophic Realism, in which the world and thoughts are connected by words, just as Creation and God's thoughts of Creation are connected by the Word—so that the "metaphysical metaphor" does indeed become "Physical" (*CP*, 301).[14] We see this sense of language stated more explicitly a few lines later in "An Ordinary Evening in New Haven":

---

[13] In reference to this poem Stevens wrote, "At the time when that poem was written my feeling for the necessity of a final accord with reality was at its strongest" (*L*, 719).

[14] It is worth noting that although Roy Harvey Pearce insists that the theological element of realism is not present in Stevens' poetry, he

CHAPTER TWO

> The dry eucalyptus seeks god in the rainy cloud.
> Professor Eucalyptus of New Haven seeks him
> In New Haven with an eye that does not look
>
> Beyond the object.
> . . . .
>   He seeks
>
> God in the object itself, without much choice.
> It is a choice of the commodious adjective
> For what he sees, it comes in the end to that:
>
> The description that makes it divinity, still speech
> As it touches the point of reverberation—not grim
> Reality but reality grimly seen. . . .
>   (*CP*, 475)

    Although he restricts it to a "possibility," Stevens' desire for such an impossible union accounts for the "presence" of God or some divine form in so many of his poems.[15] The last poem in the book entitled *The Man with the Blue Guitar* concludes with the following lines:

---

nonetheless concludes that "ultimately, existing as a mode of pure possibility [in Stevens' poetry], there was *the* poem identical with *the* man, and these in turn identical with reality" (*Continuity*, p. 407).

[15] In his concordance Thomas F. Walsh cites 35 lines in which "god" appears, 15 for "gods," and 14 for "lord." In addition, many lines including words such as "power," "influence," "good," "light," "portent," and of course "divinity" refer to some form of divinity (*Concordance to the Poetry of Wallace Stevens* [University Park: Pennsylvania State University Press, 1963]). In this respect consider the following statement: "The ultimate American poet [Stevens], searching for the ultimate American poem, has again willed that he become Adam. But Adam is by now old and weary. His burden, the burden of the world which he makes in the naming, is great—too great. . . . It is wanting to be a god—a god in a world without gods, to be sure, but a god nonetheless" (Pearce, *Continuity*, p. 419).

METAPHOR

> God and all angels, this was his desire,
> Whose head lies blurring here, for this he died.
>
> Taste of the blood upon his martyred lips,
> O pensioners, O demagogues and pay-men!
>
> This death was his belief though death is a stone.
> This man loved earth, not heaven, enough to die.
>
> The night wind blows upon the dreamer, bent
> Over words that are life's voluble utterance.
> (CP, 188)

This poem calls attention to the frustration inherent in the impossible desire for the words to speak the Word: "To say more than human things with human voice, / That cannot be." Yet, as we shall see in this chapter, language as (and in) the Logos is the extension of "life's voluble utterance" and is even for Stevens a necessary fiction, providing a sanction for the modern age in which "The idea of god [is] no longer sputtered" (CP, 184).

So despite the fact that Stevens says that the realist's sense of language "is not true," it is nevertheless a possibility that Stevens continues to explore throughout his poetic career, achieving its most poignant expression in one of his late poems, "Final Soliloquy of the Interior Paramour":

> Light the first light of evening, as in a room
> In which we rest and, for small reason, think
> The world imagined is the ultimate good.
>
> This is, therefore, the intensest rendezvous.
> It is in that thought that we collect ourselves,
> Out of all the indifferences, into one thing:
>
> Within a single thing, a single shawl
> Wrapped tightly around us, since we are poor, a warmth
> A light, a power, the miraculous influence.

CHAPTER TWO

> Here, now, we forget each other and ourselves.
> We feel the obscurity of an order, a whole,
> A knowledge, that which arranged the rendezvous.
>
> Within its vital boundary, in the mind.
> We say God and the imagination are one . . .
> How high that highest candle lights the dark.
>
> Out of this same light, out of the central mind,
> We make a dwelling in the evening air,
> In which being there together is enough.
> (*CP*, 524)

This is a poem which speaks to the human desire for "an order," "a whole," "one"—despite its various qualifications. The two boldest metaphors ("The world imagined is the ultimate good" and "God and the imagination are one," both of which describe a point of union) are modified, gently but devastatingly, by the words "think" and "say"—words that manage to undermine the unity posited in the metaphors. Similarly, the reverberating exclamation, "How high that highest candle lights the dark," reverberates precisely because, despite the candle and the light, it still is dark. Even the title presents a disclaimer for the very unity the poem evokes: that the poem is a "Soliloquy" implies isolation rather than "being there together"; that the speaker is an "*Interior* Paramour" reinforces the isolation.

Nevertheless, the "Interior Paramour" is still a "paramour," that is, a lover. And the fact that it is a lover suggests a creative union, touching, and communication, so that before the poem has ended the "paramour" is not just Stevens' internal self but a lover of the world. In this respect, one of Stevens' early poems, rare in being a "love poem," is useful here. In "Re-statement of Romance," the bleak, unconscious backdrop of night that "knows nothing of the chants of night" provides the "background" for the intense intimacy of the lovers (*CP*, 146). In "Final Soliloquy" the "poverty" of the human condition, kept present in the poem by the various qualifications or disclaimers, provides the background for another form of intimacy—"a warmth, / A light, a power, the miraculous influence." The next three stanzas build upon this intimacy (in some of Stevens' most moving and powerful lines), making a formation in language that is the "dwelling . . . / In which being there together is enough." The possibility of this dwelling is the possibility of *metaphor*—namely, that language operating in the manner of metaphor can create something real. As we have seen, the myth ("venerable and articulate and complete") is that language can name being at "the source"; rather than being disjunctive, it unites, creating reality, establishing identity in the very act of naming.

In this respect Northrop Frye's comments on metaphor in "The Realistic Oriole: A Study of Wallace Stevens" are particularly helpful. Having stated that metaphor is nothing like a simile or comparison, Frye says, "In its literal grammatical form metaphor is a statement of identity: this is that, A is B. And Stevens has a very strong sense of the crucial importance of poetic identification, 'where as and is are one' (476), as it is only there that one finds 'The poem of pure reality, untouched / By trope or deviation' (471)."[16] Or as Stevens says in "The Man with the Blue Guitar,"

> A dream (to call it a dream) in which
> I can believe, in face of the object,
>
> A dream no longer a dream, a thing,
> Of things as they are, as the blue guitar
>
> After long strumming on certain nights
> Gives the touch of the senses. . . .
>   (*CP*, 174)

Metaphor, as a means of identification, is further discussed in *Anatomy of Criticism*:

---

[16] Frye, "The Realistic Oriole," p. 170.

CHAPTER TWO

> In the anagogic aspect of meaning, the radical form of metaphor, "A is B," comes into its own. Here we are dealing with poetry in its totality, in which the formula "A is B" may be hypothetically applied to anything. . . . The literary universe, therefore, is a universe in which everything is potentially identical with everything else.

And although Frye goes on to say that "Identity is the opposite of similarity or likeness, and total identity is not uniformity, still less monotony, but a unity of various things," he also adds that, "Finally, identification belongs not only to the structure of poetry, but to the structure of criticism as well. . . . *Interpretation proceeds by metaphor as well as creation* . . ." (italics mine).[17]

Even though Stevens recognizes that a "belief in a metaphor" is "not true" and does not attain "absolute identity," he still insists that maintaining such a belief is an important part of the "act of finding / What will suffice" (*CP*, 239). In fact, as he explains in a letter to Sister M. Bernetta Quinn, it is a necessity:

> I don't want to turn to stone under your very eyes by saying "This is the centre that I seek and this alone." Your mind is too much like my own for it to seem to be an evasion on my part to say merely that I do seek a centre and expect to go on seeking it. I don't say that I shall not find it or that I do not expect to find it. *It is the great necessity even without specific identification* (italics mine). (*L*, 584)

The Necessity

As Stevens clarifies in the letter above, what is important is not necessarily reaching the "centre" (or the "point of cen-

---
[17] Frye, *Anatomy*, pp. 124-25.

METAPHOR

tral arrival") but rather the art of searching. But searching in poetry depends upon a "belief" in the possibility that we can achieve the "order," the "whole," the "one" through language. This defines the belief in metaphor—even if it is a belief that the poet recognizes as a fiction.

The "great necessity" of seeking that "centre" arises from separate (although related) areas. First, as shall be more fully considered in the next chapter, language itself, as something which defers meaning in the sign, gives rise to a nostalgia for "unicity." The

> human intellect . . . yearns for unity. Our minds want to get behind the duplicity of the proposition to a single simple apprehension of truth. . . . It develops a kind of inverse nostalgia for a vision it has never enjoyed, but which it recognizes as far superior to its own subject-predicate makeshifts.[18]

Although some theorists, such as Jacques Derrida, would say that metaphor further aggravates the problem, others, such as Walter Ong, say that metaphor helps relieve this nostalgia by bringing two things into a single vision.[19] Thus, language itself creates a need for a belief in metaphor.

Second, as is clarified in both his poetry and prose, Stevens feels a lack in the modern "age of disbelief," essentially a lack of the spiritual, that he feels poetry should fill. This concern leads to a corresponding need in Stevens for poetry to offer something "real" as a "sanction" to life:

> It seems to be elementary, from this point of view, that the poet, in order to fulfill himself, must accomplish a poetry that satisfies both the reason and the imagination. . . . [I]f the end of the philosopher is despair, the

---

[18] Mackey, "Terms and Termination," pp. 80-81. In a similar vein, Michel Benamou says that "Poets and anthropologists share the same nostalgia for origins, for a center" (p. xiii).

[19] For a discussion of the nostalgia in language, as well as of Ong's views, see Mackey, "Terms and Terminations," pp. 80-81.

end of the poet is fulfillment, since the poet finds a sanction for life in poetry that satisfies the imagination. (*NA*, 42-43)

The need for poetry to offer a "sanction" can be considered historically, since the historical events of the first half of the century led to a general atmosphere of the kind described in "Sad Strains of a Gay Waltz": "These sudden clouds of faces and arms . . . / Imposing forms they cannot describe, / Requiring order beyond their speech" (*CP*, 122). But even in his youth Stevens felt that art "must fit with other things; it must be part of the system of the world. And if it finds a place in that system it will likewise find a ministry and relation that are its proper adjuncts" (*L*, 24-25).

Stevens, then, is most interested in poetry that can "speak humanly": "It is life we are trying to get in poetry" (*OP*, 158). In a more suggestive passage from "Adagia," Stevens says, "The poet is the intermediary between people and the world in which they live and also, between people as between themselves; but not between people and some other world" (*OP*, 162). This statement reveals the desire for a unitive poetics, one that is "inter-mediary" rather than mediated, and also shows Stevens explicitly denying that poetry "connects" people to "another world" (a connection which is a form of fragmentation).

Stevens' concern for the world in which people live is perhaps curious since he was so often accused of being an aesthete, with no concern for his times.[20] Yet, according to Hayden Carruth, Stevens' aim in poetry was "above all to deal uncompromisingly with the realities of the contempo-

---

[20] Randall Jarrell, for example, says that "It is the lack of immediate contact with lives that hurts his [Stevens'] poetry more than anything else" (p. 128). Similarly, Julian Symons condemns Stevens for being frivolous in "A Short View of Wallace Stevens," *Life and Letters Today*, 26 (1940), 215-24. See also Mark Van Doren; Yvor Winters; John Crowe Ransom, "Poet without Laurels," *The World's Body* (New York: Charles Scribner's Sons, 1938), pp. 55-75.

rary world."[21] As Stevens says of the imagination in *The Necessary Angel*, "It has the strength of reality or none at all" (*NA*, 7). With this in mind, the following lines from "Montrachet-le-Jardin," written in 1942, are particularly interesting, for they deal with the harsh realities of the time, but are also written from the desire for language to touch reality—essentially from the desire that the poet could be "the deliverer // Delivering the prisoner by his words":

> To-night, night's undeciphered murmuring
> Comes close to the prisoner's ear, becomes a throat
> The hand can touch, neither green bronze nor marble,
>
> The hero's throat in which the words are spoken,
> From which the chant comes close upon the ear,
> Out of the hero's being, the deliverer
>
> Delivering the prisoner by his words,
> So that the skeleton in the moonlight sings,
> Sings of an heroic world beyond the cell,
>
> No, not believing, but to make the cell
> A hero's world in which he is the hero.
> Man must become the hero of his world.
>   (*CP*, 261)

Although Stevens recognizes that such a desire for language is a fiction, he still insists that the belief in such a fiction is necessary, enabling the poet "to help people to live their lives" (*NA*, 30).

 It is perhaps useful at this point to look at another "fiction." One of Stevens' contemporaries, Albert Einstein, posed the question of how a fiction (for him, mathematics) could still produce "such remarkably applicable conclusions": "Here arises a puzzle that has disturbed scientists of all periods. How is it possible that mathematics, a product of human thought that is independent of experience, fits so excellently the objects of physical reality? Can human rea-

---

[21] Carruth, p. 289.

CHAPTER TWO

son without experience discover by pure thinking properties of real things?" According to Morris Kline in *Mathematics: The Loss of Certainty*, there is no answer to this question unless we accept "some inner mysterious strength."[22] So too Stevens (who, as we shall see, was troubled by the "loss of certainty" in the modern age) explores in many of his poems the question of how language, which is "never the thing but the version of the thing" (*CP*, 332), still "is the making of the world"; how language, which "is not / The thing described," but rather "an artificial thing that exists, / In its own seeming," still offers "A text"

> More explicit than the experience of sun
>
> And moon, the book of reconciliation,
> Book of a concept only possible
>
> In description, canon central in itself,
> The thesis of the plentifullest John.
> (*CP*, 344-45)

Even at the end of his life, Stevens insists that there is no answer to this question, unless it is to embrace some "power, the miraculous influence," a conclusion which is quite similar to Kline's "inner mysterious strength."

In an early essay much admired by Stevens (see *L*, 694), Bernard Heringman cites Stevens' statement that the poet " 'creates the world to which we turn incessantly and without knowing it and that he gives to life the supreme fictions

---

[22] Einstein, cited in Morris Kline, *Mathematics: The Loss of Certainty* (New York: Oxford University Press, 1980), p. 340; from *Sidelights on Relativity* (1921). In relation to Stevens' and Einstein's "fictions," Northrop Frye makes a suggestive remark in *Anatomy of Criticism*: "Both literature and mathematics proceed from postulates, not facts; both can be applied to external reality and yet exist also in a "pure" or self-contained form. Both, furthermore, drive a wedge between the antithesis of being and non-being that is so important for discursive thought. The symbol neither is nor is not the reality which it manifests" (p. 351).

without which we are unable to conceive of it,' " and concludes that Stevens' "passage has double relevance to his theme of the intersection of imagination and reality: socially, in that the poet thereby helps men to live their lives; aesthetically, and ontologically, in that poetry thereby constitutes a greater reality."[23] The desire Stevens feels for poetry to constitute a greater reality is the desire for poetry to satisfy the mind (or spirit) in what he calls "The epic of disbelief" which he says "Blares oftener and soon" and "will soon be constant" (*CP*, 122). Early in his journals, we can find a similar reaction to the "want of faith": "I wish that groves still *were* sacred—or, at least, that something was. . . . I grow tired of the want of faith—the instinct of faith" (*L*, 86). But, as he writes years later, "It is the belief and not the god that counts" (*OP*, 162).

It thus became Stevens' purpose to write "Of Modern Poetry," not according to the notions of the Imagists or any other contemporary notions about poetry, but to try to find what would satisfy that "want" in the modern age[24]:

> The poem of the mind in the act of finding
> What will suffice. It has not always had
> To find: the scene was set; it repeated what
> Was in the script.
>   Then the theatre was changed
> To something else. Its past was a souvenir.
> It has to be living, to learn the speech of the place.
> It has to face the men of the time and to meet
> The women of the time. . . .

---

[23] Bernard Heringman, "Wallace Stevens: The Use of Poetry," *ELH*, 16 (1949), 326-27. Heringman cites Stevens from the 1942 publication of "The Noble Rider and the Sound of Words," in *The Language of Poetry*, ed. Allen Tate (Princeton: Princeton University Press, 1942), pp. 120-21; and Stevens voices his approval of Heringman's article in *L*, 694-95.

[24] Note that Stevens says that "not all objects are equal. The vice of imagism was that it did not recognize this" (*OP*, 161).

CHAPTER TWO

>   It has
> To construct a new stage.
>   (CP, 239-40)

For Stevens, the "scene" that "was set" has been destroyed in the modern age; constructing a new stage meant, among other things, constructing a fiction that would fill the loss of belief in "the script" (which is also the loss of belief in the "scriptures").

Perhaps Stevens' best explanation of this need is given in "Two or Three Ideas":

> In an age of disbelief, or, what is the same thing, in a time that is largely humanistic, in one sense or another, it is for the poet to supply the satisfactions of belief, in his measure and in his style. I say in his measure to indicate that the figures of the philosopher, the artist, the teacher, the moralist and other figures, including the poet, find themselves, in such a time, to be figures of an importance greatly enhanced by the requirements both of the individual and of society; and I say in his style by way of confining the poet to his role and thereby of intensifying that role. It is this that I want to talk about today. I want to try to formulate a conception of perfection in poetry with reference to the present time and the near future and to speculate on the activities possible to it as it deploys itself throughout the lives of men and women. I think of it as a role of the utmost seriousness. It is, for one thing, a spiritual role.
> (OP, 206; read at Mount Holyoke, April 28, 1951)

In an "age of disbelief," a "want of faith" presents, ironically, a lack that necessitates the possibility of a unitive poetics in order to be filled. As Randall Jarrell says succinctly, Stevens' poetry "is obsessed with lack. . . ."[25] It is no longer possible,

---

[25] Jarrell, p. 122. Although in this particular article Jarrell is often negatively critical of Stevens' work, he is particularly astute in this comment.

for example, to believe what Alan de Lille, a major twelfth-century poet, believed—that through words we could reach the "more than human" Logos; no longer possible to believe in what Miller calls the "second theory" of poetry—that the "*logos* as being comes into the open by way of the *logos* as words . . . as dramatic action, as metaphor."[26] Yet Stevens insists upon the possibility that poetry can provide a real and necessary sanction. As Michel Benamou notes in *Wallace Stevens and the Symbolist Imagination*, "What makes Stevens a modern poet, i.e., a poet of our time, is this modern consciousness that the arts compensate for our lost belief."[27]

Stevens remains acutely aware that the search for a "centre" is impelled by a loss, by a necessity, by the fact that "we are poor." The "age of disbelief" is, in other words, a poverty, and "It is poverty's speech that seeks us out the most" (*CP*, 510). This poverty of life demands a sanction in language. Precisely because "life / Itself is like a poverty in the space of life," the speaker in "Chocorua to its Neighbor" insists on the possibility that "Of what I am, // The cry is part. My solitaria / Are the meditations of a central mind" (*CP*, 298-99). Similarly, in "Extracts from Addresses to the Academy of Fine Ideas" the "poverty" demands the possibility of a "centre":

> And naked of any illusion, in poverty,
> In the exactest poverty, if then
> One breathed the cold evening, the deepest inhalation
> Would come from that return to the subtle centre.
> (*CP*, 258)

Stevens' recognition of this poverty explains the seriousness with which he writes the following letter late in his life:

---

[26] Miller, "Theoretical and Atheoretical," p. 276.

[27] Benamou, p. 23. Consider, also, Pearce's statement in *The Continuity of American Poetry*: "In Stevens there is always in view . . . an end . . . that the poem, the creative act, must be made continually to point beyond itself to the problems of belief which its existence raises" (p. 380).

CHAPTER TWO

Isn't it the function of every poet, instead of repeating what has been said before, however skillfully he may be able to do that, to take his station in the midst of the circumstances in which people actually live and to endeavor to give them, as well as himself, the poetry that they need in those very circumstances? (*L*, 711)

However much he may recognize the limitations of language, Stevens still insists upon the possibility that language can establish itself "in the midst of the circumstances" and create that which will fill the need of those circumstances—something real, as in "The Planet on the Table":

> Ariel was glad he had written his poems.
> . . . .
>
> His self and the sun were one
> And his poems, although makings of his self,
> Were no less makings of the sun.
>
> It was not important that they survive.
> What mattered was that they should bear
> Some lineament or character,
>
> Some affluence, if only half-perceived,
> In the poverty of their words,
> Of the planet of which they were part.
>   (*CP*, 532-33)

Here language is not only an "affluence" compensating for the poverty of the planet, but the only possible affluence for the poverty of language itself, "the poverty of their words." Incapable of attaining the "one" spoken of in this poem, language is still the only means of expressing that desire. Stevens explores, then, the power of language, of metaphor, to create "a sign of meaning in the meaningless," "no sign of life but life, / Itself, the presence of the intelligible / In that which is created as its symbol" (*CP*, 529). Similarly, in "The Noble Rider and the Sound of Words," Stevens insists that "A poet's words are of things that do not exist without the words" (*NA*, 32); and in a letter to José Rodríguez Feo, he writes, "You are describing a world and by describing it you are creating it" (*L*, 495).

In these excerpts we see a faith in an Adam-like power of language to create through the act of naming—a faith that assumes there is a correspondence between the imagination and reality that is achieved in words.[28] It is precisely this "faith" (although a faith recognized as a fiction) which allows Stevens to raise in earnest the possibility of "the poet who achieved God," even though "the poet himself, still in the ecstasy of the poem that completely accomplished his purpose," would seem "a man who needed what he had created, uttering the hymns of joy that followed his creation" (*NA*, 51).

The Possibility

For Stevens metaphor is crucial (even "central") in achieving what would completely accomplish his purpose.

> In short, metaphor has its aspect of the ideal. This aspect of it cannot be dismissed merely because we think that we have long since outlived the ideal. The truth is that we are constantly outliving it and yet the ideal itself remains alive with an enormous life. (*NA*, 81-82)

Stevens' metaphors, then, are an integral part of his desire to express the ideal, a belief in the "one thing" that could

---

[28] Pearce, for example, says that in Stevens' "work . . . the continuity of the most deeply rooted tradition, . . . its Adamic phase, reaches the point of no return" (p. 376). We should clarify that although Pearce defines "Adamic" as the making of the world through the act of naming, he opposes Adamic poetry to mythic poetry, saying that the first is the poetry of man and that the second is the poetry of the Word (*Continuity*, pp. 431-32). Although such a distinction is useful for Pearce's work, it is unnecessary here; consequently I am calling creating either by words or by the Word "Adamic."

CHAPTER TWO

transcend "all our indifferences"—a desire that is made all the more poignant or "finally human" (*CP*, 504) by his acknowledgment that it "is not true." Similarly, after all the luxuriant language of *Harmonium*, Stevens closes that book with a short poem, "To the Roaring Wind," that suggests that language *cannot* express what he desires it to express:

> What syllable are you seeking,
> Vocalissimus,
> In the distances of sleep?
> Speak it.
> (*CP*, 113)

This is a poem of desire, which also means that it is a poem of frustration. Still, as we have seen, the possibility that he could "Speak it" is a necessity: "The final belief is to believe in a fiction, which you know to be a fiction, there being nothing else. The exquisite truth is to know that it is a fiction and that you believe in it willingly" (*OP*, 163). Or, as he says in "Asides on the Oboe," "The prologues are over. It is a question, now, / Of final belief. So, say that final belief / Must be in a fiction. It is time to choose" (*CP*, 250).

Occasionally, as in "Prologues to What is Possible," Stevens explores the "inhuman" consequences of realizing that desire toward unity, of reaching the "point of central arrival" that would necessarily "shatter the boat and leave the oarsmen quiet." Often, however, Stevens' metaphors celebrate *the movement of desire*, of "What is Possible." As Frank Doggett says of Stevens' prose in *The Necessary Angel* (and, as we may add, of his poems throughout his career), Stevens' language reveals a poet "fascinated with the possibility of words, with what they may create in the silence beyond the voice."[29]

For several reasons then Stevens explores the possibility that language can create in the Adamic sense—that "what we said of it became // A part of what it is . . ." (*CP*, 159).

---
[29] Doggett, *The Making of the Poem*, p. 43.

Sometimes this possibility is expressed as a desire for divinity; at other times as a desire for reality, to be "At the centre of reality, seeing it" (*CP*, 205). But in either case, it is a possibility that is Logo-centric in its conception. So, even though the "centre" of language (the "more than human" Logos) may be recognized as impossible, its possibility still elicits something that Stevens often presents as miraculous, such as the "miraculous influence" in "Final Soliloquy of the Interior Paramour" or the surprising gaiety of the poem "Of Bright & Blue Birds & the Gala Sun":

> Some things, niño, some things are like this,
> That instantly and in themselves they are gay
> And you and I are such things, O most miserable . . .
>
> For a moment they are gay and are a part
> Of an element, the exactest element for us,
> In which we pronounce joy like a word of our own.
>
> It is there, being imperfect, and with these things
> And erudite in happiness, with nothing learned,
> That we are joyously ourselves and we think
>
> Without the labor of thought, in that element,
> And we feel, in a way apart, for a moment, as if
> There was a bright *scienza* outside of ourselves,
>
> A gaiety that is being, not merely knowing,
> The will to be and to be total in belief,
> Provoking a laughter, an agreement, by surprise.
> (CP, 248)

Part of the "gaiety" of the poem comes from the ironic asides—the apostrophe, "O most miserable . . . ," and the parenthetical "being imperfect." Yet the possibility of the "exactest" moment in which there is an "agreement," a joining of the elements, words, and thinking in "belief" is a gaiety, the poem tells us, that is synonymous with total being.

Perhaps the clearest expression of this possibility occurs in the following lines from "A Primitive Like an Orb":

CHAPTER TWO

> The lover, the believer and the poet.
> Their words are chosen out of their desire,
> The joy of language, when it is themselves.
> . . . .
> It is if the central poem became the world,
>
> And the world the central poem. . . .
> . . . .
> The central poem is the poem of the whole,
> The poem of the composition of the whole.
> (CP, 441-42)

In poems such as this, Stevens is exploring the possibility that language is creative and establishes meaning, rather than merely being disjunctive. Significantly, the "central poem" is the "poem of the composition of the whole," suggesting that creation is equivalent to composing; it is an ordering of chaos, like the jar in "Anecdote of the Jar" that composes the "wilderness," so that it is "no longer wild" (*CP*, 76).[30]

Even if de Man is right and language does institute a reflective disjunction, Stevens reiterates the possibility that language as communication is union. Instead of negating or dividing in the two-part predication of the "dialectic,"[31] it is possible that language affirms and unites in a tripartite sense, making a "central" conjunction in and of itself that is, in its extension, an incarnation.[32]

---

[30] It is worth noting that Stevens counters this idea of the "composing" effect of composition in such poems as "Two Versions of the Same Poem: That Which Cannot Be Fixed" (*CP*, 353-55).

[31] Although this is taken up in the following chapter, it is worth citing now: "The word . . . is the means by which the permanance of natural entities [and of language] can be put into question and thus negated, time and time agin, in the endlessly widening spiral of the dialectic" (de Man, "Intentional Structure," p. 69).

[32] In this respect, Michel Benamou's comment on Stevens' early poems is particularly interesting: he says that they are "evolved from symbols of intimacy, hedonistic joy, and incarnation" (p. xxv). See also Adalaide Kirby Morris, *Wallace Stevens: Imagination and Faith*

Whereas the fragmenting process of language potentially severs being and meaning from the "thing itself," the "metaphoric" process of language potentially brings the "thing itself" into being through the very language. Consequently, the "thing itself" cannot be grasped through its separate parts, but only in its entirety: "In the simplest formulation, when we use a metaphor we have two thoughts of different things active together and supported by a single word, or phrase, *whose meaning is a resultant of their interaction*" (italics mine).[33] Rather than being ironic disjunction, this kind of "interaction" or unity approaches the unity of Coleridge's "infinite I AM" in which there can be no separate parts. for example, in Stevens' line, "God and the imagination are one," "God" and the "imagination" are joined in the metaphor with the word "one" *in* a fused and single entity that defies even the word "one."

The mathematical representation of this process or model of language would be "$X = Y$." As the "equals" mark indicates, there is a bridge in metaphor; and although a bridge may imply a gap, it is a gap that metaphor tends to conceal in the "interaction" that both constitutes and provides meaning. In this sense, metaphor is neither a transfer of meaning from one term to another, nor the displacement of one term (or sign) by another, but the creation of a new term that is a function of the "interinanimation" of X and Y. Metaphor, therefore, is creative, and it is creative precisely in its bridge. The "bridge" can be viewed as a function of a three-part predication which unites subject with object, word with action, being with motion in the same way that the finite is joined with the infinite in the "Word."[34]

(Princeton: Princeton University Press, 1974): "Stevens' poetic trinity is a transvaluation of the Christian trinity. In his poetic doctrine, God becomes one with the imagination; Christ becomes the poet-hero, or incarnation of imagination; and the Holy Ghost becomes the active though diffused presence of imagination in human life" (p. 5).

[33] Richards, p. 93.

[34] In relation to this subject, consider what Frye finds as the analogical level of any poem: "Here the *dianoia* of art is no longer a *mimesis*

CHAPTER TWO

Whether or not such a conception of language is fictional, it is a powerful and generative concept in Stevens' poetry, from "The Man with the Blue Guitar" to "The World as Meditation." This last poem, for instance, concludes with a stanza which, though deliberately ambiguous, suggests that the uttering of the name "Ulysses" is bringing him into being:

> She would talk a little to herself as she combed
>   her hair,
> Repeating his name with its patient syllables,
> Never forgetting him that kept coming constantly
>   so near.
> (*CP*, 521)

Although the moment of union is held off, the possibility here is that language joins the worlds of imagination and reality. Language, acting in the manner we are calling *metaphor*, brings together into being all the dichotomies inherent in consciousness—such as subject versus object, mind versus body, imagination versus reality—and thus "fulfills its highest function in naming being as a presence."[35] As de Man has pointed out, the naming of being is the poet's desire, and it is often Stevens' desire. Walsh's *Concordance*, for instance, lists forms of "to be" only "when their meaning stresses existence as such,"[36] and yet Walsh still cites 82 lines containing "being," 71 lines with "be," 42 with "is," 34 with "are," 13 with "was," 9 with "am," and 6 with "were"— all of which stress "being."

Not only does Stevens write about the possibility that language can create being, by bringing the "dream" into the

---

logou, but the Logos, the shaping word which is both reason and . . . *praxis* or creative act. The *ethos* of art is no longer a group of characters within a natural setting, but a universal man who is also a divine being, or a divine being conceived in anthropomorphic terms" (*Anatomy*, p. 120).

[35] De Man, "Intentional Structure," p. 67.

[36] Walsh, vii. Corresponding statistics on Stevens' interest in negations of being can be found in Chapter Three.

METAPHOR

"thing," as in several of the poems cited above, he also uses that possibility as the informing principle of some of his poems, such as "World without Peculiarity," a poem that contains several metaphors:

> The day is great and strong—
> But his father was strong, that lies now
> In the poverty of dirt.
>
> Nothing could be more hushed than the way
> The moon moves toward the night.
> But what his mother was returns and cries on his breast.
>
> The red ripeness of round leaves is thick
> With the spices of red summer.
> But she that he loved turns cold at his light touch.
>
> What good is it that the earth is justified,
> That it is complete, that it is an end,
> That in itself it is enough?
>
> It is the earth itself that is humanity . . .
> He is the inhuman son and she,
> She is the fateful mother, whom he does not know.
>
> She is the day, the walk of the moon
> Among the breathless spices and, sometimes,
> He, too, is human and difference disappears
>
> And the poverty of dirt, the thing upon his breast,
> The hating woman, the meaningless place,
> Become a single being, sure and true.
> 					(*CP*, 453-54)

The first several lines of this poem establish the state of "difference," even isolation, of the man. He is alienated from his father, mother, lover, the earth, even from himself, in his consciousness of his condition. In contrast, the unconscious earth, which is "justified," "complete," "an end," "enough," essentially exhibits the "abolute identity" with itself that de Man says "exists in a natural object."

CHAPTER TWO

However, in the last three stanzas of the poem there is a movement of metaphors that increasingly unites the fragmented elements until "difference disappears." At that point all the separated things of the poem, the "thing upon his breast," the "poverty of dirt," the woman, the place—all of which are meaningless throughout the first lines of the poem—are joined in the last metaphor of a "single being." The poem thus enacts its own meaning by bringing together all its discrete elements into a final "single being, sure and true."

To a large degree the creation of this "being" (implying immediacy, origination, presence—that which we have seen excluded by the disjunction inherent in the sign) is a function of the metaphors. The last three stanzas, for instance, have seven basic metaphors that become increasingly complex and inclusive. The effect of these metaphors is, potentially, to overcome the disjunction inherent in the sign and, in their "interaction," unite language with the world and even with ultimate Being. This is immediate rather than mediated, so that if the disjunction of the sign threatens to eradicate meaning, the possibility evoked here is a process of language that creates and confirms meaning. This is the "belief in a metaphor"—that meaning is created in the interaction of its own words and thus reveals "origination" at its source.

For example, in "World without Peculiarity," we are told that "the earth . . . is humanity": this is truly a joining, in the way Richards suggests, since the meaning that metaphor evokes is something that cannot be understood in its separate parts, but only in the "interaction" of the parts. Similarly, "he" is infused with the "inhuman," and "she" with the "fateful mother," the "day," and "the walk." Eventually all the elements of the poem are united by the last metaphor into one thing, the "single being," which itself cannot be grasped in the individual parts of the poem, but can only be perceived as a whole. This "being," Stevens would insist, has gained an element of reality: "There is no such thing as a metaphor of a metaphor. . . . [R]eality is the indispensable element of each metaphor. When I say that man is a god it is very easy to see that if I also say that a god is something else, god has become reality (*OP*, 179). The poem illustrates, then, the possibility that language approaches being through the "metaphoric" process of language. As it connects and unites, language posits absolute immediacy, as opposed to "absolute metaphysical distance."[37]

But, as may have been implied, this uniting process is not restricted specifically to metaphors. The metaphoric process of language described here is merely a model that describes something inherently possible in all language. In other words, in the act of language there is a connection or bridge that suggests a movement toward the absolute Word or one—even if such an "end" is finally unattainable. As Richards suggestively insists, "It is important . . . to realize how far back into the past all our meanings go, how they grow out of one another . . . and how inseparable they are from one another."[38]

The attention given to "being" in "World without Peculiarity" helps to account for why Stevens can say seriously of the seemingly playful poem "The Emperor of Ice-Cream" that "the true sense of Let be be the finale of seem is let being become the conclusion or denouement of appearing to be: in short icecream is an absolute good. The poem is obviously not about icecream, but about being as distinguished from seeming to be" (*L*, 341). The degree of seriousness with which he uses the phrase "absolute good" is perhaps more obvious if we consider his own conjunction of the words "God is good" in his discussion of metaphor and in the title of the first poem of *Transport to Summer*, "God

---

[37] The phrase is taken from Georges Poulet, *The Interior Distance*, tr. Elliott Coleman (Baltimore: Johns Hopkins University Press, 1959), p. 242.

[38] Richards, p. 30.

CHAPTER TWO

is Good. It is a Beautiful Night," and especially in the following excerpt from "The Irrational Element in Poetry":

> All mystics approach God through the irrational. Pure poetry is both mystical and irrational. If we descend a little from this height and apply the looser and broader definition of pure poetry, it is possible to say that, while it can lie in the temperament of very few of us to write poetry in order to find God, it is probably the purpose of each of us to write poetry to find the good which, in the Platonic sense, is synonymous with god. One writes poetry, then, in order to approach the good in what is harmonious and orderly. (*OP*, 222)

So, despite his reservations and qualifications, Stevens continually explores the possibility that language, operating in the manner we have described as *metaphor,* can evoke the "living ideal," even in the modern "age of disbelief." Like the chapel of "St. Armorer's Church from the Outside," which becomes the "presence of the intelligible," language becomes the reality it evokes:

> Its chapel rises from Terre Ensevelie,
> An ember yes among its cindery noes,
> His own: a chapel of breath, an appearance made
> For a sign of meaning in the meaningless,
>
> No radiance of dead blaze, but something seen
> In a mystic eye, no sign of life but life
> Itself, the presence of the intelligible
> In that which is created as its symbol.
> (CP, 529)

The Extension

As has already been stated, the ultimate extensions of metaphor, or of the possibility that language may predicate in the manner of metaphor, is unavoidably spiritual or religious in its implications—something that Stevens contemplates in such statements as "God and the imagination are one," "The poet is the priest of the invisible" (*OP*, 169) and "The mind that in heaven created the earth and the mind that on earth created heaven were, as it happened, one" (*OP*, 176). Sometimes this possibility is presented as a merging with reality and sometimes as a seeking of divinity; at other times, it simply stresses the act of creation itself. But this possibility, in its extension, depends on Logocentric assumptions about language. In his discussion of Stevens, Ralph J. Mills, Jr., calls attention to those assumptions even when Stevens attempts to transfer the creative power of the word from the realm of the divine to that of the human:

> The transfer of generative power from the divine Logos of the Prologue of St. John's Gospel to the human spirit is accomplished in "Description without Place." The world is created, we are told in this poem, not out of nothing but, we might say, *in* depth or perspective through the description of it.[39]

In "Of a Remembered Time," Stevens' business friend Wilson E. Taylor cites the excerpt from "Adagia" about the mind in heaven and on earth as an example of "the depth of his [Stevens'] religious feeling."[40] Although I find the meaning of this excerpt to be more ambiguous than Taylor does (especially when Stevens rather repeatedly claims, "I am not in the least religious" [*L*, 96]), we cannot dismiss the fact that Stevens' poetry and his discussions of poetry invite a serious regard that is essentially religious in nature.[41]

---

[39] Ralph J. Mills, Jr., "Wallace Stevens: The Image of the Rock," in Borroff, ed., *Collection*, p. 100.

[40] Wilson E. Taylor, "Of a Remembered Time," in Doggett and Buttell, ed., *Celebration*, p. 97.

[41] In this respect, it is quite provocative to consider the account of Stevens' late conversion given by Rev. Arthur Hanley in Peter Brazeau, *Parts of a World: Wallace Stevens Remembered* (New York: Random House, 1983), pp. 294-96.

CHAPTER TWO

However, according to Geoffrey Hartman, "After Marx and Freud, there is a tendency to make religion part of the problem rather than of the solution, and to expel it from the enlightened analysis of human experience. It is as if certain kinds of interpretation were exclusive. . . ."[42] So, in order to understand the religious implications of the possibility of language we have been discussing here, it is perhaps useful to look at earlier writers and what their ideas about language suggest.

Like the Romantics, Stevens is concerned with the relation between reality and imagination; and Romantic ideas about this subject, particularly those of Coleridge, offer insight into Stevens' ideas about language and suggest some of their religious ramifications. As we shall see, Stevens replaces Coleridge's belief in the imagination with the possibility of metaphor. And although Coleridge may have disparaged metaphor, deriding it as a mere operation of fancy,[43] his interest in the imagination and the "vital" power he attributes to it are much like Stevens' interest in metaphor.

As he reveals in "The Noble Rider and the Sound of Words," Stevens was familiar, at least through I. A. Richards, with Coleridge's theories:

> Dr. Richards cites Coleridge's theory of fancy as opposed to imagination. Fancy is an activity of the mind which puts things together of choice. . . . Fancy, then, is an exercise of selection from among objects already supplied by association, a selection made for purposes which are not then and therein being shaped but have already been fixed. (NA, 10-11)

Stevens goes on to say that "a work of fancy precludes it from

---

[42] Geoffrey Hartman, p. 63.

[43] Samuel Taylor Coleridge, *Lay Sermons*, ed. R. J. White, vol. 6 of *The Collected Works of Samuel Taylor Coleridge*, Bollingen Series, 75 (Princeton: Princeton University Press, 1972), p. 79.

being a work of the imagination. A glance at it shows it to be unreal" (*NA*, 11). This is an important statement insofar as it implies that a work of the imagination somehow is "real."

In Coleridge's definition of the imagination, we once again see a desire for unity that is religious in its extension. He defines the "primary imagination" as the "living power and prime agent of all human perception, and as a repetition in the finite mind of the eternal act of creation in the infinite I AM." The "secondary" imagination he considers as an "echo of the former," one which "struggles to idealize and to unify" and which is "essentially *vital*, even as all objects (as objects) are essentially fixed and dead."[44] Much as Stevens does, this earlier philosopher-poet sees the need to find a *"unified sensibility that has been lost"* (italics mine); according to Barth, it is "Coleridge's achievement" that he saw this need; "in the final analysis, there was only one way for him to find it—through religious vision."[45]

For Stevens, the way to find this lost unified sensibility is through a belief in the "Supreme Fiction," and he consequently translates Coleridge's belief in the imagination into his own terminology, one which stresses "poetry" in general and "metaphor" in particular. For example, after citing Coleridge's theory of the imagination early in *The Necessary Angel*, Stevens later writes that "Resemblance in metaphor is an activity of the imagination; and in metaphor the imagination is life" (*NA*, 73); thus, he places the "vital" power Coleridge finds in the imagination into the domain of metaphor. By the time Stevens says that metaphor is "poetry at its source" and that metaphor "has its aspect of the ideal" (*NA*, 81-82), he has managed to rewrite Coleridge's belief in the imagination as a belief in the possibility of metaphor. So,

[44] Coleridge, *Biographia Literaria*, ed. George Watson (New York: E. P. Dutton, 1975), p. 167.

[45] J. Robert Barth, *The Symbolic Imagination: Coleridge and the Romantic Tradition* (Princeton: Princeton University Press, 1977), p. 21.

whereas Coleridge synthesizes the two realms of subject and object with the power of the imagination, Stevens finds in poetic metaphors a "fusion of the two realms of Imagination and Reality."[46]

In terms of how Stevens thinks about this possibility of language, however, it is the medieval writers who most clearly parallel Stevens. Whereas Coleridge disparages metaphor, for the medievals such as Alan de Lille (and excluding, notably, the medieval nominalists) metaphor was raised as an ultimate principle for gaining knowledge, for approaching God or ultimate Being. So Stevens, in a similar fashion, raises the "activity of the imagination" that he says defines "metaphor" (NA, 73) to the level of the "mind's being, striving to realize itself in knowing itself" (NA, 10). For example, Alan de Lille claims that his words are connected to the world and even to ultimate Being. In the Prologue to *Anticlaudianus*, Alan states that his words, even in their most "literal sense," will be intimately connected to the "ears" of the world (a connection which would not be claimed by the nominalists). Moreover, Alan says that his words "will inspire the mind on the road of perfection" (which is the road to God) and that his words will teach not only of syntax but also of God. These claims are justified because, according to Alan, poetry creates—as does God—and thus follows Truth more "faithfully" than does logic.[47] In a similar vein, Stevens says, "For realist, what is is what should be" (CP, 41). Perhaps most importantly for our purposes here, in *Anticlaudianus* Alan says that God "conceives everything by means of a trope and by way of a figure. . . ."[48] Thus, language in the poetic, metaphoric process is contem-

---

[46] Heringman, p. 330.

[47] Alan of Lille, *Anticlaudianus*, tr. James J. Sheridan (Toronto: Pontifical Institute of Medieval Studies, 1973), pp. 40-42, 49.

[48] Ibid., p. 141.

METAPHOR

poraneous with the creation of reality rather than being divorced from reality.

I do not want to over-medievalize Stevens, particularly since he was "horrified" by being compared to some of the medieval artists and philosophers. As he says to Henry Church in a letter dated November 10, 1942, he had seen a circular that some publisher had sent out

> in which, after listing sundry eccentricities of Giotto and Duns Scotus and St. Augustine, he (or, rather, she) went on to say that NOTES TOWARD A SUPREME FICTION exhibited many symptoms of these. The thing horrified me, but there is nothing to do about it. I can only protest my innocence. (L, 428)

Nevertheless, the medieval conviction that God's thoughts about creation and creation are connected by the Logos (and that our thoughts about the world and the world are connected by our words) is not essentially different from Stevens' suggestion that words not only "create the world" but approach the "living ideal."

In the same year that Stevens wrote the letter cited above, he wrote "Certain Phenomena of Sound."[49] The concluding lines of this poem clearly exhibit Stevens' entertaining the possibility that language itself creates reality:

> A sound producing the things that are spoken.
>
> Eulalia, I lounged on the hospital porch,
> On the east, sister and nun, and opened wide
> A parasol, which I had found, against
> The sun. The interior of a parasol,

---

[49] Despite the fact that I am prescinding "deconstructive" aspects of Stevens' work from this chapter, it is probably useful to consider the word "parasol" ("para-sol") in relation to Derrida's discussion of the "heliotrope" in "White Mythology," especially the sections "Ellipsis / Eclipse of the Sun" and "The Flowers of Rhetoric: The Heliotrope," pp. 29-60.

CHAPTER TWO

> It is a kind of blank in which one sees.
> So seeing, I beheld you walking, white,
> Gold-shined by sun, perceiving as I saw
> That of that light Eulalia was the name.
> Then I, Semiramide, dark-syllabled,
> Contrasting our two names, considered speech.
> You were created of your name, the word
> Is that of which you were the personage.
> There is no life except in the word of it.
> I write *Semiramide* and in the script
> I am and have a being and play a part.
> You are that white Eulalia of the name.
> (CP, 287)

To my mind, these lines, of all Stevens' lines, most clearly illustrate the creation of being in the *logos*—not only in metaphor (although we are calling this process of language *metaphor*) but clearly in the "sound producing the things that are spoken."

With some qualifications, Joseph N. Riddel says something quite similar about Stevens in his essay on Stevens and Whitman:

> [M]etaphors proliferate in both essays and poetry and suggest an elemental vision by which one can once more like the old Adam possess the world in naming it. The poet at least re-enacts this ritual every time he approaches the mundane with a fresh vision and a refreshing word. If poetry cannot penetrate to Logos, as Whitman believed, it can and does bring order and delight by the very act of renewing our cognizance of the human condition.[50]

Frye takes a similar observation about Stevens one step further:

---

[50] Joseph N. Riddel, "Walt Whitman and Wallace Stevens: Functions of a 'Literatus,' " *South Atlantic Quarterly*, 56 (1962), 506-20; reprinted in Borroff, ed., *Collection*, p. 41.

The theoretical postulate of Stevens' poetry is a world of total metaphor, where the poet's vision may be identified with anything it visualizes. For such poetry the most accurate word is apocalyptic, a poetry of "revelation" (344) in which all objects and experiences are united with a total mind.[51]

Or, as Stevens himself says in *Opus Posthumous*, "After one has abandoned a belief in god, poetry is that essence which takes its place as life's redemption" (*OP*, 158).

In "The Well Dressed Man with a Beard," Stevens raises the possibility that after all the "things denied" have "Slid over the western cataract," there could still be "One thing remaining, infallible," "a speech / Of the self that must sustain itself on speech" and that this one thing "would be / Enough." This is essentially the "central" myth, which is the myth of the Logos, that is, the infallible, permanent word that establishes meaning in a world of change. But for Stevens this myth is only a possibility: as he says in the concluding line of the poem, "It can never be satisfied, the mind, never" (*CP*, 247).

If the positive extension of the movement toward unity in language is the divine Logos, the negative extension is the obliteration of the individual as it becomes amorphous in the "One." This, as we have seen, is recognized by Stevens when he says, "The metaphor stirred his fear" (and accounts to some degree for the nominalists' objections to the realists' ideas about language). The negative extension is not merely that individual words may lose their identity as they are subsumed into the Logos, but that individual people may lose their identities as they are subsumed into language. This fate is precisely the fate of the hero in "Examination of the Hero in a Time of War":

> Say that the hero is his nation,
> In him made one, and in that saying

---

[51] Frye, "The Realistic Oriole," p. 173.

CHAPTER TWO

> Destroy all references. This actor
> Is anonymous and cannot help it.
> (CP, 279)

This "hero" sounds much like Hegel's "hero" in *Reason in History*, and his fate here (which is to become annihilated in the anonymity of the "one") suggests the reason that Kierkegaard reacted so negatively to Hegel's ideas.[52] In other words, "The world reduced to one thing"—to cite one of Stevens unpublished aphorisms—would indeed be a reduction: "Wishing to become whole, the self ends in the ultimate alienation."[53]

Such a paradoxical state is seen in the ninth section of "Things of August":

> A text of intelligent men
> At the centre of the unintelligible,
> As in a hermitage, for us to think,
> Writing and reading the rigid inscription.
> (CP, 495)

The attempt to write "A new text of the world," even if it "is a text that we shall be needing" (CP, 494-95), means attempting to arrive at a "centre" wherein it is possible to make the "unintelligible" intelligible; but, as the poem says, such a state is "As in a hermitage," which is alienated, and the text rather than being intelligible becomes "rigid."

Ultimately, whether viewed positively or negatively, the extension of the movement toward unity in terms of lan-

---

[52] Compare the "hero" in Stevens' poem to the "world-historical individual" of Hegel's *Reason in History*, tr. Robert S. Hartman (Indianapolis: Bobbs-Merrill, 1953; rpt. 1978), p. 43.

[53] The previously unpublished aphorism is cited by A. Walton Litz in "Particles of Order: The Unpublished *Adagia*," in Doggett and Buttel, eds., *Celebration*, p. 74. The quotation that follows next in the text above is taken from Helen Regeuiro, *The Limits of Imagination: Wordsworth, Yeats, Stevens* (Ithaca: Cornell University Press, 1960), p. 163.

guage is silence: as Stevens says, "Poetry is a search for the inexplicable" (*OP*, 173). According to Helen Regeuiro in her discussion of Stevens, the attempt to create or to call into being in language ends in a frustrated silencing of language caused by the disjunction between language and the world: "[W]ords conceived in the mode of being of the natural object are conceived 'in silence.' The attempted creation of reality ends in a silencing of the word in face of a reality it cannot name, order, or 'conceive.' "[54] But even if it were possible to overcome this disjunction, the resulting union would again impose silence: "But the voice of union [words with reality] is also a voice of silence, a 'sunken voice' that suggests the dissolution of the self in the natural world."[55] However, as we have seen, the positive name for this silence is the silent name of God. But even if imaged positively, the poet, like the bells in "To an Old Philosopher in Rome," is "unwilling that mercy should be a mystery / of silence" (*CP*, 510).

In one of his earliest and best poems, "Sunday Morning," we find Stevens as unwilling for "mercy" to be a "mystery of silence" as he is in his late poems:

> What is divinity if it can come
> Only in silent shadows and in dreams?
> . . . .
> Divinity must live within herself:
> . . . .

---

[54] Regeuiro, p. 178. Such a silencing would also be the effect if de Man's "poetic intent" were realized: "It would follow then, since the intent of the poetic word is to originate like the flower, that it strives to banish all metaphor, to become entirely literal" ("Intentional Structure," p. 68). Derrida makes a similar statement in "White Mythology": "If there were only one possible metaphor (a dream at the basis of philosophy), if the play of metaphor could be reduced to a family circle or group of metaphors, that is, to a 'central,' 'fundamental,' or 'principal' metaphor, there would no longer be any true metaphor" (p. 70).

[55] Regeuiro, p. 190.

CHAPTER TWO

> Death is the mother of beauty; hence from her,
> Alone, shall come fulfilment to our dreams
> And our desires.
> (*CP*, 67-69)

Ultimately Stevens' desire is not the "absolute identity" that we began with, whether that is the "poem of pure reality" or the "more than human" but rather the desire "To speak humanly." Nonetheless, part of Stevens' genius is that he recognizes that within the "human speech" there stirs a desire for the "more than human"—essentially a desire for divinity in language, even if it is impossible to achieve. And as the seminal "Notes toward a Supreme Fiction" shows, its impossibility does not prevent Stevens from imagining the possibility of such an "absolute."

> The poem refreshes life so that we share,
> For a moment, the first idea . . . It satisfies
> Belief in an immaculate beginning
>
> And sends us, winged by an unconscious will,
> To an immaculate end.
> . . . .
> It is possible, possible, possible. It must
> Be possible.
> . . . .
>   To find the real,
> To be stripped of every fiction except one,
>
> The fiction of an absolute—Angel,
> Be silent in your luminous cloud and hear
> The luminous melody of proper sound.
> (*CP*, 382, 404)

The Restraint

We cannot forget that this "fiction of an absolute" is for Stevens a fiction, a possibility beyond the realm of language, born from the desire created by the absolute's being unattainable in words. As he also says in "Notes toward a Supreme Fiction," "the priest desires. The philosopher desires. // And not to have is the beginning of desire" (*CP*, 382). Isabel McCaffrey maintains that "Stevens' voyage toward the possible . . . is also a voyage to the center. . . . The final syllable at the center is, of course, unutterable. . . . On this side of ultimate limit, limits are approached but never achieved. . . ."[56] The sheer insistence that "It is possible, possible, possible" indicates a frustration, even a sadness, about the fact that this desire cannot ultimately be fulfilled.

Similarly, the overstatement of "The Poem that Took the Place of a Mountain" calls attention to the same frustrations:

> There it was, word for word,
> The poem that took the place of a mountain.
> . . . .
> It reminded him how he had needed
> A place to go to in his own direction,
> . . . .
> For the outlook that would be right,
> Where he would be complete in an unexplained
>   completion:
> . . . .
> Where he could lie and, gazing down at the sea,
> Recognize his unique and solitary home.
>   (*CP*, 512)

The overstatement of the opening two lines is humorously evocative and is part of the warmth of this late poem. But even the "solitary" nature of the "home," if the desire to "be complete" were realized, points to a larger sadness, an isolation beyond the human should the "point of central arrival" prove attainable.

As much as it is necessary for Stevens to explore the pos-

[56] Isabel McCaffrey, "A Point of Central Arrival: Stevens' *The Rock*," *ELH*, 40 (1974), 611.

CHAPTER TWO

sibility that language could achieve absolute identity, it is necessary for him to provide restraints against that possibility. Bloom says that "Stevens' grammar is as disjunctive as his syntax tends to be conjunctive. His syntax affirms: his grammar is heavily conditional and reductive. . . ."[57] As we have seen, in "The Qualified Assertions of Wallace Stevens," Helen Vendler shows how Stevens' various ways of qualifying his assertions keep his poetry from becoming "doctrine." In terms of this particular chapter, it might be more appropriate to call the qualifications, "dis-claimers," thereby calling attention to the fact that often Stevens' strategy is to negate the very unity that he seeks to evoke. Thus, as already seen, he checks such sweeping assertions as "God and the imagination are one" with disclaimers such as "We say." Similarly, many of the forms of qualifications that Vendler describes, such as the use of "modal auxiliaries," "questions," "infinitives," or the "aspectual 'seems,' "[58] are disclaimers of the very "centre" or point of unity that Stevens has encouraged many of his poems to claim. One particular form of qualification that she discusses—"not X but Y"—is of particular interest when we consider the analysis given in *A Grammar of Metaphor*. According to Christine Brooke-Rose, one term's being "equated with two quite different things" causes a "logic of 'disbelief'" by calling attention to the disbelief we usually suspend when reading literature: the result is "incongruity."[59] In a somewhat similar vein, Helen Vendler makes the following remarks in reference to Stevens' poem "Not Ideas about the Thing but the Thing Itself":

[T]he title embodies one of Stevens' typical formulas, "not X but Y," which appears in a frequency far beyond the normal throughout Stevens' work, and seems to be

[57] Bloom, *Poems of Our Climate*, p. 406.
[58] Vendler, "Qualified Assertions," p. 168.
[59] Christine Brooke-Rose, *A Grammar of Metaphor* (London: Secker & Warburg, 1958), p. 113.

METAPHOR

another case of the left hand subtracting what the right hand gives. (We are reminded by the "not-but" formula that what we might be impelled to call The Thing has been said on imposing authority to be merely Ideas About the Thing, a fact we might not have recalled if we were not so reminded.)[60]

Sometimes, however, the disclaimers are more integral—and therefore the more unsettling—to the poem than mere manipulations of grammar. For example, in "A Primitive Like an Orb," Stevens raises the possibility (already cited) that the "central poem became the world, // And the world the central poem." But against this possibility, the poem concludes:

> That's it. The lover writes, the believer hears,
> The poet mumbles and the painter sees,
> Each one, his fated eccentricity,
> As a part, but part, but tenacious particle,
> Of the skeleton of the ether, the total
> Of letters, prophecies, perceptions, clods
> Of color, the giant of nothingness, each one
> And the giant ever changing, living in change.
> *(CP,* 443)

The "giant of nothingness" as the "total of letters" is a figure for the point at which union becomes annihilation. As such, it is ripe for deconstruction. However, as Stevens makes clear, this is not necessarily a negative movement, but the point necessary for "changing" and "living in change."

In a similar fashion, Stevens evokes a moment of magnificent union in "The Idea of Order at Key west":

> It was her voice that made
> The sky acutest at its vanishing.
> . . . .

---

[60] Vendler, "Qualified Assertions," pp. 175-76.

CHAPTER TWO

> And when she sang, the sea,
> Whatever self it had, became the self
> That was her song, for she was the maker.

He then tempers that magnificence with the fact that the words are only "portals, dimly-starred," "ghostlier demarcations" (even if they are "keener sounds" [*CP*, 129-30]).

Even when he explores the possibility in language of achieving pure identity, Stevens always returns to the "human speech," which is incapable of the "predicate of bright origin," with a variety of intentional disclaimers. He recognizes that what Derrida calls "differance" is necessary for the play of human language. The possibility that union could prevent the play of language accounts for why Stevens can ask for

> a shape of life described
> By another shape without a word.
> Mulberry, shade me, shade me awhile—
>
> With nothing fixed by a single word.
> *(OP,* 114)

The poetics that such a desire involves—and the poem from which the excerpt above is taken, in particular—will be discussed more fully in the following chapter. At this point, it is enough to say that for Stevens there would be only a static (and dead) ideal without the "differance"—both as a principle of language and as a principle of life. Such an imagined state causes him to ask the disturbing question of "Sunday Morning": "Is there no change of death in paradise?" (*CP*, 69), and to answer it twenty-three years later in "The Poems of Our Climate":

> The imperfect is our paradise.
> Note that, in this bitterness, delight,
> Since the imperfect is so hot in us,
> Lies in flawed words and stubborn sounds.
> *(CP,* 194)

METAPHOR

The "imperfect," then, is the "mercy" or "grace" that saves us from annihilation in the one:

> The last island and its inhabitant,
> The two alike, distinguish blues,
> Until the difference between air
> And sea exists by grace alone,
> In objects, as white this, white that.
> (*CP*, 235)

In "Notes toward a Supreme Fiction," after saying that "Two things of opposite natures seem to depend / On one another," Stevens clarifies his statement with the following lines:

> as a man depends
> On a woman, day on night, the imagined
>
> On the real. This is the origin of change.
> Winter and spring, cold copulars, embrace
> And forth the particulars of rapture come.
> (*CP*, 392)

Heringman says that this passage "epitomizes the dichotomy, synthesis, and at least an aspect of the supreme fiction which arises in synthesis."[61] Ultimately, however, the emphasis lies less on the unity than on the "things of opposite natures": the uniting embrace may be a creative, even rapturous synthesis, but it is dependent upon the difference.

It is the recognition of this fact that accounts for the lines that follow the lines with which I headed this chapter.

> Professor Eucalyptus said, "The search
> For reality is as momentous as
> The search for god." It is the philosopher's search
>
> For an interior made exterior
> And the poet's search for the same exterior made
> Interior: breathless things broodingly abreath

[61] Heringman, p. 333.

CHAPTER TWO

> With the inhalations of original cold
> And of original earliness.
> (*CP*, 481)

However much Stevens may explore the desire for language to call into being, he recognizes that such identification, the point of *origination*, must be "breathless" and "cold." It is because Stevens prefers the "finally human" (*CP*, 504) that he says to know "that what it believes in is not true" is "the nicer knowledge of / Belief." We can see the necessity, both of the restraint and of the possibility, of the search for a "centre" summarized succinctly in the following stanza:

> If ever the search for a tranquil belief
>   should end,
> The future might stop emerging out of the past,
> Out of what is full of us; yet the search
> And the future emerging out of us seem to be one.
> (*CP*, 151)

CHAPTER THREE

FRAGMENTATION

The sounds of the guitar
Were not and are not. Absurd. The words spoken
Were not and are not. It is not to be believed.
(CP, 525)

The law of chaos is the law of ideas,
Of improvisations and seasons of belief.
(CP, 255)

The civil fiction, the calico idea,
The Johnsonian composition, abstract man,
Are all evasions like a repeated phrase,
Which, by its repetition, comes to bear
A meaning without a meaning.
(OP, 65)

IN THE INTRODUCTION to her translation of Jacques Derrida's *Dissemination*, Barbara Johnson cites the following as one of the assumptions made in a "deconstructive reading": "certain levels of any rigorous text will engender a systematic double mark of the insistent but invisible *contradiction or differance (the repression of) which is necessary* for and in the text's very elaboration" (italics mine).[1] The irony of the "double mark" in the passage—that is, the parenthetical expression—is intentional, making visible the "invisible contradiction" of that particular text. This contradiction cor-

[1] Barbara Johnson, introduction to Jacques Derrida, *Dissemination*, tr. B. Johnson (Chicago: University of Chicago Press, 1981), p. xvi.

responds to the two different senses of language with which we are concerned.

Read with the parentheses, this passage informs us that it is necessary to repress our knowledge of "differance" in order to make meaningful statements at all; we must focus on the joining of word to word and suppress our awareness of the fact that words are only signs and not unequivocal in meaning. Thus it might be argued, the previous chapter, in its attempt to describe a unitive poetics, illustrates the tendency to repress "differance," a tendency that the deconstructionists would say is necessary in order for the text to elaborate itself. We have engaged in this repression because, as we have seen, it is one of the repressions in which Stevens himself engages as he strives to find a poetics that "will suffice."

If in elaborating Stevens' sense of metaphor, we have given a prime example of repressing "differance," in this chapter we wish to examine the repression of unity, which Johnson's passage also says is "necessary." If we read her statement without the parentheses, we find that "differance . . . is necessary for . . . the text's very elaboration." In other words, if a text is to be meaningful, language must be able to separate itself from the "One" and delineate distinctions. That things are meaningful only if distinct is one of the primary axioms of linguistics.[2] Edmund Leach, who combines his training in linguistics with his training in anthro-

---

[2] See M. H. Abrams, *Glossary of Literary Terms*, 4th ed. (New York: Holt, Rinehart, 1981). Derrida's arguments against "presence" in language are derived from Saussure's *Linguistics in Literary Criticism*, specifically Saussure's "view that both the spoken and written elements (the *signifiers*) and the meanings (the *signifieds*) . . . owe their identity, not to their own positive or objective features, but to their *differences* from other speech-sounds, written marks, or conceptual significations" (p. 39). Compare this to Saussure's observation in the *Course in General Linguistics*: "The linguistic signifier . . . is not [in essence] phonic but incorporeal—constituted not by its material substance but the differences that separate its sound-image from all others" (cited in Derrida, *Of Grammatology*, p. 53).

pology, says that in order for us to gain knowledge and self-awareness, it is necessary for us to make distinctions in our language and in our physical world by repressing our perception of the continuity in language and the world. According to him, our "normal perception displays only a continuum." Language as something which imposes "differance" by naming thus becomes a necessary instrument for discrimination:

> we have to train our perception to recognize a discontinuous environment. . . . We achieve this second kind of trained perception by means of a simultaneous use of language and taboo. Language gives us the names to distinguish the things; taboo inhibits the recognition of those parts of the continuum which separate the things.[3]

The deconstructionists would point out that the "taboo" or separation is already an inherent part of language itself.

The purpose of this chapter is to explore that point of separation. We will examine, in relation to Stevens, the necessity of repressing the desire for unity which we have already discussed and offer another perspective for understanding language, one that sees *fragmentation* rather than the unifying tendency of *metaphor* as necessary for meaning. In so doing, we will describe the possibility of a disjunctive, instead of a unitive, poetics. And, as we shall see, exploring such a possibility is another way in which Stevens searches for a poetics that "will suffice." The fact that Stevens does explore both possibilities accounts for the reason, as J. Hillis Miller correctly notes, that it is possible for critics to

> develop radically different notions of Stevens' aims as a poet. . . . It can be shown that Stevens believes all poetry is metaphor, and that he believes all metaphors are factitious. At times he is unequivocally committed to

[3] Edmund Leach, "Anthropological Aspects of Language: Animal Categories and Verbal Abuse," in *New Directions in the Study of Language*, ed. Eric H. Lenneberg (Cambridge: MIT Press, 1964), p. 35.

bare reality. At other times he repudiates reality and sings the praises of the imagination. . . . For each position and for its antithesis there are fully elaborated poems or parts of poems. . . . After the disappearance of the gods the poet finds himself in a place where opposites are simultaneously true. It seems that this situation can be dealt with in poetry only by a succession of wild swings to one extreme or another, giving first one limit of the truth, then the other.[4]

There is an essentially ironic assumption behind this second "truth"—that things (including ideas) are known and therefore become "real" only if they are made distinct, that identification is essentially synonymous with separation. The irony that the deconstructionists find is that the act of discriminating through language (that is, the attempt to say anything) further defers knowledge and reality since language is only a system of signifiers which can never coincide with the signified: "The notion of the sign always implies within itself the *distinction between* signifier and signified . . ." (italics mine).[5] Thus language, which marks this separation, creates a nostalgia for unity that can never be attained:

> différance makes the opposition of presence and absence possible. Without the possibility of différance, the desire of presence as such would not find its breathing-space. That means by the same token that this desire carries in itself the destiny of its non-satisfaction. Différance produces what it forbids, makes possible the very thing that it makes impossible.[6]

This second perception of language and its possibilities (even impossibilities) demands a different kind of poetry than that described in the last chapter. It is a poetry of the "violent mind," to use a phrase from "Farewell to Florida."

[4] Miller, "Poetry of Being," p. 89.
[5] Derrida, *Of Grammatology*, p. 11.
[6] Ibid., p. 143.

In that poem, the first poem in *Ideas of Order* and the first poem after *Harmonium*, Stevens regards the unity he sought in many of the earlier poems as a seduction by a female, even a suffocation by a mother, that has left him in a kind of unthinking, unconscious "hedonism."[7] It is evident that Stevens can regard such unconscious, unpredicated totality as a "freedom" and does again in *Parts of a World*: "It was how he was free. It was how his freedom came. / It was being without description" (*CP*, 205). However, in "Farewell to Florida" Stevens regards it negatively and seeks a poetry removed from the luxuriance of *Harmonium*, asking for a poetry of the independent mind:

> Her mind will never speak to me again.
> I am free.
> . . . .
> Her mind had bound me round.
> . . . .
> How content I shall be in the North to which I sail
> And to feel sure and to forget the bleaching sand . . .
> . . . .
> To be free again, to return to the violent mind
> That is their mind, these men, and that will bind
> Me round, carry me, misty deck, carry me
> To the cold, go on, high ship, go on, plunge on.
>   (*CP*, 117-18)

However, freedom as independence ruptures union and annihilates the "One-ness" formerly described since, as Paul de Man notes, any "beginning implies a negation of permanence."[8] In this respect, it is interesting that Stevens wrote the following to William Carlos Williams: "[T]o fidget with points of view leads always to new beginnings and in-

---

[7] See Janet P. McCann, "French Flowers: Baudelaire and Wallace Stevens" (Ph.D. diss., University of Pittsburg, 1974), pp. 23-26.

[8] De Man, "Intentional Structure," p. 68.

cessant new beginnings lead to sterility."[9] Thus, the "violent mind" also implies fragmentation, infinite change, even chaos—so that ultimately it is true that the "law of chaos is the law of ideas" and that the law of ideas is the law of chaos.

It is important, however, to stress again that although I am presenting these two tendencies (or necessities) of language as if they were diametrically opposed, they are in fact mutually dependent and mutually explanatory. Moreover, as at least one critic has noted, "concepts in Stevens' mind grew binately."[10]

So, despite the chronological development implied by "Farewell to Florida" in relation to *Harmonium*, the oscillations in Stevens' thoughts about language are not necessarily chronological at all. Rather, the oscillations are the poles of possibilities made necessary throughout his poetic career from thinking deeply about language:

> That the glass would melt in heat,
> That the water would freeze in cold,
> Shows that this object is merely a state,
> One of many, between two poles. So,
> In the metaphysical, there are these poles.
>   (*CP*, 197)

Thus, although Frank Doggett may be correct when he says that "A characteristic of Stevens' mind was its tendency to adopt first one and then another contrary point of view,"[11] we should keep in mind Miller's conclusion that Stevens' poetry "is not dialectical, if that means a series of stages which build on one another . . . in some version of the Hegelian sequence of thesis, antithesis, synthesis. . . . To escape such oscillation Stevens must find a way to write poetry

---

[9] Stevens, letter to Williams, included in the latter's "Preface," *Kora in Hell* (Boston: Four Seas, 1920), p. 15; cited in Morse, *Poetry as Life*, p. 79.

[10] Doggett, *The Making of the Poem*, p. 16.

[11] Ibid., p. 126.

which will possess simultaneously both extremes."[12] In the next chapter I hope to show that Stevens finds in similes a way to do just that.

That Stevens apparently, if not intentionally, contradicts himself by countering the "rage to order" (*CP*, 130) with the "law of chaos" is not surprising. It is, perhaps, even expected as the necessary consequence of the restraints with which Stevens qualifies the "belief in metaphor." As he says in "Connoisseur of Chaos" (a title appropriate here):

> . . . things partake of one,
> At least that was the theory, when bishops' books
> Resolved the world. We cannot go back to that.
> The squirming facts exceed the squamous mind.
> (*CP*, 215)

The very retractions or disclaimers (dis-claimers) with which Stevens surrounds such statements as "God and the imagination are one"—statements, one assumes, such as those found in the bishops' books to which we cannot go back—imply another (although concurrent) perception of language, as well as another poetics.

The Necessity

As we have seen, what Stevens felt as a loss or as a poverty in the "age of disbelief" necessitated a belief in a fiction that would satify the mind. It is necessary, says Stevens, to "collect ourselves, / Out of all the indifferences, into one thing" and to say that it "is enough" since "we are poor" (*CP*, 524). This "poverty" demands a "belief in metaphor" as a compensation, even a sanction. But, as Stevens says, "It can never be satisfied, the mind, never" (*CP*, 247). If it is true that Stevens felt the poverty of the modern age, it is equally true that he felt the pressure of the modern age—a pressure

---

[12] Miller, "Poetry of Being," p. 89.

CHAPTER THREE

that needed to be avoided as much as the void of the poverty needed to be filled. This second pressure demands a different sense of language—what we are calling *fragmentation*.

These two needs, the need to avoid the pressure of the modern age and the need to fill its void, appear to be Stevens' overriding and personal needs, corresponding to Harold Bloom's generalized needs for a poet:

> A poem begins because there is an absence. An image must be given, for a beginning, and so that absence is ironically called a presence. Or, a poem begins because there is too strong a presence, which needs to be imaged as an absence, if there is to be any imaging at all.[13]

Bloom's statement draws attention to the essential irony in either poetic process. This irony is perhaps inescapable for the modern consciousness that, as Stevens notes, both requires what will suffice and yet refuses to be satisfied.

In relation to the preceding chapter, what is important to us is that Stevens' nostalgic desire for unity and his use of language to create the possibility of unity are born in the *absence* of belief in that unity. As Stevens says in "The Comedian as the Letter C," "In all desires, his destitution's mark" (*CP*, 31), and "The more invidious, the more desired" (*CP*, 37). Such statements sound much like Derrida, when he explains that "desire carries in itself the destiny of its non-satisfaction."[14] To want is to lack, and what is wanted is thus created by and is dependent upon that very lack: "And not to have is the beginning of desire" (*CP*, 382).

In relation to this chapter, what is important in Bloom's statement is the suggestion that Stevens' desire for fragmentation and his use of language in its interest arise both from and against "too strong a presence," what Stevens calls the "pressure of reality." In a late poem, "Madame La Fleurie,"

[13] Bloom, *Poems of Our Climate*, p. 375.
[14] Derrida, *Of Grammatology*, p. 143.

the heavy pressure of reality is pictured as something that "Weight[s] him, weight[s], weight[s] him" (*CP*, 507). In an earlier poem, "Motive for Metaphor," this pressure is called "The weight of primary noon, / The ABC of being," the "arrogant, fatal, dominant X" which gives a "motive for metaphor" that attempts to "shrink" from the pressure of reality instead of approaching its presence (*CP*, 288).

The first of Bloom's beginnings for poetry demands, as we have seen, an Adamic use of language that calls into being in the act of naming, whereas the second one demands a use of language which calls away from being. A consideration of a few other sets of polarities described by others in their discussions of language reveals the ways in which Stevens does and does not agree with the deconstructionists.

Although the deconstructionists do not wish to work within polarities since thinking "in terms of dichotomies or polarities" is to make Logocentric assumptions,[15] we can say nevertheless that the deconstructive ideas about the "sign" are in many ways opposed to the Adamic or Logocentric assumptions about language. Against Logocentric assumptions about language, Derrida advances his theory of the sign and shows that the sign is already the possibility of its own repetition and that meaning is always already deferred. It is thus particularly apt that Stevens writes that fictions and ideas "All are evasions like a repeated phrase, / Which, by its repetition, comes to bear / A meaning without a meaning" (*OP*, 65).

Though not a deconstructionist, Gerald L. Bruns makes a somewhat similar division in *Modern Poetry and the Idea of Language*. He gives the name "Orphic" (rather than "Adamic") to the first use of language: it is the

> idea of poetic speech as the ground of all signification . . . [in which the] sphere of activity is governed by a mythical or ideal unity of word and being, and whose

---

[15] Derrida, as summarized by Barbara Johnson in her introduction to *Dissemination*, p. viii.

power extends therefore beyond the formation of a work toward the creation of the world.

The other use of language he calls "hermetic"—the purpose of which is to "displace or arrest the function of signification": "the poet's activity is toward the literary work as such, that is, the work as a self-contained linguistic structure."[16] When he says that this form of poetic language "displace[s] . . . signification," Bruns is quite close to agreeing with the deconstructionists. The deconstructionists, however, would argue that it is impossible to have a "self-contained linguistic structure" and insist that *all* signification already displaces signification (or meaning).

Stevens' poetry often seems to correspond to such ideas. Certainly the frequent self-reference of his poems, as in "Notes toward a Supreme Fiction," "Add This to Rhetoric," "The Poem that Took the Place of a Mountain" or "Of Modern Poetry," seems at times to indicate the desire for a "self-contained linguistic structure." At the same time, such self-reference often appears intentionally to undercut the possibility of meaning and to trace the abyss (to use Derrida's vocabulary).

Even if such critics as J. Hillis Miller and Joseph N. Riddel are right in saying that Stevens' poetry exposes the "abyss," Stevens does not always seek to do so. It is important to note that Stevens employs the fiction of another "myth" (which is not exactly deconstructive) to contradict the Adamic myth of language. Janet McCann chooses the word "Satanic" to describe this second fiction about language. According to her, Stevens writes two kinds of poetries: the "Adamic" and the "Satanic." As opposed to the "Adamic," which "seeks oneness with God, with nature, and/or with others" and "reaches out from the self to the other," the "Satanic" form is inward, having "not awareness

---

[16] Gerald L. Bruns, *Modern Poetry and the Idea of Language: A Critical and Historical Study* (New Haven: Yale University Press, 1974), p. 1.

of the self and of the self's possibilities, but knowledge of some kind of damnation."[17] It is true that we feel a sense of damnation in some of Stevens' poetry, as in the following lines from "Esthétique du Mal":

> Panic in the face of the moon—round effendi
> Or the phosphored sleep in which he walks abroad
> Or the majolica dish heaped up with phosphored fruit
> That he sends ahead, out of the goodness of his heart,
> To anyone that comes—panic, because
> The moon is no longer these nor anything
> And nothing is left but comic ugliness
> Or a lustered nothingness.
> (CP, 320)

Such a feeling of estrangement, nothingness, even panic, may well correspond to the feeling we have when we contemplate the abyss in language. But to use the word "Satanic" is to use a word with negative connotations that I do not wish to attribute to the second process of language we are considering. If I am thus far indulging in a logocentric operation by talking of language in terms of "dichotomies or polarities," I wish to avoid as far as possible the logocentric tendency to make the second "negative, corrupt, undesirable."[18]

Therefore, as opposed to the possibility that the poet (or human) can call into being through what is often termed an "Adamic" use of language, I would say that Stevens entertains the possibility of being able to call away from and out of being in what I shall term an "Augustinian" use of language. In using the word "Augustinian" in this sense, I am not referring to the stereotype of St. Augustine's conception of language—that human language is meaningful only insofar as it is grounded in the divine Logos. Rather, I am ap-

---

[17] McCann, p. 17.

[18] Summary of deconstructive views in Johnson's introduction to *Dissemination*, p. viii.

CHAPTER THREE

pealing to a sense of Augustine's use of language that emerges in his *Confessions*, perhaps nowhere more clearly than in the ninth chapter of the tenth book in which he describes a conversation with his mother:

> [W]e were talking alone together and our conversation was serene and joyful. *We had forgotten what we had left behind and were intent on what lay before us.* . . . Our conversation led us to the conclusion that no bodily pleasure . . . was worthy . . . even of mention. . . . [O]ur thoughts ranged over the whole compass of material things in their various degrees, up to the heavens themselves. . . . Higher still we climbed, thinking and speaking all the while. . . . At length we came to our own souls and passed beyond them to that place of everlasting plenty, where you feed Israel forever with the food of truth.[19]

The implication here is that there is a division between language and the world that allows Augustine to transcend the world to the Word by speaking of the things of the world and, consequently, speaking them away. Such a sense of language appears often in Stevens' poetry: as we shall see in this chapter, Stevens employs the fiction that language can alter, resist, or evade reality.

I should clarify that referring to these two processes of language as Adamic and Augustinian appeals to the Logocentric sense of language that Derrida wishes to deconstruct. The Adamic use of language rather obviously depends upon Logocentric assumptions, including the nostalgic idea of original unity between the Logos and Being. As such, the Adamic use of language essentially attempts a restoration. The Augustinian use of language is perhaps less obviously Logocentric: it depends upon the idea of a post-Babelian state in which words no longer di-

---

[19] St. Augustine, *Confessions*, tr. R. S. Pine-Coffin (Baltimore: Penguin, 1961), p. 197.

rectly signify the world and, consequently, upon a state in which the world interferes with the perception of the Word. The Augustinian idea of using language in order to erase the world for the purpose of perceiving the Word has its own nostalgic desire for a Logocentric unity. Even the possibility that words *could* distance the world—and, in Stevens, the possibility that words could resist the "pressure of reality"— implies a connection, although an ironically inverted one, between the world and words. As such, this use of language is a redemption; and, as Stevens notes, "Poetry is a means of redemption" (*OP*, 160).

It is not the purpose of this study, however, to examine fully the various sub-categories of the ways in which Stevens counters the desire for unity (or the "belief in metaphor") with a desire for fragmentation. To place them under the category of fragmentation is to describe one of the "poles" in Stevens' perceptions of language. Just as Stevens uses metaphor as a creative possibility, he uses fragmentation as a creative possibility. At times, this second possibility seems to illustrate deconstructive ideas about language; at other times there is a deliberate "Augustinian" desire. However much we may agree with Derrida's insights into language and with his own desire to deconstruct some of the Logocentric assumptions that have informed writings (and criticism), it is obvious that Stevens at least felt not only a nostalgic need to replace a lost unity but also a simultaneous need to displace a fallen world.

Perhaps Stevens' best-known statement of this second need is his conclusion to the 1942 essay, "The Noble Rider and the Sound of Words":

> The mind has added nothing to human nature. It is a violence from within that protects us from a violence without. It is the imagination pressing back against the pressure of reality. It seems, in the last analysis, to have something to do with our self-preservation; and that, no

CHAPTER THREE

doubt, is why the expression of it, the sound of its words, helps us to live our lives. (NA, 36)

Here language, as the expression of the imagination, is (ironically) presented not as something that can re-unite us with reality by filling an absence, but as something that can preserve us from reality by creating an absence.

Considering the historical context of his life, it is understandable that in 1941 when he wrote this essay, Stevens would feel the need to resist or evade the "pressure of an external event or events on the consciousness" that was threatening to exclude "any power of contemplation" (NA, 20). As examples of such external events, he lists "a whole generation and . . . a world at war," news of "Europe, Asia and Africa all at one time," ultimately a "war-like whole" that has become potentially suffocating in its extremity (NA, 20-21). "Reality," Stevens says, has become

> violent and so remains. This much ought to be said to make it a little clearer that in speaking of the pressure of reality, I am thinking of life in a state of violence, not physically violent, as yet, for us in America, but physically violent for millions of our friends and for still more millions of our enemies and spiritually violent, it may be said, for everyone alive.
>
> A possible poet must be a poet capable of resisting or evading the pressure of reality of this last degree, with the knowledge that the degree of today may become a deadlier degree tomorrow. (NA, 26-27)

From this perspective, we have a certain insight into the pathos of the following lines from "Madame La Fleurie": "It was a language he spoke, because he must, yet did not know. / It was a page he had found in the handbook of heartbreak" (CP, 507). We also have a different response than we had in the last chapter to the desire for "The Poem that Took the Place of a Mountain" or to the feeling that informs the following lines:

> Ariel was glad he had written his poems.
> . . . .
> Other makings of the sun
> Were waste and welter
> And the ripe shrub writhed.
>
> His self and the sun were one
> And his poems, although makings of his self,
> Were no less makings of the sun.
> (*CP*, 532)

Stevens, then, feels not only the need for poetry to find what will suffice to replace belief, but also the need for what will suffice to displace the world.[20] It is consequently possible to read the same poems and to discover traces of both needs operating simultaneously: as Stevens says himself, "Poetry is a poetic conception, however expressed. A poem is poetry expressed in words. But in a poem there is a poetry of words. Obviously, a poem may consist of several poetries" (*OP*, 163).

The fact that this second desire is as imperative as the first explains in part why on the one hand Stevens can say that poetry "enhances the sense of reality" (*NA*, 77) and on the other hand can say without condemnation that the "poetic process is psychologically an escapist process" (*NA*, 30). We should note that in another essay, "The Irrational Element in Poetry," Stevens contrasts escapism with "resistance," thereby making this second purpose of poetry aggressive rather than regressive:

> We have a sense of upheaval. We feel threatened. We look from an uncertain present toward a more uncertain future. One feels the desire to collect oneself against all this in poetry as well as in politics. . . . The

---

[20] In this respect, consider F. O. Matthiessen's observation in 1947: "All of Stevens' later work has been written against the realization that we live in a time of violent disorder" ("Wallace Stevens at 67," *New York Times Book Review*, 20 April 1947, p. 4).

CHAPTER THREE

trouble is that the greater the pressure of the contemporaneous, the greater the resistance. Resistance is the opposite of escape. The poet who wishes to contemplate the good in the midst of confusion is like the mystic who wishes to contemplate God in the midst of evil. There can be no thought of escape. . . . Resistance to the pressure of ominous and destructive circumstance consists of its conversion, so far as possible, into a different, an explicable, an amenable circumstance. (*OP*, 225)

In this passage Stevens provides a different "motive for metaphor" than that discussed in Chapter Two, as well as a different reason for saying, "God and the imagination are one"—that is, the desire to convert (rather than to converge with) our circumstances.

The need to resist the contemporaneous, if not to escape its violence, also offers some insight into a curious paradox in Stevens' poetry. His poetry, so often concerned with the relation of the imagination and reality, seldom deals with what most of us would call the "real world": his poems are highly esoteric, often abstract or fabulous and have little to do with the social situations of his time. In fact, the early reviewers of Stevens' work often criticized him for his lack of social awareness.[21] Even Delmore Schwartz, who in 1940 defends Stevens against this charge by discussing the "poet's sense that something catastrophic is happening to

---

[21] See, for example, William Carlos Williams' review of *Man with the Blue Guitar and Other Poems* in *The New Republic*, 93 (17 November 1937), 50; Julian Symons; Jarrell, who says that it "is the lack of immediate contact with lives that hurts his [Stevens'] poetry more than anything else" (p. 128); and William Empson, rev. of *Selected Poems* in *The Listener*, 48 (26 March 1953), 521. We should also note that others did defend Stevens's poetry, saying that it did have social significance. See Harriet Monroe, "He Plays the Present," *Poetry*, 47 (1935), 153; Robert Fitzgerald, "Thoughts Revolved," *Poetry*, 51 (1937), 153-57.

the society in which he lives," still finds that "there are no human beings in his poems."[22]

At the same time, one "real-life" figure, that of a soldier, makes an erratic appearance throughout his work, appearing in "Notes toward a Supreme Fiction," "Description without Place," and "Repetitions of a Young Captain," as well as in the titles, "Poems from 'Lettre d'un Soldat,'" "The Death of a Soldier," and "A Woman Sings a Song for a Soldier Come Home." In addition, as early as 1914, Stevens sent several "battle-sketches" to *Poetry*, four of which were published.

In "Repetitions of a Young Captain," Stevens gives his reason for this curious paradox: "On a few words of what is real in the world / I nourish myself. I defend myself against / Whatever remains" (*CP*, 308). The soldier is the "violent" figure necessary for a defense against the violent pressures of the modern age who reveals Stevens trying "to speak humanly" in a different way from that described in the last chapter. As such the soldier is also an example of the desire Stevens announces in "Farewell to Florida" when he asks "to be free again / To return to the violent mind."[23]

In "Extracts from Addresses to the Academy of Fine Ideas," the soldiers mark the acute point where men resist (and are defeated) by the "evil" of reality and dissolution:

---

[22] Delmore Schwartz, "The Ultimate Plato with Picasso's Guitar," *The Harvard Advocate*, 127, 3 (1940), 12, 14. In this last statement Schwartz says he is also paraphrasing Howard Baker. See "Wallace Stevens and Other Poets," *Southern Review*, 1 (1935), 373-89, in which Baker defends Stevens' poetry at length.

[23] In contradistinction to my suggestion here, Marianne Moore finds that the soldier in "Notes toward a Supreme Fiction" is a figure for the "violence from without" that "gives rise to the violence within" ("There Is a War That Never Ends," *Kenyon Review*, 5 [1943], 147). With regard to Stevens' concern with war, note that his "Prose Statement on War" was originally included in *Parts of a World*, although it was deleted from the *Collected Poems*. The "Statement" is reprinted in *PM*, 206 (see also the note at *PM*, 402).

CHAPTER THREE

> How can
> We chant if we live in evil and afterward
> Lie harshly buried there?
>
> If earth dissolves
> Its evil after death, it dissolves it while
> We live. Thence come the final chants, the chants
> Of the brooder seeking the acutest end
> Of speech: to pierce the heart's residuum
> And there to find music for a single line,
> Equal to memory, one line which
> The vital music formulates the words.
>
> Behold the men in helmets borne on steel,
> Discolored, how they are going to defeat.
> (CP, 259)

Though Stevens may wish at times to "pierce" it, the "heart's residuum" is much like Derrida's "*supplément*"; that is, it is both " 'an addition' and 'a substitute' " which prevents and postpones the certainty of meaning. It is also like Derrida's "*remainder* which is added to the subsequent text and which cannot be completely summed up within it."[24] As Stevens says in "Notes toward a Supreme Fiction," "It knows that what it has is what is not" (CP, 382). If this seems contradictory, it is no more so than a "belief" in what is known to be a fiction.

Perhaps a more telling absence than the loss of belief in the modern age (more telling because, unlike "belief," it remains unspoken) is the absence in Stevens' work of the largest "sign" of destruction in his world—the atomic bomb. Despite its catastrophic violence, Stevens rarely refers to it in his prose or his poetry. I can find only two instances in which Stevens explicitly mentions the atomic bomb.[25] The

---

[24] See *Dissemination*, pp. xiii, 9.

[25] See *L*, 620, 839: "I cannot say that there is any way to adapt myself to the idea that I am living in the Atomic Age and I think it a lot of nonsense to try to adapt oneself to such a thing." (Even in this in-

absence of such an extremely violent object is a mark of the "too heavy" presence (such as Bloom envisions as a source for poetry) that Stevens attempts to overcome in the act of de-scribing or re-marking the violence of reality through and in his poems. We can say, then, of language used for this purpose what Stevens says of the imagination; that it "consumes and exhausts some element of reality" (*OP*, 173).

In summary, it is possible to say that real war obviously "weighs" on Stevens, dictating for him a war between the world and the imagination, even a war within language itself. In this respect the following lines from "Man and Bottle," written in 1940, are particularly suggestive:

> It [the mind] has to content the reason
>   concerning war,
> It has to persuade that war is part of itself,
> A manner of thinking, a mode
> Of destroying, as the mind destroys,
>
> An aversion, as the world is averted
> From an old delusion. . . .
>   (*CP*, 239)

We can see evidence of such a war in the most famous of Stevens' passages in which the soldier appears, the unnumbered "coda" that concludes "Notes Toward a Supreme Fiction":[26]

---

stance, Stevens seems to suppress his reaction to the atomic bomb.) Consider a similar observation made by Samuel French Morse: "The first edition of *Harmonium* suppressed any reference to the war" (*Wallace Stevens: Poetry as Life* [Indianapolis: Pegasus, 1970], p. 145).

[26] In reference to some of Stevens' shorter poems, Doggett says that it is "typical of Stevens' mode of composition that after presenting his ideas . . . he concludes the poem with an expository passage that explains" what had preceded it (*Making of the Poem*, p. 74). We can apply the same principle to Stevens' longer poems, so that the unnumbered passage which concludes "Notes toward a Supreme Fiction" should be particularly important, offering a sort of summary and explanation of the entire poem. (I am calling such a passage a "coda.")

CHAPTER THREE

> Soldier, there is a war between the mind
> And sky, between thought and day and night. It is
> For that the poet is always in the sun. . . .
> . . . .
> It is a war that never ends.
>
> Yet it depends on yours. The two are one.
> . . . .
> Monsieur and comrade,
> The soldier is poor without the poet's lines,
>
> His petty syllabi, the sounds that stick,
> Inevitably modulating, in the blood.
> And war for war, each has its gallant kind.
> (*CP*, 407)

It is easy to understand why Stevens needed to entertain the possibility that the "world of words" (*CP*, 345) could resist or evade the "pressure of reality" when we consider the violent atmosphere during Stevens' life. It is, however, a view of language that Stevens probably would have entertained even without those violent conditions.

Stevens' need for language to defend against the contemporaneous "pressure of reality" is much like his need for poetry to displace belief, rather than fill the void of its loss, when belief takes the form of *dogma*: "Loss of faith," he says, "is growth" (*OP*, 172). Although he says, "I do seek a centre and expect to go on seeking it" (*L*, 584), the emphasis is on the seeking, not on a static belief. As he insists to Bernard Heringman, "I have no wish to arrive at a conclusion" (*L*, 710). We know from such poems as "Sunday Morning" that a static "centre," presented in the form of eternity, is more deadly than death, presented there as a form of change. Similarly, Stevens feels the need for "*seasons* of belief" (italics mine), for belief is found for him in the seeking, in the questioning, in that which engages the mind, not in doctrine or dogma that ceases to be thought about. As he writes in a letter to Sister M. Bernetta Quinn, "I have been fitted into too many philosophic frames. As a philosopher one is expected to achieve and express one's center . . . and it is poetry that I want to write" (*L*, 753). So, even though Stevens insists that "there must be a certain amount of didactic poetry, or a certain amount of didacticism in poetry" (*L*, 302-3), Helen Vendler is quite right to complain when "what was a diffident suggestion in the poetry becomes . . . 'doctrine' . . . in the hands of his critics."[27]

We can see the attempt to disrupt dogma in "A High-toned Old Christian Woman." In that poem Stevens does not attempt to replace the old woman's dogmatic views of "the moral law" with any others. Instead, he wishes to shock the old woman with the "opposing law" in order to keep the fictions alive and "winking": "This will make widows wince. But fictive things / Wink as they will. Wink most when widows wince" (*CP*, 59). Similarly, "The Latest Freed Man" is the man who can escape the "doctrine" of "this landscape" (even if in that poem "freedom" is also an escape from language, or "being without description" [*CP*, 204-5]).

In contrast to the deadening stasis of dogma, movement in thought, and therefore fiction, keeps belief alive. As a result, ironically it is possible for the "law of chaos" to engender "seasons of belief," and it is possible for Stevens to say in "Someone Puts a Pineapple Together" that "The incredible gave him a purpose to believe" (*NA*, 85). Similarly, Stevens concludes "Flyer's Fall," the short poem about the man who "escaped the dirty fates," with the statement that "We believe without belief, beyond belief" (*CP*, 336).

In terms of his own life, the account given by his daughter in *Souvenirs and Prophecies* indicates the intensity with which Stevens at times needed to shun the external world and to create a world in words. As Holly Stevens points out, with an excerpt from one of Stevens' letters, " 'At home, our house was rather a curious place, with all of us in different parts of it, reading.' " She explains that her father had been

---

[27] Vendler, "Qualified Assertions," p. 163.

CHAPTER THREE

raised in a family in which his father remained consistently aloof, even from the children. As an illustration, she cites Stevens' letter describing his own father: " 'The greater part of his life was spent at the office; he wanted quiet and, in that quiet, to create a life of his own,' " and concludes that "If that was true of my grandfather . . . it certainly was true of my father and of our house as I grew up; we held off from each other—one might say that my father lived alone."[28]

These personal notes point to at least part of the negative extension of the possibility that language can distance the world: that isolation is inherent in the replacement and displacement of the world with words. In a late and poignant poem, "As You Leave the Room," Stevens considers this negative extension and asks whether living so much in a world of language has been worth what he has lost by doing so: "I wonder, have I lived a skeleton's life, / As a disbeliever in reality, // A countryman of all the bones in the world?" (*OP*, 117). This poem corresponds in thought, though not in tone, to a letter written to José Rodríguez Feo in 1948:

> Pehaps I am beginning to think permanently, and without regard to the weather, that one gets nowhere by reading. . . . Is not a meditation after soup of more consequence than reading a chapter of a novel before dinner? (*L*, 599)

Nevertheless, much of the time, as his own poetry testifies, Stevens needed that "quiet place" created by language in which to "live his life." This accounts, I think, for that fact that so little of the "real world" and so very little of his private life are revealed in his poetry. Thus, although Stevens

---

[28] Holly Stevens, *Souvenirs and Prophecies: The Young Wallace Stevens* (New York: Knopf, 1977), p. 4. Stanley Kunitz suggests something of this isolation in the chapter "The Vice-President of Insurance" in his *A Kind of Order, A Kind of Folly* (Boston: Atlantic, Little, Brown, 1975): "Wallace Stevens was so fine and rare a poet, such a dazzling virtuoso on the keyboard of language, that he became one with his instrument: the man disappeared" (p. 233).

at times might desire to be free from words, might desire the "freedom" of "being without description," he also desired the freedom that words gave him from the "pressure of reality," even in his own home. As he says in "The Man with the Blue Guitar":

> Poetry is the subject of the poem,
> From this the poem issues and
>
> To this returns. Between the two,
> Between issue and return, there is
>
> An absence in reality,
> Things as they are. Or so we say.
> (*CP*, 176)

This is the possibility. Instead of a desire for language to achieve an "agreement with reality" (*NA*, 54), implying, again, an immediacy central to a unitive poetics, these various needs give rise to a desire for language to defend against reality, displace the world, unsettle belief, all of which imply a rupture inherent in a mediating or a disjunctive poetics. Language becomes, then, for Stevens a way of evading the very "centre" that was sought.

The Possibility

Sometimes Stevens sees language as an "evasion" of, or "resistance" to, reality. Sometimes he conceives of it as the means for avoiding a "doctrine" or a "definition" and keeping "it . . . unfixed" (*NA*, 34). At other times, he uses it as an ironic way of establishing identity by removing existing fictions. In reference to "An Ordinary Evening in New Haven," for example, Stevens writes, "It is not a question of grim reality but of plain reality. The object is of course to purge oneself of anything false" (*L*, 636). Language which achieves these ends demands a possibility that we are calling

CHAPTER THREE

fragmentation, the common denominator being that language avoids union.

Although the possibility that language can divide from, and even annihilate, being[29] may imply a metamorphosis or conversion of reality, at times this movement is seen more clearly as a radical departure, even an erasure of reality. Mr. Homburg, for example, has the idea "To think away the grass, the trees, the clouds, / Not to transform them into other things" (*CP*, 517). Although in that poem Stevens ironically refers to it as one of "the more irritating minor ideas," such an idea is clearly in the Augustinian mode. Ultimately, however, language as fragmentation can be an opening of the abyss, a recognition that by the "repetition" inherent in language, it "comes to bear / A meaning without a meaning." Thus, this second possibility of language implies a disjunctive poetics that is in essence a mediation, at best a metamorphosis, and an infinite deferral *in potentia*.

We have already seen such *fragmentation* perceived as necessary, "Required, as a necessity requires" (*CP*, 503). If there were absolute unity, if "this end and this beginning" were "one" (*CP*, 506), there would be no gap, no time or space in which to articulate or elaborate. As Derrida says, the "differance" is necessary for elaboration. For the same reason Georges Poulet says that if all is joined, "Nothing any longer subsists but a moment and an indefinite perpetual place, horrible *soil*, in which one is *caught*—caught in a 'dreadful sensation of eternity.' "[30] Stevens says much the same thing far more eloquently in "Somnambulisma": "Without this bird that never settles," without this bird that "thinks of settling, yet never settles," we would have "a geography of the dead" (*CP*, 304). Language, like the bird,

---

[29] This is the negative aspect of the "second theory" of poetry that Miller describes in "Theoretical and Atheoretical", i.e., that "the *logos* captured in language" is "the annihilation of the *logos* as the hidden one" (p. 277).

[30] Poulet, p. 255.

FRAGMENTATION

must not settle: it must be able to separate from the One in order to create, ironically, the "chaos" of uncertainty and questioning that in turn allows "seasons of belief."

Even the "theory of poetry" (*NA*, vii), Stevens insists, must not ultimately be defined: "I am evading a definition. If it is defined, it will be fixed and it must not be fixed. . . . To fix it is to put an end to it. Let me show it to you unfixed" (*NA*, 34). Similarly, in "Banjo Boomer," Stevens asks for "nothing fixed by a single word" (*OP*, 114).

In a particularly subtle way, Stevens exhibits the corresponding disjunctive poetics in the poem, "Add This to Rhetoric":

> It is posed and it is posed.
> But in nature it merely grows.
> Stones pose in the falling night;
> And beggars dropping to sleep,
> They pose themselves and their rags.
> Shucks . . . lavender moonlight falls.
> The buildings pose in the sky
> And, as you paint, the clouds,
> Grisaille, impearled, profound,
> Pftt. . . . In the way you speak
> You arrange, the thing is posed,
> What in nature merely grows.
>
> To-morrow when the sun,
> For all your images,
> Comes up as the sun, bull fire,
> Your images will have left
> No shadow of themselves.
> The poses of speech, of paint,
> Of music—Her body lies
> Worn out, her arm falls down,
> Her fingers touch the ground.
> Above her, to the left,
> A brush of white, the obscure,
> The moon without a shape,

CHAPTER THREE

> A fringed eye in a crypt.
> The sense creates the pose.
> In this it moves and speaks.
> This is the figure and not
> An evading metaphor.
>
> Add this. It is to add.
> (*CP*, 198-99)

Initially this poem appears to prefer reality (the sun not altered by language, but simply the sun or "What in nature merely grows") to the somewhat irritating and disappointing "evasion" of the "way you speak." (The irritation is signalled by "Shucks" and "Pftt," which interrupt the rhetoric.) However, the poem then enacts the evasions language makes (and marks), even when it says that it is "not / An evading metaphor." The sun, for example, is never the sun, but "bull fire," and the woman, never a woman, but a "pose." The poem illustrates that "In the way you speak / You arrange, the thing is posed."

The last three lines, however, complicate the meaning of the poem even more. The self-reference of the word "This" engenders a self-consciousness in the poem, in language, that distances meaning and complicates the ambiguity.[31] Even the word "figure" implies a representation and, therefore, is not the "thing itself"; so that even by saying, "This is the figure and not / An evading metaphor," Stevens calls attention to a disjunction that *is* an "evading metaphor." As

---

[31] As Owen Barfield says, "As consciousness develops into self-consciousness, the remembered phenomena become detached or liberated from their originals and so, as images, are in some measure at man's disposal" (*Saving the Appearances: A Study in Idolatry* [New York: Harcourt, n.d.] pp. 126-27). So, too, when the language of a poem becomes self-conscious, its own words become detached and the things to which it refers are in some measure at the poem's disposal. Such a situation is potentially an infinite regress and is precisely the situation of the "sign" (or of language) as Derrida explains it.

the poem illustrates, language can never coincide with nature.

Ultimately, when Stevens says, "Add this. It is to add" (and remember that the title is "Add This to Rhetoric," when "this" is a piece of finely ironic rhetoric), Stevens' language calls attention to the fact that not only can language never coincide with nature, it can never coincide with itself. For a number of reasons, then, Stevens entertains the possibility that language can displace the world: "The great poem is the disengaging of (a) reality" (*OP*, 169). In the following excerpt from a letter to Rodríguez Feo, Stevens declares his need for language to displace the world and to defend against reality:

> It is like changing records on a gramophone to speak of the red and the almost artificial green of mango skins and then speak of blue and white Munich. But unless we do these things to reality, the damned thing closes in [on] us, walls us up and buries us alive. (*L*, 599)

The potentially irrevocable divorce between language and the world is apparent again in one of the later essays in *The Necessary Angel*. Stevens writes that "The constant discussion of imagination and reality is largely a discussion not for the purposes of life but for the purposes of arts and letters. . . . In life what is important is the truth as it is, while in arts and letters what is important is the truth as we see it" (*NA*, 147). In its own escalating self-consciousness, the "truth" inscribed in letters and art is much like Derrida's "supplément," an addition and a substitute for the text that cannot be summed up within it:

> For it is in the essence of language to be capable of origination, but of never achieving the absolute identity with itself that exists in the natural object. Poetic language can do nothing but originate anew over and over again: it is always . . . able to posit . . . but . . . unable to give a foundation to what it posits except as an intent

CHAPTER THREE

of consciousness. The word is always a free presence to the mind, the means by which the permanence of natural entities can be put into question and thus negated, time and time again, in the endlessly widening spiral of the dialectic.[32]

In positive terms, language is the means by which the mind attains the freedom desired in "Farewell to Florida" and by which the mind defends itself against the world. "The positive name . . . of this process is freedom," according to Paul de Man, who also maintains that language "remains unique in being the only entity by means of which it can differentiate itself from the world."[33] Such "differentiation," which contains the potential for irrevocable divorce, is necessary for self-consciousness and for the elaboration of language itself. As Stevens says in "To the One of Fictive Music":

> Yet not too like, yet not so like to be
> Too near, too clear, saving a little to endow
> Our feigning with the strange unlike, whence springs
> The difference that heavenly pity brings.
> (CP, 88)

Just how "difference" is a principle of language is explained in "Description without Place." In this poem Stevens raises the possibility that language (in the form of description) can be

> an expectation, a desire,
> A palm that rises up beyond the sea,
>
> A little different from reality:
> The difference that we make in what we see
>
> And our memorials of that difference. . . .
> . . . .

---

[32] De Man, "Intentional Structure," p. 69.
[33] De Man, "Rhetoric of Temporality," pp. 202, 196.

> The future is description, without place,
> The categorical predicate, the arc.
> (*CP*, 344)

Compared to "The Idea of Order at Key West," in which language in the form of song creates itself, the world, and the place and makes them "acutest," the preceding lines illustrate the fragmenting potential of language. The poetics implied is, in fact, a de-scription, an un-writing of the first poetics we explored. These lines invite and anticipate a deconstructive reading, an unfolding of the gap inscribed within the text, such as found in some of the more recent discussions already mentioned.

Put in mathematical symbols, the appropriate description of this model of language is $X \neq Y$. As the slashed line visually suggests, unity is broken by language as it speaks itself; that is to say, language is divided from itself in the gap between the signifier and signified. The break can be conceived of as a function of a two-part predication (as opposed to the three-part predication of metaphor) which divides subject from object, word from act, being from motion. In many of his poems Stevens entertains the possibility of such a "breaking" in all language, whether or not a negating word such as "not," "never," or "no" appears. But since the model, "X does *not* equal Y," describes a particular characteristic intrinsic to all language, it will be convenient to examine Stevens' use of negations.

One of the basic strategies of Stevens' "evasion" or describing is the use of negatives as a distancing device. This device appears in his poetry from the 1921 poem, "The Snow Man," who "beholds / Nothing that is not there and the nothing that is" (*CP*, 10),[34] to the 1954 poem, "A Clear

---

[34] Here is a place where Stevens' letters do not support my point since Stevens says that "The Snow Man" is "an example of the necessity of identifying oneself with reality in order to understand it and enjoy it" (*L*, 464). It is hard for me to picture the man with the "mind of winter" enjoying reality. The situation created in that poem seems

CHAPTER THREE

Day and No Memories," in which there are "No soldiers" and "No thoughts" and

> the air is clear of everything.
> It has no knowledge except of nothingness
> And it flows over us without meanings,
> As if none of us had ever been here before
> And are not now. . . .
> (*PM*, 397)

Stevens uses the word "not" so often that Thomas F. Walsh omits the word entirely from his *Concordance to the Poetry of Wallace Stevens*. For the same reason, Walsh omits the word "no" unless that word is used specifically as the opposite of "yes"; used in such a manner, "no" appears in 19 lines of Stevens' poetry. With regard to other forms of negations, we find that "none" appears in 12 lines of his poetry; "nowhere," in 9 lines; "nothingness," in 23 lines; "nothing," in 135 lines; and "never," in 137 lines.

The most "positive" aspects of negations are discussed by Kenneth Burke in *Language as Symbolic Action*: "There is an implied sense of negativity in the ability to use words at all. For to use them properly, we must know that they are *not* the things they stand for." Burke locates the "specific nature of language in the ability to use the Negative" since, as he says, nothing in nature is negative: "A ditch is as positive as a dyke, though each might be classed as a 'negation' of the other." Moreover, "Implied in the use of the negative, there is both the ability to generalize and the ability to specify."[35] The possibility suggested here is that negation ironically contains the "ability to specify" and that by purging "oneself of anything false," negation is a way of establishing identity.

---

more like the situation that de Man says is typical of Romantic and Victorian writers in which "the priority of nature is experienced as a feeling of failure and sterility" ("Intentional Structure," p. 72).

[35] Kenneth Burke, *Language as Symbolic Action* (Berkeley: University of California Press, 1966), pp. 12, 419-20, 425.

FRAGMENTATION

So, Stevens can say at the conclusion of "The Lack of Repose" that "Not yet to have written a book . . . is good, is a good" (*CP*, 303). At the same time there is the possibility that language conceived as negation, fragmentation, or as a distancing device prevents the possibility of union by unfixing or de-scribing itself.

Even though language as fragmentation does not depend upon the presence of negative words, these rather complex ideas can be seen in "Landscape with Boat," a poem laced with negative words:

> It was not as if truth lay where he thought,
> Like a phantom, in an uncreated night.
> It was easier to think it lay there. If
> It was nowhere else, it was there and because
> It was nowhere else, its place had to be supposed,
> Itself had to be supposed, a thing supposed
> In a place supposed, a thing that he reached
> In a place that he reached, by rejecting what he saw
> And denying what he heard. He would arrive.
> He had only not to live, to walk in the dark,
> To be projected by one void into
> Another.
> . . . .
> . . . He received what he denied.
> (*CP*, 242)

The most obvious fragmentation of unity or being occurs in the tenth line of this excerpt: "He had only not to live." The word "not" gramatically and semantically separates the "he" (who is "supposing" throughout) from "to live." For our purposes, the "not" then is especially appropriate for showing how language fragments being by parceling, dividing, deferring, even evading—a fact which is explored in the poem as the "he" becomes farther and farther removed from the "truth" or from "life" as the language spins out its supposi-

CHAPTER THREE

tions. As the poem says, ultimately this projection is a "void."³⁶

To a large degree, this "void" is "created" ("decreated," Roy Harvey Pearce would say)³⁷ by the negatives in the poem: "not," "uncreated," "nowhere," and "not." Such fragmenting, however, is also the necessary process for seeking the "truth" since an identity of words, thought, and being would preclude the reflection necessary for thought or language. Thus, like the negations in this poem, the words "rejecting" and "denying" call attention to the necessary division of the "he" from "truth" which occurs in the act of language—a division ironically necessary in order to "know" whatever "fiction" may be perceived as truth. "Rejecting" and "denying" consequently mean "supposing," but paradoxically they also mean "receiving." Division is ironically the only possible arrival: "He would arrive . . . He received what he denied."

Between the future/subjunctive tense of "would" and the past tense of "received" is the point of presence or truth which, as the deconstructionists would agree, cannot be presented or represented in the poem and which can be known only through deferral (which may be figured as repetition). The poem neatly enacts its own repetitions:

> It was nowhere else
> It was nowhere else

---

³⁶ Compare the situation in this poem to what Georges Poulet says of Mallarmé: "For I can affirm the existence of that which does not exist only by withdrawing existence from all that which does exist. In order to make my dream exist, I abolish the world. . . . That which denied [the external world] is denied. What was denied [the internal world] is attested. In order to create his dream, the poet has proceeded as if he were God. He has first created nothingness" (pp. 268-69).

³⁷ Roy Harvey Pearce, "Toward Decreation: Stevens and the 'Theory of Poetry,'" in Doggett and Buttel, eds., *Celebration*, pp. 286-307.

FRAGMENTATION

>   In a place
>   In a place

and substitutions;

>   its place had to be supposed,
>   Itself had to be supposed
>   a thing supposed
>   In a place supposed.

Such "differing" occurs as well in the comparative "easier" and the conditional "If," both of which a-void the "thing itself."

As the words "easier" and "if" suggest, this fragmenting tendency is not restricted to "negatives," but is a tendency of all language. One of Stevens' letters to José Rodríguez Feo is particularly useful in clarifying this point: "Are you visiting some new scene? A young man in a new scene, a new man in a young scene, a young man in a young scene—excuse my guitar" (L, 767). Since this letter is written to a particular person, it is easy to assume that in the first sentence Stevens is actually asking Rodríguez Feo if he is visiting some new place: the language would seem to bear some sort of relation to reality. The second phrase, "A young man in a new scene," still appears to have a relation to the world; it is as if Stevens is still referring to Rodríguez Feo, but is now considering him from the perspective of a third person narrator—as a "young man" instead of "you." Nevertheless, already language has made a somewhat startling switch in the situation: in the second sentence the man is not "visiting" a scene but is "in" the scene. Rapidly the "man" becomes no man, only a sign inscribed in the text and described by substitution and repetition. In a sense, the man is "in" the language; and by the time "a young man in a young scene" appears in the letter, it is obvious that the language has no direct relation to reality. Again, language is revealed to be something "Which, by its repetition, comes to bear / A meaning *without a meaning*" (italics mine) or, to use

CHAPTER THREE

Georges Poulet's phrase, "a processus of indetermination."[38]

Another strategy that Stevens uses for evading a definition and leaving his theory "unfixed" is to contradict (that is, contra-dict) his own corpus. For example, having emphatically made the "sound of the guitar" the means by which we know "things as they are" in "The Man with the Blue Guitar," Stevens says in a later poem that "The sounds of the guitar // Were not and are not. Absurd. The words spoken / Were not and are not. It is not to be believed" (*CP*, 525). Rather than being the voice of disillusionment, these lines from "The Rock" voice a counter-poetics of mediation that is deliberately raised as a possibility, ironically, in order to keep the poetry immediate. It is appropriate, then, that in "Banjo Boomer" Stevens plays an "instrument" different from the guitar he had played when playing a different poetics:

> The mulberry is a double tree.
> Mulberry, shade me, shade me awhile.
>
> A white, pink, purple berry tree.
> A very dark-leaved berry tree.
> Mulberry, shade me, shade me awhile.
>
> A churchyard kind of bush as well,
> A silent sort of bush, as well.
> Mulberry, shade me, shade me awhile.
>
> It is a shape of life described
> By another shape without a word.
> Mulberry, shade me, shade me awhile—
>
> With nothing fixed by a single word.
> Mulberry, shade me, shade me awhile.
> (*OP*, 114)

[38] Georges Poulet, *The Metamorphosis of the Circle*, tr. Carley Dawson and Elliott Coleman (Baltimore: Johns Hopkins University Press, 1966), p. 259.

Rather than being the "thing itself," in this poem "life" is merely "a shape of life," created by shadows and described, ironically, without words and by another shape. Like Plato's shadows in the cave, the shadow of the mulberry's shade is the closest we can get to this shape of life. Deferred by words and shadows, the shape is alive only insofar as it is not "fixed by a single word," just as Plato's Forms cannot be approached directly, but only through deferment.[39] The mulberry is from this perspective a figure for language itself, or at least one aspect of language with which Stevens is concerned. It illustrates the poetics of "differance," that is, language as division and deferral.

This unfixing or unsettling is a fragmenting of the kind of unity evoked in Chapter Two, and informs the strategy of such poems as "Contrary Theses, I and II," "Study of Images, I and II," "Thirteen Ways of Looking at a Blackbird," "Two Versions of the Same Poem," and "Two Illustrations That the World Is What You Make of It." This last poem ends appropriately (and ambiguously) enough with the lines: "But his mastery // Left only the fragments found in the grass, / From his project, as finally magnified" (*CP*, 515).

The Extension

The "fragments . . . as finally magnified" suggest the rather metaphysical extensions of this use of language. As already implied, there is a pathos and even a potential abyss in "fragments" (or fragmentation). But the phrase "as finally magnified" suggests that something positive occurs in this fragmentation. Among the positive possibilities of this use of language is the ability to evade a definition, to keep it unfixed since "negations are never final" (*CP*, 414). In addition, a positive possibility of this use of language is, paradoxically, establishing identity indirectly and ironically, by

[39] Plato, *The Republic*, ed. Edith Hamilton and Huntington Cairns (Princeton: Princeton University Press, 1961), Book VII.

CHAPTER THREE

separating what is fragmented or negated from the amorphous unity. So Mrs. Uruguay says: " 'I have said no / To everything, in order to get at myself' " (*CP*, 249).

As already noted, this possibility was recognized, positively, by the twelfth-century French nominalists (such as Abelard) and received negatively by their opponents, the realists. For Abelard, the dissection of the world through language in the form of dialectic as well as the dissection of language itself by his concepts of universals was a way to know, to gain knowledge, and thereby eventually to return to the Word in the form of Truth. He deemed this searching necessary, much as Stevens insists on "seeking," and rejected the simple correlation between words and things or between words and the Logos that the realists wanted to uphold.

The postitive name for this quest through language is, as we have seen, freedom. As such, it is very much like Kierkegaard's insistence upon a radical difference between the Creator and created or between the individual and such unity as Hegel envisioned. Thus, as Stevens says to Henry Church, even the "Supreme Fiction" depends upon the negation of other fictions so that it stands out clearly and individually in a sort of pristine originality achieved by fragmentation, although it is an "originality" still recognized as a "fiction": "The first step toward a supreme fiction would be to get rid of all existing fictions. A thing stands out in clear air better than it does in soot" (*L*, 431). Thus, "Farewell to Florida" calls for the freedom of the violent mind that can clear itself of the "soot" engendered by the words of previous poems. Or, as Stevens says when he "begins" "Notes toward a Supreme Fiction" (while knowing it is a fiction to "begin"):

> Begin, ephebe, by perceiving the idea
> Of this invention, this invented world,
> The inconceivable idea of the sun.
> . . . .
>
> Phoebus is dead, ephebe. But Phoebus was

> A name for something that never could be named.
> There was a project for the sun and is.
>
> There is a project for the sun. The sun
> Must bear no name, gold flourisher, but be
> In the difficulty of what it is to be.
> (*CP*, 380-81)

If the "thing itself" cannot be spoken directly without fixing it and if fragmenting is a form of establishing identity indirectly, the ultimate extension of this use of language is to speak that which "we do not speak" (*CP*, 311), to utter a "name for something that never could be named."

Several recent studies have addressed themselves precisely to this point, that is, Stevens' speaking of the unspeakable.[40] As a strategy, it has parallels with those of other writers who pre-date the deconstructionists. For example, Bernard de Clairvaux felt that humility could not be directly addressed; consequently, in *The Twelve Steps of Humility* he counts the steps of humility by recounting, in reverse order, their opposite—the twelve steps of pride.[41] Similarly, Flannery O'Connor, who intends that her rather gruesome stories show the operation of Grace, feels that grace itself cannot be shown, except by its opposite: "It's almost impossible to write about supernatural Grace in fiction. We almost have to approach it negatively."[42] Like Stevens, these writers employ strategies for speaking that which "we do not speak" and "uttering a name for something that never could be named."

But, as Stevens himself recognizes, the very separation between language and the world that makes such a strategy

---

[40] See Regeuiro, p. 148; MacCaffrey, "Ways of Truth", Miller, "Stevens' Rock"; Riddel, "Metaphoric Staging"; and Bloom, *Poems of Our Climate*.

[41] Bernard de Clairvaux, St., *The Steps of Humility and Pride*, in *Treatises II*, vol. 5 of *The Works of Bernard de Clairvaux* (Washington, D.C.: Cistercian Publications Consortium Press, 1974).

[42] Flannery O'Connor, *The Habit of Being*, ed. Sally Fitzgerald (New York: Farrar, Straus & Giroux, 1979), p. 144.

possible has, as its negative extension, the possibility of infinite regress, as in "The Bed of Old John Zeller":

> This structure of ideas, these ghostly sequences
> Of the mind, result only in disaster. It follows,
> Casual poet, that to add your own disorder to disaster
>
> Makes more of it.
> (*CP*, 326)

Although Derrida says that the "freedom" engendered by the separation and the "play" of the sign may be viewed positively, he also says it may be viewed as "catastrophe." Similarly, in reference to the "reflective disjunction" that occurs "*by means of* language," Paul de Man says that although the "positive name . . . of this process is freedom," such disjunction "engenders a temporal sequence of acts of consciousness which is endless. . . . [The] irony is not temporary . . . but repetitive, the recurrence of a self-escalating act of consciousness."[43]

The "freedom" created by language, then, is also an entrapment:

> Freedom is like a man who kills himself
> Each night, an incessant butcher, whose knife
> Grows sharp in blood.
> (*CP*, 292)

In its attempt to displace the world, defend against the pressure of reality, this "freedom" transfers meaning out of the world and in to itself alone. The negative extension of this sense of language is suggested in the following lines from "Description without Place":

> Thus the theory of description matters most.
> It is the theory of the word for those
>
> For whom the word is the making of the world,
> The buzzing world and lisping firmament.

[43] De Man, "Rhetoric of Temporality," pp. 196, 202.

> It is a world of words to the end of it,
> In which nothing solid is its solid self.
> *(CP, 345)*

With nothing solid, with no ground, language comes to be meaningless noise in a void—what the twelfth-century realists called the *flatus vocis*. Although this section of the poem ultimately valorizes language, the lines cited above point to the underlying possibility that the fragmenting process of language may transfer meaning out of the world and into the "world of words" alone.[44] In the acutest sense, it is a translation.

In summary, to perceive of language as divisive, even when used as a defense or as a strategy of expression, is potentially to open the great abyss, to become conscious of "the terror of discontinuity."[45] The effect is to usurp meaning not only out of the world, but also out of language, so that "meaning . . . can then consist only in the *repetition* . . . of a previous sign with which it can never coincide."[46] Or, as Stevens says in the conclusion to "Esthétique du Mal," meaning becomes a "dark italics" that "Speech . . . could not propound" *(CP, 326)*. The negative extension of the possibility of language as fragmentation is to leave us (and meaning) in a metaphysical void. Ultimately we can say of language what Stevens says of the mind: that it is

> the terriblest force in the world, father,
> Because, in chief, it, only, can defend
> Against itself. At its mercy, we depend

---

[44] Compare this to what de Man says of ironic language: it "splits the subject into an empirical self that exists in a state of inauthenticity and a self that exists only in the form of a language that asserts the knowledge of this inauthenticity" (ibid., p. 197). As Derrida has shown, all language (not just ironic language) is already "split," so that language itself leads to this situation.

[45] Hartman, *Wordsworth's Poetry: 1787-1814* (New Haven: Yale University Press, 1964, 1971), p. 169.

[46] De Man, "Rhetoric of Temporality," p. 190.

CHAPTER THREE

<blockquote>
Upon it.
(<i>CP</i>, 436)
</blockquote>

Like the "civil fiction" or other fictions (all of which are "evasions like a repeated phrase"), language "comes to bear / A meaning without a meaning." This is, of course, the extension that Derrida and his followers recognize and reiterate. The idea that language itself is already fragmented from itself in an endless series of signs that can never coincide with their referents leaves us potentially without any meaning and without the ground for belief in anything—even the fiction of belief or the belief in a fiction. So Stevens implies when, after saying that "What / One believes is what matters," he goes on to say that "One would be drowned in the air of difference, / Incapable of belief, in the difference" (*CP*, 258).

The Restraint

However, just as Stevens refuses to accept fully the possibility of absolute unity, so he also refuses to accept fully the possibility of absolute distance. The "Augustinian" pose—the suggestion that language *could* distance or change the world—is itself a resistance to the abyss. In addition, just as Stevens qualifies statements of belief in unity with disclaimers, so he also qualifies statements of pure fragmentation with what we might call *reclamations*, which reassert or reclaim something that the language as *fragmentation* has given up.

In "Prologues to What Is Possible," for instance, the first section of the poem reveals that the lure of language, of the "syllable without any meaning," is something which causes utter isolation and removes the man "beyond his recognizing." No wonder the "metaphor stirred his fear." But the second section of the poem, beginning with the word "unless," is a reclamation of that isolation and raises the possibility of belonging and of union:

> The metaphor stirred his fear. The object
>   with which he was compared
> Was beyond his recognizing. By this he knew
>   that likeness of him extended
> Only a little way, and not beyond, unless
>   between himself
> And things beyond resemblance there was this
>   and that intended to be recognized. . . .

The sense of communion then grows throughout the rest of the poem until "vocabulary" and "what was real" join in an act of revelation and creation:

>   . . . to which he gave
> A name and privilege over the ordinary of his
>   commonplace—
>
> A flick which added to what was real and its
>   vocabulary,
> The way some first thing coming into Northern
>   trees
> Adds to them the whole vocabulary of the South,
> The way the earliest single light in the evening
>   sky, in spring,
> Creates a fresh universe out of nothingness by
>   adding itself,
> The way a look or a touch reveals its unexpected
>   magnitudes.
>   (*CP*, 516-517)

"Adding itself" in "magnitudes" (like "fragments . . . as finally . . . magnified") is the positive possibility of "Add This to Rhetoric." The qualification which follows the word "unless" reclaims the possibility of meaning in much the same fashion that the lines "yet the absence of imagination had / Itself to be imagined" reclaims the imagination and transcends the bleak picture of the "silence of a rat come out to see" and the "blank cold" (*CP*, 502-3). As he insists, this was "Required, as a necessity requires."

Stevens engages in a different, more complex form of reclamation in "Extracts from Addresses to the Academy of Fine Ideas":

> The wind blew in the empty place.
> The winter wind blew in an empty place—
> There was that difference between the and an,
> The difference between himself and no man,
> No man that heard a wind in an empty place.
> It was time to be himself again, to see
> If the place, in spite of its witheredness, was still
> Within the difference.
> (*CP*, 255)

Such a possibility of the "difference between the and an" reclaims the nothingness of "The Snow Man" who becomes a "No man" hearing the wind in an empty place. Such lines essentially deconstruct what Pearce calls the "decreative" movement in Stevens' work, so that he can find himself again, "still / Within the difference."

The ambiguity of the word "still" points to the integrity of Stevens, who does not attempt to hide from anxiety inherent in self-consciousness. A comparison of "First Warmth" and "As You Leave the Room" is revealing here. The first poem says,

> I wonder, have I lived a skeleton's life,
> As a questioner about reality,
>
> A countryman of all the bones of the world?
> Now, here, the warmth I had forgotten becomes
>
> Part of the major reality, part of
> An appreciation of a reality;
>
> And thus an elevation, as if I lived
> With something I could touch, touch every way.
> (*OP*, 89-90)

FRAGMENTATION

The second poem begins with four allusions to earlier poems, including the "one / About the mind as never satisfied" and says that these "are not what skeletons think about." The poem then continues with, "I wonder, have I lived a skeleton's life, / As a disbeliever in reality." Although Stevens undercuts the despairing tone by saying that skeletons do not think about the poems he has written, including the one about the "mind as never satisfied," he also increases the despairing tone by changing "questioner about reality" to "disbeliever." Similarly, the "warmth I had forgotten" in the first poem is replaced by the "snow I had forgotten" in the second poem. And, whereas the concluding lines of the first poem raise the possibility that he is now living in touch with an original warmth, the second one undercuts that possibility by adding that "Nothing has been changed" (by the poem) "except what is / Unreal." However, the following clause, "as if nothing had been changed at all" (OP, 117), further complicates the ambiguity and raises the possibility that something has been changed by and in the language. This complication is, of course, one of the things that makes the second poem superior to the first. The other is the depth created by the ruthless question the second poem asks: whether living in poems has not been a kind of death. However, the restraint has been an inherent part of the poem since the opening lines, in which Stevens quietly reminds us that skeletons do not think. Ultimately, the poem reclaims something of the "finally human" despite its ruthless questioning.

Kenneth Burke says that

> however important to us is the tiny sliver of reality each of us has experienced firsthand, the whole overall "picture" is but a construct of our symbol systems. To meditate on this fact until one sees its full implications is much like peering over the edge of things into an ultimate abyss. And doubtless that's one reason why,

though man is tyically the symbol-using animal, he clings to a kind of naive verbal realism. . . .[47]

As we have seen, Stevens does not attempt to cling to a naive verbal realism. But if he is not a naive realist, neither is he a naive nominalist; he recognizes the positive and negative extensions of both ways of thinking about language. In this respect, Coleridge will offer a final point of comparison.

In the early chapters of the *Biographia Literaria*, Coleridge evolves a philosophy based on a rather Manichean set of dichotomies. His stated desire is for union with the "*one & invisible*,"[48] but the philosophy he has evolved precludes this and leaves him trapped in the gulf created by and between his own divisions. In what de Man calls a "defensive strategy that tries to hide from this negative self-knowledge,"[49] Coleridge introduces a fictitious letter which he claims a friend sent (and which Coleridge wrote himself) that asks Coleridge to omit the rest of his philosophical treatise from the *Biographia Literaria*:

> *I do not hesitate a moment in advising and urging you to withdraw the Chapter from the present work, and to reserve it for your announced treatise on the Logos or communicative intellect in Man and Deity. . . . You have been obliged to omit so many links from the necessity of compression, that what remains looks . . . like the fragments of the winding steps of an old ruined tower. . . . Be assured, if you do publish this chapter in*

[47] Burke, p. 5.

[48] Coleridge, letter to John Thelwall, 14 October 1797, in *English Romantic Writers*, ed. David Perkins (New York: Harcourt, Brace & World, 1967), p. 523. Note also the following statement from the *Biographia*: "But if we elevate our conception to the absolute self, the great eternal I Am, then the principle of being, and of knowledge, of idea, and of reality, the ground of existence, and the ground of the knowledge of existence, are absolutely identical" (p. 152).

[49] De Man, "Rhetoric of Temporality," p. 191. (Here de Man is referring to Coleridge and other Romantic poets.)

the present work, you will be reminded of Bishop Berkeley's Siris, *announced as an* Essay on Tar-Water, *which beginning with Tar ends with the Trinity, the omne scibile forming the interspace. I say in the present work. In that greater work to which you have devoted so many years, and study so intense and various, it will be in its proper place.*

Immediately after the passage above, Coleridge inserts the "main result" of the unfinished treatise, proclaiming the imagination as the "infinite I AM."[50] The "letter" is an attempt to hide the gap between the philosophy of dichotomies and the desire for a theory of unity.[51] Stevens, however, does not attempt to hide (from) that gap; rather, he explores it throughout his poetry—in part through the reclamations of fragmentation and disclaimers of the belief in metaphor which keep both vibrating in their possibilities.

[50] Coleridge, *Biographia*, pp. 166, 167.
[51] Consider what Poulet has to say about such a situation: "Coleridge is not unaware of the grave dangers which are implied by an illimitable expansion of thought. A thought without boundaries is, in effect, a thought without coherence" (*Metamorphosis of the Circle*, p. 105). Coleridge, as we have seen, badly wants coherence; hence his definition of the Imagination.

CHAPTER FOUR

SIMILE

> It is as if in a human dignity
> Two parallels become one, a perspective, of which
> Men are part both in the inch and in the mile.
> *(CP, 508)*

> It is like a new account of everything old.
> *(CP, 529)*

> It was like
> A new knowledge of reality.
> *(CP, 534)*

IN 1940 STEVENS wrote an important series of letters to Hi Simons in which he provided glosses for several of his poems. In relation to this study, Stevens' gloss on the eleventh section of "The Man with the Blue Guitar" is of particular interest:

> The chord destroys its elements by uniting them in the chord. They then cease to exist separately. On the other hand, discord exaggerates the separation between its elements. . . . As between reality and the imagination, we look forward to an era when there will exist the supreme balance between these two, with which we are all concerned. The idea can be extended socially, but this is not what is intended. It can also be extended in philosophy, but, again, this is not what is intended. *(L, 363)*

SIMILE

The idea can also be extended in terms of language, which perhaps is intended, given the context of a poem so obviously concerned with language and what it creates (rather than with music or a guitar). The "chord," then, corresponds to the process of language that we have examined under the rubric *metaphor*: in its movement toward unity, the "chord" destroys its individual elements. As we have seen, the loss of distinction is the negative extension of the movement toward unity in *metaphor*. The "discord" corresponds to that process of language we have termed *fragmentation*: in its divisive movement it exaggerates the separation between the elements, potentially annihilating any relation between them in the difference. As Stevens clarifies in the letter above, neither the "chord" nor the "discord" alone will suffice; rather, what is needed is a "supreme balance." So, despite what seems to be a slight preference for "discord" (since the poem says, "It is the chord that falsifies," whereas "The discord merely magnifies" [*CP*, 171]), Stevens still desires a balance between language as fragmentation and language as metaphor, as well as between the imagination and reality. It is this desire for a "balance" that causes him to place the "restraints" on both processes of language that we have examined thus far.

In "The Man with the Blue Guitar" the speaker further clarifies that the "balance" cannot be static, that it must "not quite rest":

> So it is to sit and to balance things
> To and to and to the point of still,
>
> To say of one mask it is like,
> To say of another it is like,
>
> To know that the balance does not quite rest,
> That the mask is strange, however like.
>   (*CP*, 181)

CHAPTER FOUR

He does not desire a "supreme balance" so perfectly balanced that it reaches "the point of still": such a point would be the kind of static perfection that he has rejected throughout his poetry. As we have seen him say in "Connoisseur of Chaos," the idea that "opposite things partake of one" is something "We cannot go back to" (*CP*, 215). But even though he does not want a perfect balance, neither does he want a complete imbalance: such a condition would be a meaningless fragmentation that we have also seen him reject. What Stevens ultimately desires is neither language as metaphor, nor language as fragmentation, not even their perfect balance, but rather a way of writing that reveals and sustains both possibilities of language at once while exposing their relation. As he also says in "Connoisseur of Chaos,"

> And yet relation appears,
> A small relation expanding like the shade
> Of a cloud on sand, a shape on the side of a hill.
> (*CP*, 215)

The Relation

In respect to this relation, the next letter that Stevens wrote to Hi Simons, dated August 27, 1940, is especially apposite:

> When I was a boy I used to think that things progressed by contrasts, that there was a law of contrasts. But this was building the world out of blocks. Afterwards I came to think more of the energizing that comes from mere interplay, interaction. Thus, the various faculties of the mind co-exist and interact, and there is as much delight in this mere co-existence as a man and a woman find in each other's company. This is rather a crude illustration, but it makes the point. Cross-reflections, modifications, counter-balances, complements, giving and taking are illimitable. They make things inter-dependent, and their inter-dependence sustains them and

gives them pleasure. While it may be the cause of other things, I am thinking of it as a source of pleasure, and therefore I repeat that there is an exquisite pleasure and harmony in these inter-relations, circuits. (*L*, 368)[1]

Defining this "relation," and yet keeping the definition "unfixed," is one of the major "projects" of Stevens' poetry. "Definitions," he insists, "are relative. The notion of absolutes is relative" (*OP*, 158).

We consequently find the possibility of this supreme, yet unresting "relation" throughout Stevens' poetry; as for example, in the concluding lines of "Study of Images II":

> As if, as if, as if the disparate halves
> Of things were waiting in a bethrothal [*sic*] known
> To none, awaiting espousal to the sound
>
> Of right joining, a music of ideas, the burning
> And breeding and bearing birth of harmony,
> The final relation, the marriage of the rest.
>   (*CP*, 464-65)

The "marriage" in this poem, like the pleasurable "co-existence" that "a man and a woman find in each other's company," is a figure for the "supreme balance" or "final relation" that Stevens ultimately desires in his poetry: as he says here, this balance is a "*sound // Of right joining.*" And whether or not such a figure is a "crude illustration," as he says in the letter above, it is one he frequently uses in his poetry to make "the point"—as he does again in 1942 in "Notes toward a Supreme Fiction":

>   Perhaps
> The truth depends on a walk around a lake,

---

[1] The last word of this letter is particularly to the point. Given the word "energizing" that appears earlier in the letter, "circuits" probably means something like electrical circuits, in which energy is created by the interaction of positive and negative poles.

CHAPTER FOUR

> A composing as the body tires, a stop
> To see hepatica, a stop to watch
> A definition growing certain and
>
> A wait within that certainty, a rest
> In the swags of pine-trees bordering the lake.
> Perhaps there are times of inherent excellence,
>
> As when the cock crows on the left and all
> Is well, incalculable balances,
> At which a kind of Swiss perfection comes
>
> And a familiar music of the machine
> Sets up its Schwärmerei, not balances
> That we achieve but balances that happen,
>
> As a man and woman meet and love forthwith.
> (*CP*, 386)

Obviously by 1940 when Stevens was writing to Hi Simons, if not by 1937 when he wrote "The Man with the Blue Guitar," Stevens was consciously creating poetry out of "modifications" and "counter-balances." But I think that we can take him seriously when he says that he had not believed in the compartmentalized "law of contrasts" since he was a boy: throughout Stevens' poetic career he remained interested in the "counter-balances" and "modifications" that two possibilities of language provide for each other. As the "restraints" discussed in Chapters Two and Three suggest, there is always in Stevens the tendency to search for a "supreme balance" between opposing desires. In fact, without the sections called "restraints," and especially without the restraints that the preceding two chapters place on each other, Chapters Two and Three could be regarded as exemplifying the "law of contrasts" that Stevens came to regard as mechanical ("building the world out of blocks"). However, ultimately Stevens is interested, in terms of language, in exposing the relationship—even the necessary relationship—between the two possibilities of language that

SIMILE

we have examined. As such, he is not a poet of doctrine or even of doctrines, but as Frank Kermode says, "a poet of thresholds."[2]

Stevens sustains the precarious thresholds of possibility through several different means, including the various types of modifications that we have called reclamations and disclaimers. However, as he suggests in his letter to Simons, he does not wish to entertain first one possibility, then another: that is merely the mechanical "law of contrasts." We may infer from the words "interplay," "interaction," "inter-dependence," and "inter-relations" that Stevens desires the simultaneous sustaining of both "poles." This is the conclusion that J. Hillis Miller also reaches when he notes that it became important for Stevens to find a way to write poetry that would avoid "a succession of wild swings to one extreme or another, giving first one limit of the truth, then the other. To escape such oscillation Stevens must find a way to write poetry which will possess simultaneously both extremes."[3]

It is particularly instructive, then, to examine two of Stevens' lesser known poems in which he is very obviously trying to create an "energy" or "interaction" between opposing elements, as the titles "Desire & the Object" and "This as Including That" may suggest. The first of these, first published in 1942, presents two possibilities for the origin of desire:

> It is curious that I should have spoken of Raël,
> When it never existed, the order
> That I desired. It could be—
>
> Curious that I should have spoken of Jaffa
> By her sexual name, saying that high marriage
> Could be, it could be.
> . . . .

---

[2] Kermode, "Dwelling Poetically in Connecticut," in Doggett and Buttel, eds., *A Celebration*, p. 265.
[3] Miller, "Poetry of Being," p. 89.

CHAPTER FOUR

> Consider that I had asked
> Was it desire that created Raël
>
> Or was it Jaffa that created desire?
> The origin could have its origin.
> It could be, could be.
>
> It could be that the sun shines
> Because I desire it to shine or else
> That I desire it to shine because it shines.
> <div align="right">(<i>OP</i>, 85)</div>

In questioning the origin of desire, even the origin of "origin," this poem asks whether desire is created out of an absence in reality, demanding an "order," or a presence in reality. The possibility evoked by the "or else" and the subjunctive "could be" of the last stanza is that the "origin" may never be ascertained, but that in either case the "desire" and the "object" are joined in the "I" (the human) of the poem. Yet, if the concluding stanza seems a little flat, even a little mechanical, it is because the structure of the poem, which presents first one desire and then the other, is itself somewhat mechanical; the structure of the poem still follows the "law of contrasts" rather than sustaining the interplay of the opposing possibilities.

In "This as Including That," dated ca. 1944-1945, we see Stevens using a different approach to resolve a similar problem:[4]

> This rock and the dry birds
> Fluttering in blue leaves,
>
> This rock and the priest,
> The priest of nothingness who intones—
>
> It is true that you live on this rock
> And in it. It is wholly you.

[4] Samuel French Morse assigns this date to the poem; see *OP*, 299.

SIMILE

> It is true that there are thoughts
> That move in the air as large as air,
>
> That are almost not our own, but thoughts
> To which we are related,
>
> In an association like yours
> With the rock and mine with you.
>
> The iron settee is cold,
> A fly crawls on the balustrades.
> <div style="text-align:right">(<i>OP</i>, 88)</div>

As in "Desire & the Object," this poem attempts to describe the relation between the human (and his perceptions) and the world. Like the first poem, it offers different ways of perceiving that relationship, including the stated unity that the rock "is wholly you." The rest of the poem, however, explains that relationship in a series of complex relations that come together in the one word "like," which makes the following "relations":

> we are related to thoughts that are in the
>   air and almost not our own (which suggests that
>   they are our own)
> in an association similar to
> your association with the rock
> (in an association similar to)
> my association with you.

Despite the stated unity in the third couplet, these relations never imply identity, that "this" *is* "that." As the title announces, the nature of "relation" revealed in this poem remains "This *as* Including That." Consequently, despite the connection between "us" and thoughts, or between the person addressed and the rock, or between two people, there is always in the poem the simultaneously stated difference between them, a difference also stated by the word "like." The concluding lines of the poem perhaps suggest the "cold" and unsettling emptiness of the world without the human ability to fill it with relations, to say that "it is like." Yet, as in "The Man with the Blue Guitar," there remains a certain estrangement, "however like." As in "The Course of a Particular," even "though one says that one is part of everything," ultimately "There is a conflict, there is a resistance involved" (*OP*, 96). The resistance, however, does not deny that "relation appears / A small relation expanding. . . ." The crucial movement of "This as Including That," then, is enacted in a complex simile that neither exaggerates the separation nor dissolves the individual elements in its unity. Like Stevens' analogy of the co-existence of men and women, the simile provides a point of intimacy that is contingent upon the separation.

Stevens increasingly came to rely on similes and the related form "as if" to sustain this difficult "relation" that he desired, as they afforded him a way to sustain simultaneously the interplay and inter-dependence of the possibilities of language as metaphor and language as fragmentation. The relatively simple model of the simile, then, will prove particularly useful for understanding the paradoxical nature of language in Stevens' poetry. Simile "satisfies" where the models given in Chapters Two and Three do not because it sustains the interplay of the two *as* one and at once. Invoking the gap that is both the point of fragmentation and the point of union, the simile combines both tendencies of language we have discussed and consequently provides the best model for understanding the form and action of Stevens' poetic language as it attempts to expose itself. Whereas metaphor attempts to conceal that gap (with the unspoken unity of tenor and vehicle), simile attempts to reveal that gap. Therefore, a problem in metaphor which Richards notes is not a problem in simile: "Something which is obvious and true of the whole metaphor and its meaning thus lends an illusory plausibility to a false view of the correspondence of vehicle to tenor."[5] In simile, however, one

---

[5] Richards, p. 133.

thing is said only to resemble another, never to *be* another; the two are always two and yet are joined *as* one by that resemblance. On the other hand, fragmentation tends to exaggerate the gap or separation, as does "discord." Simile, however, neither obscures nor exaggerates that gap, but rather (to use Heidegger's vocabulary) most clearly calls into it.

Consequently, the model of the simile best reveals the latent tension of language in Stevens' poetry, not because it does something which metaphor or fragmentation cannot do, but because it more obviously does what both already do—fragment and unite. The simultaneous sustaining of both poles is made by positing, semantically, an identity even as this identity is denied: "This formula, then, states that reality as given, the particular, is *compared* with something whose impossibility and unreality is at the same time admitted."[6] Although Hans Vaihinger is referring to the phrase "as if," this statement describes simile equally well: it equates one thing with another (as metaphor obviously does), while dividing one thing from another (as fragmentation most obviously does).

The "as if" formula therefore offers a convenient way for understanding how a double statement is made simultaneously in the single "like" or "as" of a simile. In addition, the "as if" has the advantage of containing a logical division between the words "as" and "if" that corresponds to the distinction between metaphor and fragmentation. So, before examining Stevens' similes in detail, I wish first to look at

[6] Hans Vaihinger, *The Philosophy of "As If". A System of the Theoretical, Practical and Religious Fictions of Mankind*, tr. C. K. Ogden (London: Routledge & Kegan Paul, 1924; rpt. 1949), p. 93. The *Philosophy* was first published in German in 1911; and although Stevens could read German, I think it more likely, given the quotations from Stevens and Vaihinger cited below, that if Stevens did read the *Philosophy*, it was in the English translation. I have also discussed the possible connection between the two writers in "The 'Form / And Frame' of 'As if' in Wallace Stevens," *American Poetry* 3 (Spring 1986), 34-50.

CHAPTER FOUR

Stevens' use of the phrase "as if" in relation to Vaihinger's *The Philosophy of "As If."* As we have already seen Stevens say of the "final relation" he desires, it is *"As if, as if, as if the disparate halves / Of things were waiting in a bethrothal [sic] known / To none, awaiting espousal to the sound // Of right joining."*

The "As If"

I cannot prove that Stevens was directly influenced by Vaihinger's work, although there is a high probability of indirect influence through George Santayana. According to Joel Porte, Santayana owned and had heavily annotated a 1922 copy of *Die Philosophie des 'Als Ob,'* and he suggests that Stevens and Santayana may have communicated about the subject (although we have no proof of that communication) or that Stevens may have been influenced in this regard through Santayana's works, such as the 1923 *Scepticism and Animal Faith.*[7]

[7] In response to my letter, Joel Porte answered: "As a matter of fact, Santayana's own copy of *Die Philosophie des 'Als Ob,'* heavily annotated, bears the imprint of Leipzig, 1922. It is possible that Stevens and Santayana communicated on this matter, but there is no evidence of such communication so far as I know. If Santayana influenced Stevens in this regard it could have come through Stevens' reading of Santayana's own works, such as *Scepticism and Animal Faith* (1923)" (Feb. 4, 1982).
I should add that Santayana's copy of Vaihinger, now held at Georgetown library, is not heavily annotated at any of the points I will cite below. This fact further supports the suggestion that Stevens may have been influenced by Vaihinger directly. In this regard, we should also note that Frank Kermode asserts that Stevens took his "general doctrine of fictions" from "Vaihinger, from Nietzsche, perhaps also from American pragmatism" (*The Sense of an Ending: Studies in the Theory of Fiction* [New York: Oxford University Press, 1966], p. 37). This assertion is accepted by Frank Lentricchia, *After the New Criticism* (Chicago: University of Chicago Press, 1980), pp. 53-56.

Certainly Santayana himself influenced Stevens: their acquaintance at Harvard is well known, and so is the fact that "To an Old Philosopher in Rome" was written upon the occasion of Santayana's death.[8] It thus seems likely that Santayana, who had read Vaihinger, may have at least indirectly introduced Stevens to Vaihinger's ideas. But even if we can never discover any direct knowledge of Vaihinger by Stevens, Vaihinger's *Philosophy* appears to be a manifestation of what can be described as a general outlook current during the early part of the twentieth century. Stevens says, for example, that when he attended Harvard what "was called the will to believe" that which "we know to be untrue" was a major topic of discussion in Cambridge (L, 443). Einstein, as we have already seen, discusses a similar topic, and in this regard we find Vaihinger making a statement about fictions that is quite similar to Einstein's:

> If, therefore, subjective events depart from reality and alter it either by subtracting from or adding to it, and if, in spite of this, correct practical results are obtained and the final outcome of thought tallies with reality—from these two contradictory statements there arises the important problem: How does it happen that although in thinking we make use of a falsified reality, *the practical result still proves to be right?*[9]

The widespread concern with thought and fiction also appears in Santayana's *Scepticism and Animal Faith*.[10] Einstein's comment, Vaihinger's philosophy, Santayana's work, Stevens' poetry, the topic of discussion at Cambridge all

---

[8] See the several letters in which Stevens refers to Santayana, especially L, 481-82, 637, 761-62. These are also cited in *Souvenirs and Prophecies*, pp. 68-69, along with Stevens' record of an evening with Santayana, written in Stevens' copy of Santayana's *Lucifer*.

[9] Vaihinger, p. 159.

[10] George Santayana, *Scepticism and Animal Faith: Introduction to a System of Philosophy* (New York: Charles Scribner's Sons, 1923).

point to a general interest during the time about the nature and importance of fictions.[11]

However, there are certain rather striking parallels between Vaihinger and Stevens which suggest that there may have been a direct influence of *The Philosophy of "As If"* on Stevens, even if we cannot prove it. Considering the fact that Vaihinger focuses his entire philosophy on the phrase "as if" and considering that the phrase is, as Vendler has noted, characteristic of Stevens, it might be useful to list some of the more striking points of similarity.

In addition to Stevens' and Vaihinger's general tendencies to oppose dogma and fictions and to prefer the latter, there are several points in Vaihinger's work that are nearly identical to some of Stevens' ideas. For instance, Vaihinger writes that

> The 'As If' world . . . is far more important [than the "so-called real or actual" world] for ethics and aesthetics. This aesthetic and ethical world of 'As If,' the world of the unreal, becomes finally for us a world of values which, particularly in the form of religion, must be

[11] The topic of conversation at Harvard stems from William James, *The Will to Believe: And Other Essays in Popular Philosophy* (New York: Longmans, Green & Co., 1923), pp. 1-31 (first published, after being delivered orally at Harvard, in 1896). James in turn cites Wilfrid Ward, "The Wish Believe," *Witnesses to the Unseen* (New York: Macmillan, 1893). In addition, note the necessary fiction of Joseph Conrad's *Heart of Darkness* (1902) as a literary analogue to this concern. We might also consider the early nineteenth-century writings of Jeremy Bentham on the theory of fictions. C. K. Ogden, translator of Vaihinger's *Philosophy*, tells us that Bentham's work on fictions was added to Vaihinger's library in 1932 and that Vaihinger had hoped to supervise its translation into German before his death. Both Vaihinger and Ogden seem to have regarded Bentham's emphasis on the "linguistic factor in the creation of fictions" as being especially salient (see Vaihinger, pp. v-vi). Note also the brief discussion of Vaihinger in Ogden's edition of *Bentham's Theory of Fiction* (London: Kegan Paul, Trench, Trubner, 1932), pp. xxxi-xxxii.

sharply distinguished in our mind from the world of becoming.[12]

This statement corresponds to a large degree with Stevens' "need" for poetry to provide an essentially spiritual sanction for life. Also, similar to Stevens' insistence that the "belief in a metaphor" be recognized as "not true" is Vaihinger's assertion that a "true fiction" is "always accompanied by the *consciousness* that the fictional idea, the fictional assumption, has no real validity."[13]

In addition, Stevens' "need" for poetry to protect us from the "pressure" of an increasingly violent reality corresponds to Vaihinger's observation in *The Philosophy*: "The organism finds itself in a world of contradictory sensations, it is exposed to the assaults of a hostile external world, and in order to preserve itself, it is forced to seek every possible means of assistance, external as well as internal. In necessity and pain mental evolution is begun. . . ."[14] Similarly, Stevens' statement that the imagination is a "violence within" pressing back against a "violence without" resembles Vaihinger's remark that the "special character of a fiction is not only its arbitrariness but also its violence. Violence must be done not only to reality but (in real fictions) also to thought itself."[15]

Finally, Stevens' insistence that the imagination have "the strength of reality or none at all" has a counterpart in Vaihinger: "[T]he psyche is, of course, always tied down by the actual sequence and co-existences of sense-data. If the creation of fictions is to be of value we must always be able to find our way back to actuality again"; and "Although the

[12] Vaihinger, p. xlvii.

[13] Ibid., p. 80.

[14] Ibid., p. 12. This point of similarity, as well as the following one in the text, has also been noted by Lentricchia (pp. 53 ff.), who in turn is following Kermode, *Sense of an Ending*.

[15] Vaihinger, p. 98.

course of thought deviates from that of reality, thought tends constantly to reunite with reality."[16]

Given these parallels, it is perhaps all the more significant that ultimately Vaihinger respects political and scientific fictions and has a somewhat disparaging attitude toward both religious and aesthetic fictions, as made evident in the following remark: "Plato's mythical fictions are a very good type of fiction. The *as if* is here very clearly in evidence. Yet, on the whole, they are far more in the nature of poetic similes than scientific fictions. At best they are of equal value logically and ethically with the tropic fictions of modern theologians."[17] I think we can assume that this opinion is not confined to Vaihinger; the modern world-view has been increasingly a scientific world-view. From this perspective, Stevens' poetic enterprise, both in his poetry and in his theorizing about poetry, can be seen as a modern defense of aesthetic fictions and particularly of poetry as the "supreme fiction."

Nevertheless, Vaihinger's analysis of the phrase "as if" is particularly helpful in explaining how Stevens found a mode of expression that could simultaneously sustain the opposing poles of language. Vaihinger tells us, in the "Autobiographical" section of his work, that his early training in the grammar of Latin prepared him for his work in the philosophy of "as if": "The double conjunction 'As if' was not mentioned, but it was this accurate logical training which later enabled me to recognize in the grammatical formation 'As if' the Fiction which has such logical significance." He goes on to add that Schiller's philosophical treatises were also very important in the development of his philosophy: "I understood his [Schiller's] theory of play as the primary element of artistic creation and enjoyment; and it had great influence on the development of my thought, for later on I recognized in play

[16] Ibid., pp. 55-56, 158.
[17] Ibid., pp. 137-38.

SIMILE

the 'As if', as the driving force of aesthetic activity and intuition."[18]

The reason that the phrase "as if" carries so much weight for Vaihinger is that it manages to combine two contradictory statements in such a way that both statements are formally maintained: in essence, it manages to combine the two directions of language that we have discussed. According to Vaihinger, the two words "as" and "if" represent two "unheard" clauses:

> First we have—this lies in the "as"—quite clearly an equating of two terms. . . . But to this primary thought another secondary one is added [this lies in the "if"], which is expressed by the conditional phrase. The form of this conditional statement affirms that the condition is an unreal or impossible one. . . . The case is posited but, at the same time, its impossibility is frankly stated.[19]

Consequently, in the word "as" there is an unheard equation that "X is Y" (my example). Yet in the "if" there is an unheard conditional "If X were Y" in which there "lies the assumption of a condition and indeed . . . of an impossible case."[20] Thus, "X does not equal Y." Using mathematical symbols, the "as if" makes the following logical contradiction:

$$X = Y$$

$$\text{If Y, then X}$$

$$X \neq Y$$

The phrase "as if" is particularly revealing for Stevens' work, for not only does it combine the movement of language toward unity in the "as" (or unheard equation) and the movement toward fragmentation in the "if" (or unheard

[18] Ibid., p. xxv.
[19] Ibid., pp. 258-59.
[20] Ibid., p. 92.

conditional); it is also particularly appropriate for maintaining a recognized fiction as a formal possibility. As Vaihinger says, the paradoxical effect of the phrase "as if" is that "In spite of its unreality or impossibility the assumption is still formally maintained"; and, as Helen Vendler has pointed out, the logic in Stevens' poetry is the logic of a sleight-of-hand man.[21]

The phrase "as if," then, in Stevens' poetry brings together the unitive and disjunctive processes of language in a precarious threshold of impossible possibility—perhaps nowhere more clearly or more poignantly than in "To an Old Philosopher in Rome." The poem begins with a "threshold," a place in which opposing forces interact:

> On the threshold of heaven, the figures in the
>   street
> Become the figures of heaven, the majestic
>   movement
> Of men growing small in the distances of space,
> Singing, with smaller and still smaller sound,
> Unintelligible absolution and an end—
>
> The threshold, Rome, and that more merciful
>   Rome
> Beyond, the two alike in the make of the mind.
> It is as if in a human dignity
> Two parallels become one, a perspective, of which
> Men are part both in the inch and in the mile.
>   (CP, 508)

[21] Ibid., pp. 92-93; Vendler, "Qualified Assertions," p. 175. Michel Benamou has a somewhat different interpretation of Stevens' "as if" than the one I am suggesting: "The iconoclastic aspect of Symbolism merits attention. To Mallarmé's 'comme si' repeated in *Le Coup de dés* corresponds Stevens' 'as if,' by which the poet seemed to remind himself that symbols are not to be confused with things as they are" (p. xv). In addition, Morse states that the "as if's" in poems such as "An Ordinary Evening in New Haven" discourage philosophical explications of Stevens' poetry (*Poetry as Life*, p. 213).

SIMILE

The "threshold" between the "afflatus of ruin," the real Rome of "poverty" and "misery," and the "more merciful Rome / Beyond" is clearly created by the first "as if" in the poem. Throughout the poem Stevens reiterates that it is *as if* the "poverty" and the "celestial possible" (*CP*, 509) come together "in a human dignity," in human perspective, and in his words. As such, the poem is not merely about the relationship between the imagination and reality, but about language itself and the contradictions that are necessary in order for language to search a "possible for its possibleness" (*CP*, 481).

Structurally, the poem begins with a grand statement of unity between the real world and the world "beyond." But after several stanzas in which this possibility is reiterated, the poem reminds us of the "misery" and "poverty" of this actual world:

> Impatient for the grandeur that you need
>
> In so much misery; and yet finding it
> Only in misery, the afflatus of ruin,
> Profound poetry of the poor and of the dead,
> As in the last drop of the deepest blood,
> As it falls from the heart and lies there to be seen,
>
> Even as the blood of an empire, it might be,
> For a citizen of heaven though still of Rome.
> It is poverty's speech that seeks us out the most.
> It is older than the oldest speech of Rome.
> This is the tragic accent of the scene.
> (*CP*, 509-10)

After this reminder, the poem then concludes by showing and creating *in language* the relationship between the celestial possible and tragic reality. The poem ends with this especially resonating statement:

> He stops upon this threshold,
> As if the design of all his words takes form

CHAPTER FOUR

> And frame from thinking and is realized.
> (*CP*, 511)

In this final "as if," as in the first one in the poem, lies the meaning of the poem, for it is there that the contrasting elements interact and become interdependent. In the "as if," in the human perspective that language allows, there is an equation between the world of change and misery and the ideal world of unity that, simultaneously, is pronounced as impossible. As such, it is the "as if" itself that is the "form" and "frame" of the poem.

Given that Stevens wrote this poem upon the occasion of Santayana's death, the most painful, but perhaps most revealing lines of the poem are the following:

> The bells keep on repeating solemn names
>
> In choruses and choirs of choruses,
> Unwilling that mercy should be a mystery
> Of silence.
> (*CP*, 510)

These lines suggest that to some extent the poem is an attempt to show how language, which can never fully touch this world or the world "beyond," is nonetheless merciful. The first stanza of this poem supports this suggestion, for it immediately calls attention to the diminishment and dissolution of the human—and his sounds—in the all-encompassing unity of heaven. The "majestic movement" of the "figures in the street" as they become the "figures of heaven" is a movement "Of men growing small in the distances of space." And although the men are "Singing," they sing "with smaller and still smaller sound" in this movement toward unity until there is an "Unintelligible absolution and an end—." This "end" is offered as a compensation for the emptiness and poverty of life, which themselves lead to a sort of silence:

SIMILE

> It is poverty's speech that seeks us out the most.
> . . . .
> And you—it is you that speak it, without speech.

This end, however, is undesirable; it is the "unintelligible absolution." Thus, we indeed have a "tragic" sense of the way Santayana speaks "poverty's speech . . . without speech."

The poem then declares that it (and the bells) is "Unwilling that mercy should be a mystery / Of silence." Neither the real world's poverty, nor the imagination's richness, language is nevertheless the only possible relation and the only possible (sound of) meaning. Between what is figured here as the emptiness of death and the unity of heaven, language like life itself finds the space to move. The "as if" is crucial to this movement, for it continually asserts possibilities of unity that are simultaneously denied. As such, it is the "as if" itself which is the "form / And frame" of this poem. Appropriately, the poem concludes with the image with which it began, the "threshold" which is an image for language itself.

The "as if," then, becomes a major way Stevens both evokes and counters the silence at either end of the movement toward unity or disjunction. In both his late and his early poetry, speech-without-speech is on the semantic level the subject and is enacted by "as if's." For example, in addition to this 1952 poem, we find that in 1923, in "Two Figures in Dense Violet Night," Stevens makes a very similar statement:[22]

> Speak, even, as if I did not hear you speaking,
> But spoke for you perfectly in my thoughts,
> Conceiving words,

[22] Note that this poem, "Two Figures in Dense Violet Night" (*CP*, 85-86) appears as "Two Figures in Dense Violet Light" on p. 85 of *PM*; see Brogan, "Stevens' 'Two Figures in Dense Violet Night,' " *American Notes & Queries*, 23 (1984), 49-50.

CHAPTER FOUR

> As the night conceives the sea-sounds in silence. . . .
> *(CP,* 86)

The union or intimacy evoked between these two figures, as well as their utter separation, by the phrase "as if," is beyond paraphrase, although we can rather lamely point out that despite the separation admitted by the "as if" their absolute intimacy is still formally maintained by the "as if."

Although Stevens' interest in simultaneously sustaining the interplay of contrasting forces is evident in this early poem, it is after writing the letters to Hi Simons cited above that his use of the "as if" increases dramatically. Between 1938 and 1940, for example, Stevens was using the phrase only .17 times per page, or not quite twice in every ten pages of poetry. But after 1940, when he wrote the letters to Simons, there is a dramatic rise in the frequency with which the phrase occurs, so that by the end of his life, Stevens was using the phrase .40 times per page, perhaps to the most purpose in "To an Old Philosopher in Rome." With these facts in mind, it is particularly interesting to read the following lines from "Notes toward a Supreme Fiction" (1942), a poem in which Stevens is very clearly trying to make language the ground of the interplay between opposing elements. In the following lines, Stevens uses several means, including the "or's" and the subjunctive "might," to sustain opposing possibilities, but none so powerfully as he uses the "as if":

> If MacCullough himself lay lounging by the sea,
>
> Drowned in its washes, reading in the sound,
> About the thinker of the first idea,
> He might take habit, whether from wave or phrase,
>
> Or power of the wave, or deepened speech,
> Or a leaner being, moving in on him,
> Of greater aptitude and apprehension,

SIMILE

> As if the waves at last were never broken,
> As if the language suddenly, with ease,
> Said things it had laboriously spoken.
>   (*CP*, 387)

It is as if, after 1940, Stevens found in the "as if" a way of speaking with ease that which he had been speaking with labor before.

As important and as interesting as the phrase "as if" is in Stevens' work, similes are even more so. The phrase "as if" explains how two opposite tendencies in language can be stated and sustained simultaneously; yet ultimately similes are even more integral to Stevens' structure and style than the "as if." Stevens does not use simile as a mere comparison or as a weakened metaphor, but rather (like his use of "as if") as a way of *sustaining and entertaining contradictory possibilities at once.* In Stevens' poetry at least, similes are a way of exposing language, both in its tendency to unite and in its necessarily simultaneous tendency to divide. The advantage that similes have over the "as if" is that by combining these two poles in one word, in "like" or "as," similes most clearly reveal the interaction of these two poles of language at once and *as* one. We can consequently say of simile what Stevens says in "Le Monocle de Mon Oncle," that "This trivial trope reveals a way of truth" (*CP*, 16).

In this respect one more point in Vaihinger's *The Philosophy of "As If"* is especially apt: "In this elementary mechanism, the formation of a similarity-centre, lies the secret of all fictions, whether they be simple like the artificial classifications, or complicated like the idea of infinity."[23] Such a "centre" is described in "Artificial Populations":

> The center that he sought was a state of mind,
> Nothing more, like weather after it has cleared—
> Well, more than that, like weather when it has
>   cleared

---
[23] Vaihinger, p. 104.

CHAPTER FOUR

And the two poles continue to maintain it.
(*OP*, 112)

This "center" is both a presence and an absence, expressed by the similes as the "*sound* // Of right joining."

Simile

As we have seen, the extension either of language as metaphor or of language as fragmentation, considered alone, is ultimately destructive rather than creative: the extension of either process of language alone is to end in silence—either the silence of dissolution inherent in total union or the silence of the void inherent in total fragmentation.[24] Because the possibility of total union is necessarily unspeakable, the name of God is conceived as ultimately unspeakable; and even if the man in "Prologues to What Is Possible" could finally speak that syllable of exact completion, such speech "would shatter the boat and leave the oarsmen quiet." Similarly, in "To an Old Philosopher in Rome," the union of the real world and "heaven" means diminishing sound and finally an "end." On the other hand, the possibility of total fragmentation is also unspeakable, which is why Chaos is also conceived as something ultimately silent, and why the extension of the man's negative suppositions in "Landscape with Boat" is "not to live" but "To be projected by one void into / Another." The consequence of this fact for poetry such as Stevens' which explores language in its own language is that both processes of language must be maintained at once. Thus, Stevens is interested in achieving the "supreme balance" or in using the disclaimers and reclamations that sustain both processes of language.

Silence, then, is the curious ground of language in Ste-

[24] Consider what Bruns has to say about Mallarmé: "Silence, we may say, signals for Mallarmé the presence of beauty; or, again, in silence the mystery of nothingness . . . breaks in upon man" (p. 113).

139

vens' poetry, as others, such as Isabel MacCaffrey or Helen Regeuiro, have noted. The recent studies, however, have tended to de-emphasize what Roy Harvey Pearce calls the "capacity to mean" and to emphasize the negative or "abysmal" aspects in Stevens' poetry.[25] Miller, for example, says that "each term in 'The Rock' . . . is a catachresis for something which has not, cannot have, a proper name. That something is the abyss. . . ."[26] In a similar manner, Isabel MacCaffrey says that in "Le Monocle de Mon Oncle," "we sink deeper into the well of the unconscious, into an extraordinarily visceral sequence of appeals to voiceless sensation."[27]

We should note, however, that Stevens conceives of silence as the creative *source* of both processes of language, as well as their ultimate failure. For example, in "Two Figures in Dense Violet Night," the perfect speech is figured as the silence of pure union (of man and woman, speech and thought), like the night's serenade, which is itself conceived in silence. In a similar fashion, the silence engendered by separation in "On the Road Home" is also conceived of as creative:

> "Words are not forms of a single word.
> In the sum of the parts, there are only the parts."
> . . . .
> It was at that time, that the silence was largest
> And longest, the night was roundest,
> The fragrance of autumn warmest,
> Closest and strongest.
> (*CP*, 204)

---

[25] Pearce, *Continuity*, p. 431: "Thus, in recent times particularly, the basic style of both the Adamic and the mythic poem has derived from the poet's concern to declare that language, in spite of all that we may do to it, is inherently meaningful—no matter what the ultimate source of meaning—because poems made out of it can manifest its capacity to mean."

[26] Miller, "Stevens' Rock and Criticism as Cure," p. 29.

[27] MacCaffrey, "Ways of Truth," p. 198.

In both poems, the background of silence provides the creative ground.

Thus, silence in Stevens' poetry is both the source and the failure of either direction of language, the source and end of the unitive and disjunctive poetics—essentially the condition and constraint necessary for the movement of language. In reference to music and "all sonority," Gisèle Brelet says something quite similar:

> Music is born, develops, and realizes itself within silence: upon silence it traces out its moving arabesques, which give a form to silence, and yet do not abolish it. A musical work, like all sonority, unfolds between two silences: the silence of its birth and the silence of its completion. In this temporal life where music perpetually is born, dies, and is born again, silence is ever its faithful companion. . . .[28]

In other words, in language silence is the threshold, the place where "It is as if . . . / Two parallels become one," the gap that is necessary for both the point of union and the point of separation and especially for their interaction.

In the August 27, 1940, letter to Hi Simons in which he rejects the "law of contrasts" in favor of the "energizing that comes from mere interplay, interaction," Stevens provides an analogy for this gap or threshold. As an illustration of "part of what" he is "talking about," he cites a review of Seurat: "In the comparison of aesthetic opposites . . . and the slight divergence of likenesses, he sees the source of all artistic beauty" (L, 369).[29] What Stevens ultimately desires in language is a speech that achieves the poetry of the "artistic beauty" described above, a language that will speak the

---

[28] Gisèle Brelet, "Music and Silence," *La Revue Musicale* 22 (1946), 169-81; reprinted in *Reflections on Art: A Source Book of Writings by Artists, Critics, and Philosphers*, tr. and ed. Susanne K. Langer (Baltimore: Johns Hopkins University Press, 1958), p. 103.

[29] Anthony Newmarch, "Seurat," *Apollo*, 32 (1940), 11-12; cited in L, 369.

seeming impossibility of diverging likeness (or converging differences) simultaneously. It is a desire much like Wordsworth's desire to show "similitude in dissimilitude, and dissimilitude in similitude."[30] What is perhaps even more suggestive is the actual style of Seurat's paintings. From a close perspective, "pointillism" will be seen only as different spots of color (which is something like the effect of language as fragmentation).[31] From a more distanced perspective, the different spots of color will appear to blend into a single color that is different from the individual spots (now no longer seen) and which results from their "interinanimation" (like language as metaphor). Michel Benamou, we should note, finds that Stevens used a similar technique of painting "repeatedly" in his poetry: "One element in the 'broken color' of the Impressionist is that the eye transforms two colors into a single tone. Stevens used this device repeatedly. A lemon is 'yellow-blue, yellow-green.' "[32] But, as the canvas illustrates, this diverging or blending of color is part of the same nature which either annihilates or exaggerates the "gap," in the representation itself, much as Stevens says that the "chord" and "discord" do.

One final analogy can be seen in Michelangelo's painting of the Creation of Adam on the Sistine Chapel ceiling. That small empty space between the pointing finger of God and the raised finger of Adam has long been recognized as one of the most powerful "spaces" in art. It is powerful precisely because it exposes the necessary separation between God and Adam in order for Adam to exist and, simultaneously, the necessary connection between them in order for the

---

[30] William Wordsworth, "Preface to the Second Edition of the *Lyrical Ballads*" (1800) in Perkins, p. 328.

[31] I find it interesting that what we have come to call "pointillism" was called "Divisionism" by Seurat himself. See H. S. Janson and Joseph Kerman, *A History of Art & Music* (New York: Harry N. Abrams, n.d.), p. 177.

[32] Benamou, p. 18.

CHAPTER FOUR

Creator to *impart* life. As such, the "gap" in that painting calls attention to the ultimate paradox, evoking the unspeakable mystery of life itself.

So, too, does language when it calls attention to its own "gap" in which there must be at once a similar separation and joining, the gap of "final relation," as Stevens calls it, in which these seemingly opposite tendencies of language can interact. The best of Stevens' poetry exposes just this paradoxical gap, its silence, and it is through his experimentation with "as if's" and especially with similes that he accomplishes his purpose. In its form the "as if" itself contains that gap: as Vaihinger notes, the "apodosis [in the phrase 'as if'] is . . . concealed and suppressed. It lurks *unheard between the 'as' and the 'if'* " (italics mine).³³ We might, then, draw the conclusion that the "as if" provides the best model for understanding certain aspects of Stevens' language. However, the gap is silence, and the poet in particular is "Unwilling that mercy should be a mystery / Of silence." Consequently, it is in the similes that Stevens finds a form of writing that not only exposes the gap that metaphor tends to conceal and that fragmentation tends to exaggerate, and that not only exposes the inter-relation of these two processes of language, but also speaks as a *sound* of silence. In other words, in similes Stevens finds the closest possible *sound* of that necessary gap in language, its silent threshold.

Heidegger calls this paradoxical gap a "stillness": *"Language speaks as the peal of stillness. . . . Language, the peal of stillness, is, inasmuch as the dif-ference [which he also says is equivalent to "intimacy"] takes place."*³⁴ Stevens,

---

³³ Vaihinger, p. 258.

³⁴ Martin Heidegger, *Poetry, Language, Thought*, tr. Albert Hofstadter (New York: Harper & Row, 1971), p. 207. For a discussion of the relation of Heidegger to Stevens, see Kermode, "Dwelling Poetically in Connecticut," pp. 256-73, and Thomas J. Hines, *The Later Poetry of Wallace Stevens: Phenomenological Parallels with Husserl and Heidegger* (Lewisburg: Bucknell Univeristy Press, 1976).

SIMILE

however, conceives of this gap as silence: like "Phoebus," every word is "A name for something that could never be named" (*CP*, 381), so that language, the peal of silence, is, only insofar as the silent gap or relation of difference and unity takes place. This "pealing" is not confined to actual similes but is true of what we have called metaphor and fragmentation as well, even if they tend to obscure that fact. As Heidegger also says, language "calls into a nearness. But even so the call does not wrest what it calls away from the remoteness, in which it is kept by the calling there."[35]

Although Heidegger is speaking of all language, his statement is particularly appropriate for Stevens' "Vacancy in the Park"—a poem rarely discussed in Stevens criticism, but which Stevens placed in his *Collected Poems* immediately after "To an Old Philosopher in Rome," and which is powerfully evocative in its similes. Given its title and its subject, this poem is clearly vulnerable to deconstruction. Yet the poem resists its own latent abyss, affirming the power of language to mean. Structured almost entirely by similes, this small poem exposes a linguistic gesturing toward "identity" (naming at the source of being) and a simultaneous rupturing in the sign (naming as the erasure of being)—in sum, language that announces its own displacement while paradoxically assuming continuity:

> March . . . Someone has walked across the snow,
> Someone looking for he knows not what.
>
> It is like a boat that has pulled away
> From a shore at night and disappeared.
>
> It is like a guitar left on a table
> By a woman, who has forgotten it.
>
> It is like the feeling of a man
> Come back to see a certain house.

---

[35] Heidegger, pp. 198-99. I will take up the fragmentation inherent in metaphor and the joining inherent in fragmentation in the concluding chapter.

> The four winds blow through the rustic arbor,
> Under its mattresses of vines.
> (*CP*, 511)

What might be called the whole Romantic problem of presence/absence, immediacy/mediation "traced" in this poem turns out to be the problem of language itself. The similes most obviously reveal the "calling" that "calls into itself... here into presence, there into absence"[36] characteristic of the whole poem. Essentially, the poem addresses or speaks to the gap—the silence.

The three similes all compare the indefinite "it" to something which is both there and not there, repeating the kind of union and division made in the word "like" itself.[37] For instance, in the clause, "It is like a boat," the word "it" is *irrevocably* divorced from the boat by the word "like," even as "like" joins "it" to the boat. Similarly, "it" both is and is not a guitar, is and is not a feeling. In other words, the similes make the kind of three-part predication found in metaphor wherein the thing itself can be understood only through the creative synthesis of subject and object or, as here, of subject and complement; and the similes also make the kind of two-part predication found in fragmentation wherein the thing itself is shattered into the "things themselves," or into "this thing" and "that thing." Yet, as revealed in the one word "like," these two predications happen at once: metaphor thus becomes fragmentation; fragmentation, metaphor. This "merging and dividing like language itself" is the subject of the poem.[38] In fact, the rest of the poem merely extends what is implicit in "It is like a boat." Even the title suggests that something is its opposite—that a vacancy (or absence) is a presence *in* the park.

This paradox can be traced throughout the poem, though it seems especially ironic, given Jacques Derrida's termi-

---

[36] Ibid., p. 199.

[37] MacCaffrey finds similar indefinite "its" characteristic of Stevens' poetry ("Ways of Truth," p. 216).

[38] The expression is taken from Burke, p. 407.

SIMILE

nology, that the "telling" tracks or footprints presumably left in the snow are in fact never named in the poem.[39] The "vacancy" begins with the word "March," which initially suggests the month of March and spring; immediately, however, the word suggests the activity of marching since "Someone has walked across the snow." The word, therefore, is ambiguous in a particulary appropriate way. Whether marking the passage of winter into spring, of nothingness into creation, or indicating someone's passing, a presence moving into absence, the word is an affirmation and a negation at once—as is the empty and silent space in the poem filled by the ellipsis. A similar dual motion is revealed in the image of someone's having walked across the snow in which someone who is absent is evoked as a presence. In addition, this someone is (or was) looking for something, but for something "he knows not."

The latent tension of language and of the poem's subject becomes more obvious and extreme in the expanded similes. Not only do the root similes ("It is like a boat," etc.) simultaneously connect and sever, equate and negate, but the things to which "it" is compared in the expanded similes continually evoke an image as a presence only to veil it again in a receding temporal void. For example, the boat, seen vividly pulling away from the shore, finally cannot be seen: it has "disappeared." The boat is a "presence sheltered in absence."[40] What is a boat that has disappeared *like*? How can that be spoken, except in silence? How can "It" be like that boat, unless it speaks that silence? The answer given in the poem is that "It is like a guitar left on the table"—a guitar which is there, but not there, since it has been "forgotten" or erased in the mind of the woman. Similarly, the man "Come back" to a "certain house" is both where he was and, of course, not where he was since the present can never co-

---

[39] The word "trace" (with its play on "track") is important to Derrida's "Differance."

[40] Heidegger, p. 199.

incide with the past. Over and over the poem calls up something as it annihilates that something or replaces it with a different "presence" that is also revealed as not there. Continually, the poem speaks to that gap between the calling up and the annihilation, between the identification and the negation: over and over the poem speaks to the silence of that gap.

The oneness and nothingness, the merging toward and moving away, have been implied all along by the nebulous "it" of the poem. The "It" is the vacancy in the park, or the "March . . . ," or the whole sensation of someone's having walked across the snow looking for something unknown, or the answer to what is unknown—or all of these. All of these call up the silence, the gap or "supreme balance" between positing and negating, uniting and dividing.

The silence reaches its fullest expression in the last two lines of the poem which, being syntactically different from the preceding lines, serve as the poem's coda. "It" is the "four winds" blowing from the opposing corners of the earth, arriving at a central point, but a point that is nonetheless a gap, figured in the poem as something that merges into one and into nothing. The arbor, a place sheltered by trees, especially by vines, is itself "rustic" (or made of bark-covered branches). Thus, the place is made of, shaded by, and described by the same thing—the vines. It is, therefore, an image of "oneness," such as is posited in "Prologues to What Is Possible." Yet the winds blow to this center "through it" and "under" the "mattresses of vines" as if the arbor were both a roof and a bed. Where those two become one is the same as where the four winds meet—at the center which is not a center, but the threshold, the gap, the silence: "The intimacy . . . is present in the separation of the between; it is present in the dif-ference."[41]

[41] Ibid., p. 202. I have discussed both this coda and the poem as a whole in relation to the problem of temporality, in "Wallace Stevens'

As the whole of Stevens' poem suggests, it is not merely the similes which speak to the silence. Using the relatively simple model of the simile as a starting point, the poem emerges as complex language about the nature of language that is represented in its own similes. And Stevens' genius emerges as the ability to speak so exceedingly well to that nature, the silence.

With the insight into Stevens' use of similes that "Vacancy in the Park" provides, we are in a position to understand better the complexity and significance of similes in Stevens' other poetry. For example, even in Stevens' earliest major poem, "Sunday Morning" (1915), similes are an integral part of several key passages. The first stanza of that poem, for instance, contains the following lines:

> The pungent oranges and bright, green wings
> Seem things in some procession of the dead,
> Winding across wide water, without sound.
> The day is like wide water, without sound,
> Stilled for the passing of her dreaming feet
> Over the seas, to silent Palestine,
> Dominion of the blood and sepulchre.
> (CP, 67)

In addition to the obvious simile beginning with "like" in the passage above, the verb "seem" functions essentially as a simile: it suggests a relation while avoiding either total identity or total disjunction. Thus, Stevens' use of similes and forms of similes reinforces the concern of the poem, the "interplay" of the "real" world and some ideal world. As in "To an Old Philosopher in Rome," the thought of heaven in "Sunday Morning" evokes silence and stillness—the undesirable end of unity. As Stevens asks in the next stanza, "What is divinity if it can come / Only in silent shadows and in dreams?" The poem, however, seeks to affirm the world

---

'Vacancy in the Park' and the Concept of Similitude," *Wallace Stevens Journal*, 10 (1986), 9-17.

CHAPTER FOUR

of time and change, most acutely in the line, "Death is the mother of beauty." It is thus especially appropriate that the woman contemplating the heaven of "Sunday Morning" thinks that the "oranges" and "things" of this world only *seem like* that other world: from the opening stanza there is an understated difference between the two worlds, so that this world is finally not still, silent, or "without sound."

Again, Stevens uses the verb "seem" as a simile, asking in the third stanza if "the earth" shall "seem all of paradise that we shall know?" The answer is given in the fourth stanza: there is no place of paradise "that has endured / As April's green endures; or will endure / Like her remembrance of awakened birds" (birds which " 'test the reality / . . . by their sweet questionings' ").

The sixth stanza then completes the transformation implied by the similes of the opening stanza, the question of the third stanza, and the similes of the fourth. Rather than the earth's being an image for paradise, paradise is a reflection of earth:

> Is there no change of death in paradise?
> Does ripe fruit never fall? Or do the boughs
> Hang always heavy in that perfect sky,
> Unchanging, yet so like our perishing earth,
> With rivers like our own that seek for seas
> They never find, the same receding shores
> That never touch with inarticulate pang?
> (*CP*, 69)

Although the similes imply a difference between this "perishing earth" and perfect paradise, they sustain a necessary relation, for it is through the idea of a paradise not present that we can recognize and prefer the paradise or beauty in earth. The poem then offers an alternative "devotion" to the traditional devotion of Sunday morning: the "boisterous" chant "to the sun, / Not as a god, but as a god might be, / Naked among them, like a savage source" (*CP*, 70). The similes thus sustain the interaction of opposing possibilities throughout the poem, exposing the relation between ideas of union and of separation, even in "the source." It is fitting, then, that the poem concludes with the pigeons' "Ambiguous undulations as they sink, / Downward to darkness, on extended wings" (*CP*, 70). The final image reinforces the "interplay" which not only serves as the subject of the poem, but as the effect of language as well: "In the end, as the pigeons inscribe their transient motions in air, their calligraphy is read as elusively ambiguous by the poet seeking significance, and doctrinal choice dissolves in mystery."[42] As Stevens says in *The Necessary Angel*, "The ambiguity that is so favorable to the poetic mind is precisely the *ambiguity favorable to resemblance*" (*NA*, 79; italics mine).

As important as similes are in "Sunday Morning," however, they remain fairly sparse in *Harmonium*, which contains the poems written between 1915 and 1924. It is thus particularly interesting that similes figure to a large degree in the last poem Stevens wrote that was included in the second edition of *Harmonium*, "Sea Surface Full of Clouds" (1924). This poem is a tour de force of changing perspectives and verbal presentations of representations: the five different ways of seeing the sea "In that November off Tehuantepec" created in the five sections of the poem are as dependent upon the sounds of the words as on the semantics: "poetry is words; and . . . words, above everything else, are, in poetry, sounds" (*NA*, 32). For such an early poem, "Sea Surface Full of Clouds" contains an unusual number of similes, all of which refer to the way clouds are seen in their reflection in water. Most importantly for us, the action of the similes in the poem is then explained in the last three lines, which themselves contain a simile:

> Then the sea
> And heaven rolled as one and from the two
> Came fresh transfigurings of freshest blue.
> (*CP*, 102)

---

[42] Vendler, "Stevens and Keats," p. 174.

CHAPTER FOUR

Throughout the poem, the sea and sky are *as* one in the surface reflections; they remain divided ("two") but related. It is precisely that ambiguous point of relation, figured in the poem through similes, which is the subject and substance of the poem. The resultant procreation is the product of the creative interaction of seemingly opposed elements, like the relation of a man and woman that Stevens uses so often. No wonder then that in "Study of Images II," the "espousal to the sound // Of right joining" results in "the burning / And breeding and bearing birth of harmony, / The final relation, the marriage of the rest."

At this point in his career, Stevens had his well-known dry period. After the initial publication of *Harmonium* in the early 1920's, he does not seem to have written in earnest again until 1934, when he wrote "The Idea of Order at Key West." The period from 1933 to 1937, which is the *chronological* center of his writing years, shows a rise in Stevens' use of the "as if" and of similes, including the use of an unfinished simile for the title of one of his poems, "Like Decorations in a Nigger Cemetery." Each of the fifty short sections of this poem can consequently be considered as possible completions of that simile. For our purposes, the tenth one is especially apt:

> Between farewell and the absence of farewell,
> The final mercy and the final loss,
> The wind and the sudden falling of the wind.
> (*CP*, 152)

This section, cited here in its entirety, has no subject (except the unfinished simile of the title), no verb, no predication, no presence. There is just the "between" that is nonetheless presented in language.

The problem of presentation and representation, which is the problem of the latent tension in language, reaches an acute stage in "The Man with the Blue Guitar" (1937). Obviously similes are at the center (if we can call it that) of the problem; and "The Man with the Blue Guitar" contains sev-

SIMILE

eral, including the self-referential lines cited earlier in this chapter:

> So it is to sit and to balance things
> To and to and to the point of still,
>
> To say of one mask it is like,
> To say of another it is like,
>
> To know that the balance does not quite rest,
> That the mask is strange, however like.

But the problem of presentation and representation is further complicated by the poem's relation to Picasso's art, to which Stevens refers as "this 'hoard / Of destructions' " (*CP*, 173) and which itself deals with the problem of presentation and representation.[43]

Consequently, the "as" of the expression "Things as they are," reiterated throughout the poem, is extremely complex, yet certainly powerful and generative for Stevens in this poem. It is hard, then, to accept this particular "as" as merely a conjunction, although grammatically it serves that function often in the poem, as it does in the opening lines:

> The man bent over his guitar,
> A shearsman of sorts. The day was green.
>
> They said, "You have a blue guitar,
> You do not play things as they are."
>
> The man replied, "Things as they are
> Are changed upon the blue guitar."
>
> And they said then, "But play, you must,
> A tune beyond us, yet ourselves,

---

[43] Although he probably got the phrase "hoard of destructions" from Picasso, Stevens says that he "had no particular painting of Picasso's in mind" when he wrote this poem (*L*, 783, 786). It is generally agreed, however, that Picasso's work is the "source" of "The Man with the Blue Guitar" (see Pearce, *Continuity*, p. 429).

CHAPTER FOUR

> A tune upon the blue guitar
> Of things exactly as they are."
> (*CP*, 165)

Always about the edges of this conjunction, and especially so given the semantic content of this poem, there is the sense of "as" as a simile. We find this dual sense of "as" in Stevens' prose as well; for example, in the 1941 "Noble Rider and the Sound of Words":

> The subject-matter of poetry is not that "collection of solid, static objects extended in space" but the life that is lived in the scene that it composes; and so reality is not that external scene but the life that is lived in it. Reality is things as they are. (*NA*, 25)[44]

In light of Stevens' poetic development, it seems especially fitting that not only does this poem describe the "chord" and "discord," as well as the desire for the "supreme balance" explained in the letter to Hi Simons with which we began this chapter, but that beginning with the poems written immediately after writing this one, there is a dramatic rise in Stevens' use of both similes and "as if's" that continues throughout the rest of his poetic career. It is as if the problem of language as something unitive or disjunctive becomes clarified in the "as" of this poem and that thereafter Stevens gains a certain freedom to explore and exploit his own insights into his own use of language.

We might, then, disagree with Northrop Frye's statement in "The Realistic Oriole" that "A world of total simile . . . would be a world of total monotony" and that "a world of total metaphor is the formal cause of poetry."[45] What Stevens' poetry suggests, even though he is reticent about using the word "simile," is that the relation of language to the world and to itself is best explained and expressed in simile.

---

[44] Although first published in 1942, the essay was delivered by Stevens at Harvard in 1941 (see *L*, 386).

[45] See Frye, "The Realistic Oriole," p. 170.

SIMILE

So, too, we find that other discussions of Stevens' similes tend to overlook the vital function of simile in his poetry. For example, in reference to "Domination of Black," Helen Regeurio says, "The simile undercuts the possibility of oneness, and the similarity serves only to underline the strangeness that exists between the inner and outer worlds." She further asserts that "consciousness of similarity . . . undercuts all real correspondence. . . . The seeming undercuts the capacity for being."[46] Although the simile may well undercut the possibility of oneness, or being, or correspondence, it is also the means of positing their possibility. For Stevens, simile is far more than an expression of separation: it is the expression of the necessary and "final relation."

In the three years between the publication of *The Man with the Blue Guitar* and the writing of the letters to Hi Simons, Stevens obviously continued to explore the problem of the latent tension in language. We find, for example, that in this period he wrote several of the poems cited in earlier chapters, including "The Poems of Our Climate" (1938), which not only asserts like "Sunday Morning" that "The imperfect is our paradise," but also like "Sea Surface Full of Clouds" uses an image or "reflection" as its point of departure:

>   Clear water in a brilliant bowl,
>   Pink and white carnations. The light
>   In the room more like a snowy air,
>   Reflecting snow.
>   (*CP*, 193)

Although the poem first presents this image as a perfect and stagnant "world of white and snowy scents" (*CP*, 194), the "imperfect" or the "flaw" is contained in the word "like." Since the simile is not identity, the "never-resting mind" (*CP*, 194) still finds it possible to move, to search. Fittingly, the poem concludes with the following lines:

[46] Regeuiro, pp. 152, 151.

CHAPTER FOUR

> The imperfect is our paradise.
> Note that, in this bitterness, delight,
> Since the imperfect is so hot in us,
> Lies in flawed words and stubborn sounds.
> (*CP*, 194)

In the same year, Stevens also wrote "The Glass of Water," which says, as we recall, "So, / In the metaphysical there are these poles." Stevens also wrote "Add This to Rhetoric" during this period, as well as the "Connoisseur of Chaos," which asserts, "And yet relation appears," and which begins, appropriately enough, with the following lines used to head this study:

> A. A violent order is disorder; and
> B. A great disorder is an order. These
> Two things are one. (Pages of illustrations.)

In 1940 Stevens wrote "Of Bright & Blue Birds & the Gala Sun" and "Landscape with Boat," poems that we have observed as examples of the desire for union and the desire for fragmentation in Stevens' language. It is worth noting that both poems contain similes and "as if's" in key passages and thus are not completely one-sided. "Of Bright & Blue Birds," for example, describes the moment of union and of gaiety in terms of the moment "In which we pronounce joy *like* a word of our own" and further declares that in that moment "we feel . . . *as if* / There was a bright *scienza* outside of ourselves" (italics mine). The effect of the simile and the "as if" is to sustain the awareness of separation even as participation is being asserted. Similarly, the meaning of "Landscape with Boat" is kept in suspension by the "as if" and the simile of the following lines: "It was not as if the truth lay where he thought / Like a phantom, in an uncreated night."

Finally, "Of Modern Poetry," which clearly expresses the latent tension in language with which Stevens is concerned,

SIMILE

also appeared in 1940. In the simile in which poetry is compared to an actor on a stage, Stevens again turns to the problem of presentation and representation previously explored in "The Man with the Blue Guitar":

> It has to be on that stage
> And, like an insatiable actor, slowly and
> With meditation, speak words that in the ear,
> In the delicatest ear of the mind, repeat,
> Exactly, that which it wants to hear, at the sound
> Of which, an invisible audience listens,
> Not to the play, but to itself, expressed
> In an emotion as of two people, as of two
> Emotions becoming one.
> (*CP*, 240)

Again, we find division becoming related "as" one. The complicated movement between unity and fragmentation here is appropriate, given the fact that the poem must enact its own "interaction" in order to "suffice." Since repetition precludes immediacy, the actor who presents a representation to an audience is divided from himself by having to "repeat" what he wants to hear. Yet at the "sound" the actor is united to the audience, which is, of course, the actor himself "in the mind" that in turn hears "itself." This complex relation of the dichotomy and wholeness of the self is "expressed" "*as* . . . two / Emotions becoming one." But this is also a complexity contained within and sustained by the governing simile that says that poetry is *like* an actor. "Of Modern Poetry," then, is one of the most succinct expressions of the interaction that Stevens demands of his poetry.

In 1941-1942, we reach the "textual" median of Stevens' work, so called because he wrote as much poetry in the next thirteen years as he did in the preceding twenty-five. Stevens' increasing interest in "as if's" and similes is quite noticeable: from 1938-1940, Stevens was using the "as if" .17 times per page; "like," .50; and "as," .92. From 1941-1942, he used "as if" .28 times per page; "like," .72; "as," 1.15. And

CHAPTER FOUR

from 1943 to 1946, Stevens was using the "as if" .33 times per page, "like," .87; and "as," .91. The change is even more obvious if these figures are compared with the corresponding figures for 1915-1919: .02, .69, and .35. In 1942, Stevens wrote "Notes toward a Supreme Fiction," which both Morse and Pearce regard as the culmination of Stevens' poetry.[47] The poem's success depends to a large degree, I think, on Stevens' ability to unfold the implications of the opposing tendencies in language that we have been exploring and to sustain the relationship between the two poles.

We have already seen, for example, Stevens describing his desire for the "incalculable balances" in terms of a simile: "As a man and woman meet and love forthwith." And, as we have also noted, the next group of lines in the poem's first major section, "It Must Be Abstract," concludes with "As if the waves at last were never broken, / As if the language suddenly, with ease / Said things it had laboriously spoken." Both the simile and the "as if" posit an identification in language that is simultaneously denied; consequently, they provide the form and expression of the kind of unresting "balance" that Stevens envisions as the "Supreme Fiction."

In the next major section of the poem, "It Must Change," we find the lines already cited in Chapter Three show that ultimately Stevens was interested in the "difference":

> Two things of opposite natures seem to depend
> On one another, as a man depends
> On a woman, day on night, the imagined
>
> On the real. This is the origin of change.
> Winter and spring, cold copulars, embrace
> And forth the particulars of rapture come.

---

[47] In his biography of Stevens, Samuel French Morse says that "Notes toward a Supreme Fiction" remains "the culmination of his [Stevens'] thought, of the life of his mind" (p. 180). Roy Harvey Pearce calls Stevens' "attempts to evoke the Supreme Fiction" the "apogee" of "the continuity of American poetry" (*Continuity*, p. 382).

SIMILE

In view of what we have seen Stevens to mean by "inter-dependence" and "interaction," we can now more fully appreciate the complex set of contradictory possibilities that are created by the words "seem" and "as" above. The relation, which depends upon a simultaneous point of separation and joining, is further amplified in the next lines of the poem:

> Music falls on the silence like a sense,
> A passion that we feel, not understand.
> Morning and afternoon are clasped together
>
> And North and South are an intrinsic couple
> And sun and rain a plural, like two lovers
> That walk away as one in the greenest body.
> (*CP*, 392)

Even if the mysterious and paradoxical nature of the "relation" that Stevens creates in his poetry is something that we cannot fully "understand," still it is felt "like a sense." More importantly, there is music in this relation, so that even if it does resist understanding, its mystery does not remain a "mystery of silence." And, although the last two lines cited above suggest that finally we may be aware of "difference" or plurality, they also suggest that it is possible to recognize in that difference the necessary condition for joining without dissolution in unity.

In "It Must Give Pleasure," Stevens summarizes this recognition and acceptance:

> The nothingness was a nakedness, a point
>
> Beyond which thought could not progress as thought.
> He had to choose. But it was not a choice
> Between excluding things. It was not a choice
>
> Between, but of. He chose to include the things
> That in each other are included, the whole,
> The complicate, the amassing harmony.
> (*CP*, 403)

CHAPTER FOUR

Such a perception of the relation between, or "of," the "nothingness" and the "whole" is itself a function of language. Between the nothingness that fragmentation potentially means and the silent whole that language as metaphor potentially means is a gap, a "nakedness," that is not identical either with the nothingness or with the silent whole, but that is the unspeakable condition necessary for both and for their interaction as one. It is this mysterious point of relation that both allows meaning and which questions the validity of meaning. As Stevens says in "An Ordinary Evening in New Haven," it is indeed "A difficulty that we predicate." However, as the insistence on the "choice of" in the passage above suggests, by the time Stevens wrote this poem he had less anxiety about this condition than when he wrote "Like Decorations in a Nigger Cemetery," in which he emphasized the "between." By choosing "of" rather than "between," Stevens indicates acceptance rather than an anxiety, an acceptance achieved, I think, through the insights that Stevens gained about language in his own poetry.

"Notes toward a Supreme Fiction" concludes, as noted, with a "coda," four lines of which are particularly to the point:

> The two are one.
> They are a plural, a right and left, a pair,
> Two parallels that meet if only in
>
> The meeting of their shadows. . . .
> (*CP*, 407)

Although "shadows" could imply deferral and fragmentation and although "The two are one" states a unity, these lines, even without a simile or an "as if," finally emphasize neither one. Both are sustained as possibilities that, in their interaction, indeed come to bear a relation.

Throughout the rest of his poetic career, Stevens' use of similes (and "as if's") becomes even more prominent, and the problem of the latent tension in language that was in his poetry all along, that was clarified in "The Man with the Blue Guitar," and then codified in "Notes toward a Supreme Fiction," is unfolded again and again in different forms of expression. For example, "Chocorua to its Neighbor," written in 1943, contains this paradoxical simile: "There lies the misery . . . that life / Itself is like a poverty in the space of life." The simile identifies "life" as an absence in life, an identification which is simultaneously a form of unity and a form of fragmentation. "Somnambulisma," also written in the same year, contains the image of the bird "That thinks of settling, yet never settles," with "wings" that "keep spreading and yet are never wings" (*CP*, 304). And in 1944, Stevens wrote "The Creations of Sound," which concludes with the lines:

> We do not say ourselves like that in poems.
> We say ourselves in syllables that rise
> From the floor, rising in speech we do not speak.
> (*CP*, 311)

Written in the same year, "Esthétique du Mal" uses similes and "as if's" in order to explore "negation" as if it were "true" (*CP*, 319, 323). In the next year Stevens wrote "The Pure Good of Theory" in which he says, notably, that "to speak of the whole world *as* metaphor" (italics mine) is to know that one's "belief" is "not true."

Hereafter, Stevens' use of similes and the "as if" in key passages of important poems becomes far too frequent to enumerate. We should note, however, that simile and "as if's" are very important in "Credences of Summer," "Someone Puts a Pineapple Together," and "The Auroras of Autumn," the last of which contains the following lines: "It is like a thing of ether that exists / Almost as predicate" (*CP*, 418).

In 1948 Stevens wrote "A Primitive Like an Orb." Given the acceptance in "Notes toward a Supreme Fiction" of the "nakedness" (the gap) that is both the "nothingness" and "The whole" and yet not identical to either one, we have a

CHAPTER FOUR

certain insight into how the "giant of nothingness" can be the "total of letters" without leaving us completely in a meaningless abyss. As Stevens insists, the "giant" is "ever changing, *living in* change" (italics mine). The poem also asserts, "It is / As if the central poem became the world, // And the world the central poem." The paradoxical nature of the subject of the poem—the "instant of speech" which "is and / . . . is not and, therefore is" (*CP*, 440)—is explored and explained throughout by "as if's" and similes. As the poem says, "Oh as, always too heavy for the sense / To seize, the obscurest as" (*CP*, 441). The title of this poem, containing the word "like," is thus especially appropriate.

Although the 1949 "An Ordinary Evening in New Haven" is far too long and complex to be considered fully here, it is summarized in what the poem calls "the intricate evasions of as":

> This endlessly elaborating poem
> Displays the theory of poetry,
> As the life of poetry. A more severe,
>
> More harassing master would extemporize
> Subtler, more urgent proof that the theory
> Of poetry is the theory of life,
>
> As it is, in the intricate evasions of as.
> (*CP*, 486)

Throughout, the poem expores the "enigmatical / Beauty . . . in a total double-thing," the "several selves" that "come together as one" (*CP*, 472, 482). And, although the poem seeks to be "part of the res itself and not about it," still it remains "A difficulty that we predicate": it is "as if / . . . words of the world are the life of the world" (*CP*, 473, 474).

In 1949 Stevens also wrote "Angel Surrounded by Paysans," the poem that he chose to conclude the last of his books published separately before the *Collected Poems*. The poem's relation to a painting, like that of "The Man with the

Blue Guitar," further complicates the problem of presentation and representation as it is elaborated in his poetry.[48]

The "angel," unquestionably a highly complex figure, is equally a figure of the imagination and of reality.[49] Although he presents himself as a figure of reality, saying, "I am the necessary angel of earth, / Since, in my sight, you see the earth again," he also says that he is "a man / Of the mind, an apparition apparelled in // Apparels of . . . lightest look" (*CP*, 496-97). This angel, who is "only half of a figure of a sort," is an appropriate figure for the threshold that we have been discussing throughout this chapter: notably, the poem considers the "angel" from what seems to be two different sides of a door.

Neither the countryman nor the angel reaches through that door or reaches any resolution: the poem begins with the countryman's question, "There is / A welcome at the door to which no one comes?" and concludes with the angel's question, "Am I not . . . quickly, too quickly . . . gone?" But the fact that the angel is "surrounded" by the paysans suggests that the angel and the paysans are not on

---

[48] The painting is a Pierre Tal Coat still life ("Still Life") acquired by Stevens on September 30, 1949. Stevens gave it the title "Angel Surrounded by Peasants" and later named the poem "Angel Surrounded by Paysans" (see *L*, 649-50). For a further discussion regarding the problem of presentation and representation in Stevens, see Brogan, "Wallace Stevens: 'The Sound of Right Joining,'" *TSLL* 28 (Spring 1986), 107-20.

[49] In this respect it is interesting to see that Stevens says, "I was definitely trying to think of an earthly figure, not a heavenly figure" (*L*, 661), and that the angel is "the angel of reality" (*L*, 753). Richard Allen Blessing, however, concludes that the angel has more to do with the imagination than with reality: "That the 'angel of reality' should be 'a man / Of the mind' suggests that 'reality' may be only a necessary postulate of the imagination, that even the idea of things untainted by metaphor is a consequence of the way we feel, not of the things themselves" (*Wallace Stevens' "Whole Harmonium"* [Syracuse: Syracuse University Press, 1970], p. 122).

CHAPTER FOUR

one "side" of the other, but that the angel occupies the "center" of a circumference. This suggestion, however, does not imply a static unity, for the "center" represented by the angel is only "half seen" as an "apparition." In other words, the angel is a "figure" for the kind of gap we have been discussing. So, despite what seems to be a barrier between the angel and the countrymen, there is still the play of language which makes them inter-related and inter-dependent.

The language of the poem, then, moves by negations and assertions. The angel says, for example,

> I have neither ashen wing nor wear of ore
> And live without a tepid aureole,
>
> Or stars that follow me, not to attend,
> But, of my being and its knowing, part.
>
> I am one of you and being one of you
> Is being and knowing what I am and know.

We have seen this movement in Stevens' language before: the use of negations, as in the first four lines of this excerpt, to create a form of identity that is nonetheless "unfixed." The deliberately circular logic of the next two lines brings the separate elements together into "being" and unity.

The complicated dynamics of this poem and of the language in it reach their climactic moment in the simile which compares the earth's "tragic drone," heard through the "angel," to "liquid lingerings, / Like watery words awash; like meanings said // By repetitions of half-meanings." The power of this poem is that it presents the problem of the relation of the imagination and reality in terms of the problem of meaning, of language itself, so that ultimately the two problems represent each other. The "angel" achieves an identity, but one that is never fixed, and its pathos and its beauty are its vibrating possibilities.

In the last five years of his life Stevens attempted no poem as ambitious as "The Man with the Blue Guitar" or "Notes toward a Supreme Fiction," but during that time he wrote some of the most moving lyrics of his poetic career. A few, such as "As at a Theatre" (1950), were not published in the slim book *The Rock* that was added to the end of Stevens' *Collected Poems*. "As at a Theatre" bears an obvious relation to "Of Modern Poetry," a poem he wrote years earlier. Not only is the setting again a "theatre," but the poem again questions what would suffice to satisfy the mind: "What difference would it make," Stevens concludes, "So long as the mind, for once, fulfilled itself?" (*PM*, 362.) Like many of his poems, including "Of Modern Poetry," the poem is concerned with the problem of presentation and representation in language, but the "As" in the title and the four similes in the first stanza make the tension of the "Theatre" even more acute:

> Another sunlight might make another world,
> Green, more or less, in green and blue in blue,
> Like taste distasting the first fruit of a vine,
> Like an eye too young to grapple its primitive,
> Like the artifice of a new reality,
> Like the chromatic calendar of time to come.
> (PM, 361)

Clearly, the subjunctive verb, the qualification "more or less," the paradox of "taste distasting"—as well as the similes—all serve to sustain the unresting interplay that Stevens so consistently demands of his poetry.

Increasingly, these late poems, most of which were published in *The Rock*, have come to be recognized as Stevens' best. For example, in 1961, Pearce stated in *The Continuity of American Poetry* that "It might well be that Stevens' later poems ["ranging from 'Notes toward a Supreme Fiction' to 'The Rock' "] are not really poems; that looking so compulsively toward the decreative, they fail to be creative, fail to sustain themselves as self-contained works of art."[50] However, in "Toward Decreation," an article published in the

---

[50] Pearce, *Continuity*, p. 423.

CHAPTER FOUR

1980 *Celebration*, Pearce says that "Stevens was able in the *Rock* sequence of the *Collected Poems* to achieve what I can only call transcendence. (We can count it among our wordly blessings that he lived long enough to bring the drift of his ideas to something of a stasis.)"[51] Similarly, in the same book, Frank Kermode states that Stevens' "last poetry . . . may be his greatest."[52]

Several of the poems have been discussed in detail or in part through this study, such as "Prologues to What Is Possible," "Final Soliloquy of the Interior Paramour," "The World as Meditation," "The Planet on the Table," "The Poem that Took the Place of a Mountain," "St. Armorer's Church from the Outside," as well as "To an Old Philosopher in Rome" and "Vacancy in the Park." I believe that these poems are his best at least partly because by the time he wrote *The Rock* Stevens had found in similes and had become completely comfortable with a way of writing that allowed him to navigate "between believing too much and too little."[53] As "To an Old Philosopher in Rome" and "Vacancy in the Park" indicate, Stevens found in the "as if's" and in similes a mode of expression that "satisfies" conflicting de-

[51] Pearce, "Toward Decreation," p. 301.

[52] Frank Kermode, "Dwelling Poetically in Connecticut," p. 256.

[53] Speaking of Robert Frost and his use of language, Richard Poirier makes a statement especially applicable to Stevens: "To 'hit the right channel' between believing to little and too much is to be always more or less in carefully navigated motion"; and in fact Poirier later compares Frost to Stevens: "Frost's poetry can therefore be said to include terror without being itself terrified; it is for the most part reassuring in that it leaves us feeling more rather than less confident about our capacities. His is unlike the poetry of most of his contemporaries, except Lawrence and Stevens, because while you may make your life more complicated by reading it, you do not make your life more unmanageable. You are not led to believe that life is unintelligible or that your capacity to make sense of it merely proves your triviality" (*Robert Frost: The Work of Knowing* [New York: Oxford University Press, 1977; rpt. 1979], pp. xvi, 7-8).

sires while expressing the conflicting tendencies of language itself. By the time he wrote these last poems, Stevens had so fully explored the possibilities of this mode of expression that, in contradistinction to Joseph N. Riddel's discussion of the "dis-ease that is marked by the exile of writing," these poems are marked by ease and familiarity.

As we shall see in the next chapter, Stevens' exploration and ultimate embracing of the necessary tension in language reaches a point where he no longer needs even similes to sustain conflicting possibilities of language. As much as he uses similes and "as if's" in this period, several of the poems in *The Rock* have few or none, making their quiet understatement perhaps all the more powerful. As Samuel French Morse has noted, as Stevens' "mind mellowed, the language of his poetry grew simpler, less finicking and fastidious, but at its best no less precise than it had always been."[54] But, for our purposes here, it is enough to note that Stevens chose to conclude the final poem of his *Collected Poems*, "Not Ideas about the Thing but the Thing Itself," with a simile that summarizes his entire poetic enterprise: "It was like / A new knowledge of reality" (*CP*, 534).

The Resemblance

The concluding simile of Stevens' work inevitably raises serious questions about the relation of language to the mind and to the world. These are questions which I have attempted to exclude from this study as much as possible, although they insist on being heard around the edges. We should note, however, that the complicated tension in language itself resembles, if not determines, the complex tension between language and the world and language and the mind.[55]

---

[54] Morse, *Poetry as Life*, p. 205.
[55] As I. A. Richards puts it, the "problems" of "how language works"

CHAPTER FOUR

In this respect, Thomas Aquinas, who formulated a doctrine of analogy in his various writings, is an important figure to remember, for not only does he specifically address the relation of language to knowledge and reality, he provides an even closer point of comparison with Stevens than the other medieval writers previously mentioned. In a way that perhaps modern man might find naive, Aquinas questions the relation of language, of meaning, and the way we can know what meaning is to ultimate Being. Put simply, the problem in language that troubles Aquinas is that between words that are univocal in meaning and words that are equivocal in meaning are words that seem to be neither univocal nor equivocal. Thus, although he believes we can say, with truth and understanding, that "God is good," the meaning of "good" presents a problem, for it seems to be neither univocal nor equivocal. If predicated of God, "good" must have a meaning essentially identical with God. Yet when we say that man is good or that a pie is good, certainly "good" does not have the same meaning. But if "good" is equivocal—if it has essentially different meanings in every predication—then we have no ground for meaning or knowledge when we say "God is good."

The answer Aquinas evolves for this dilemma is elaborated in his various writings as the doctrine of analogy. In terms of this study, it is important to note that Aquinas' concept of analogy (or proportionality) bears a certain relation to Stevens' use of similes. Essentially, what Aquinas says is that for a certain category of words such as "good," meaning is in an *analogous* relation to being. Thus, as man is to God, so "good" applied to man is to "good" applied to God. The point is that while a word such as "good" means different things when predicated of different subjects, it always stands for a certain proportion between what the thing is—

---

and "thought as well" are "close together and similar and neither can be discussed profitably apart from the other" (p. 13).

its *being*—and what it should be. In this sense an analogous word has *different but related* meanings.[56]

Using mathematical symbols, the doctrine of proportionality can be described as follows:

$$\frac{A}{B} :: \frac{X}{Y}$$

Depending upon one's perspective, it is possible to emphasize the point of connection between the sets of terms above and so envision an essentially logocentric ground for meaning; or it is possible to emphasize the point of separation and to conclude that language is potentially meaningless. But this is to dissolve the individual elements in unity (as in the "chord") or to exaggerate the separation (as in "discord"). For our purposes it is most useful to recognize that Aquinas' doctrine of proportionality is itself somewhat analogous to Stevens' use of simile: like the simile, it presumes a gap that is not necessarily fragmentation, but that is necessary for the

---

[56] The doctrine of analogy is formulated in the various writings of St. Thomas Aquinas, but especially in *Compendium of Theology*, Part One, chapters 24-27 (tr. Cyril Vollart, S.J., St. Louis: B. Herder, 1947; rpt. 1958), pp. 26-28, and *Summa Contra Gentiles. On the Truth of the Christian Faith,* Book I, chapters 29-36 (tr. Anton C. Pegis, Garden City, N.Y.: Doubleday, 1955), pp. 138-50. For contemporary considerations of Aquinas' views on analogy, see the following: George P. Klubertanz, S.J., *St. Thomas Aquinas on Analogy: A Textual Analysis and Systematic Synthesis* (Chicago: Loyola University Press, 1960); Rev. Gerald B. Phelan, *St. Thomas and Analogy: The Aquinas Lecture, 1941* (Milwaukee: Marquette University Press, 1941; rpt. 1948); Dorothy M. Emmet, *The Nature of Metaphysical Thinking* (London: Macmillan, 1946); Anthony Nemetz, "The Meaning of Analogy," *Franciscan Studies,* 15 (1955), 209-23; Hampus Lyttkens, *The Analogy between God and the World* (Uppsala: Almquist and Wiksell, 1952), and Timotheus F. Barth, "Being, Univocity, and Analogy according to Duns Scotus," *John Duns Scotus, 1265-1965,* vol. 3 of *Studies in Philosophy and the History of Philosophy,* ed. John K. Ryan and Bernadine M. Bonansea (Washington, D.C.: Catholic University Press, 1965), pp. 210-62.

CHAPTER FOUR

bearing (and baring) of relation. Given this perspective, and especially when we consider other analogous theories, such as Heidegger's point of "dif-ference" and "intimacy," Stevens' use of similes in his poetry is indeed "like a new account of everything old" (*CP*, 529).[57]

Increasingly, throughout his poetry, *simile* becomes Stevens' major stylistic device for simultaneously sustaining the possibilities of language with which he is concerned and for

[57] It is of particular interest that in his explication of "Les Plus Belles Pages" (*CP*, 244-45), Stevens notes that Aquinas is "a figure of great modern interest" (*OP*, 294).
We should note, however, that whereas Frye also discusses analogy or proportionality in *Anatomy of Criticism*, his sense of analogy is somewhat different from that presented above: "On the formal level, where symbols are images or natural phenomena conceived as matter or content, the metaphor is an analogy of natural proportion. Literally, metaphor is juxtaposition; we say simply 'A;B.' Descriptively, we say 'A is (like) B.' But formally we say 'A is as B.' An analogy of proportion thus requires four terms, of which two have a common factor" (p. 124).
As with simile, analogy in Frye's theory is reducible to a displaced form of metaphor. In the view presented here, analogy is itself an analogy for certain aspects of language that we have elaborated through examining simile. Thus, we find that simile exposes a relation between language as metaphor and language as fragmentation, but it is a relation that is not reducible to resolution or synthesis. If total synthesis of these two poles of language were realized in simile, fragmentation would be reduced to identity (much as analogy is reducible to metaphor in Frye's system). Conversely, the lack of final synthesis does not mean "non-relation"; otherwise, metaphor or identity would be reduced to fragmentation. In simile we see a dialectical relationship between these two extremes in which the dialectic is undecidable; i.e., what Stevens calls the "intricate evasions of as" is a structure that iterates itself endlessly.
Finally, we should also note that whereas Aristotle discusses analogy in the *Poetics* as the most popular form of metaphor, his concern is with "proper" or "literal" meaning. Thus he finds catachresis (a four-term analogy in which only three of the terms are known) to be improper (Chapter 21).

elaborating the relation of the tension in language to the mind and to the world. *Simile* for Stevens comes to speak that "human speech" he has desired all along, that "modern poetry" which necessitates a subtle, ambiguous, even contradictory voice. As Sheehan says in a somewhat similar fashion, "Between these two extremes, reality as metaphor and reality as unknowable thing, Stevens discusses the idea of resemblance."[58] In essence, resemblance in the form of simile becomes the major trope or mode for expressing what Stevens recognizes as the ambiguity of the mind, of nature, and of their relationship, ultimately the ambiguity of language itself. In terms of the "needs" discussed in Chapters Two and Three, simile is also Stevens' major stylistic device for keeping his poetry from becoming either too dogmatic or too disillusioned.

The study of similes, then, at least in Stevens' poetry, reveals that simile is far more than a weakened metaphor or a mechanical comparison. In the unresting "balance" it creates, simile is the expression of the "act of the mind" as well as a model for the act of language itself. As suggestive and as far-reaching as Stevens' use of similes may be, an examination of it has a very specific and practical application: through what we have learned from Stevens' use of similes, we gain important insights into Stevens' use of language in what may be called his enigmatic poetry. A very early and famous poem, "Le Monocle de Mon Oncle" (1918), for example, remains puzzling from the opening "clashed edges of two words that kill" (*CP*, 13) to the "fluttering things" (*CP*, 18) of the concluding lines. And, although the general consensus may well be that in one way or another, the poem is

[58] Sheehan, p. 33. See also Joseph G. Kronick, "The Metamorphic Stevens," *Wallace Stevens Journal* 6 (1982), 3-9, in which he discusses the importance of "resemblance" in Stevens; as well as Charles Altieri, "Wallace Stevens' Metaphors of Metaphor: Poetry as Theory," *American Poetry* 1 (1983), especially pp. 36, 46, in which he discusses Stevens' use of "as."

CHAPTER FOUR

"about language and love," as A. Walton Litz has said,[59] it remains open to very different interpretations.

In two recent publications, for example, we find Harold Bloom and Isabel MacCaffrey drawing quite different conclusions about the nature of language and love in "Le Monocle de Mon Oncle." Throughout his discussion of the poem, Bloom reminds us that Stevens is concerned with language in the poem: he says, for example, that the "no, no" of the opening stanza may be the "opening tropes of extravagance."[60] Yet the particular perspective that governs Bloom's interpretation is that the poem is about erotic failure. Thus, after directing our attention to the terrible irony leveled against the "language of passion," Bloom announces that the "poem's title fools no one; 'Mon Oncle' is Stevens himself, and 'Le Monocle' is his erotic outlook in the fortieth year." This "outlook," Bloom goes on to say, is the product of desire that has been frustrated by the "two words that kill," the " 'no, no' as a sexual refusal" or by the more general frustration of Stevens' own advancing age. Bloom consequently finds that the line in the second stanza, "Shall I uncrumple this much-crumpled thing?" may refer to the "abortive first four lines of *Le Monocle*, as though Stevens kept crumpling and recrumpling his attempt at starting the poem. But more likely the question refers to Stevens' own sexual organ, with about as bitter a humor as Stevens ever attempts."

Isabel MacCaffrey, in contrast, finds a completely different relation between language and love in this poem. She states that it is possible to "reconstruct" the "skeletal system of assumptions that lie behind this poem" and consequently discover the poem's true subject, though not a subject "in any traditional sense": "The reconstruction would proceed

[59] Walton A. Litz, *Introspective Voyager: The Poetic Development of Wallace Stevens* (New York: 1972), p. 83.

[60] My summary here follows Bloom, *Poems of Our Climate*, pp. 38-43.

as follows. Poetry's most important subjects belong to 'the wordless world,' the world of Eros, who, alas (or perhaps fortunately), is dumb."[61] The "world of Eros," primarily the "well of unconscious," includes death and the "fact that Eros and Thanatos must embrace," as well as the earth, which is the "source and end of love." With this complex as the background, MacCaffrey focuses on the various stylistic techniques used in the poem to "approximate," or to "find words" for, the silent world of Eros, such as the subjunctives or conditionals, indefinite "its," and the "near miss" of something like slant-rhyme. This particular perspective allows MacCaffrey to conclude that the line, "Shall I uncrumple this much-crumpled thing?" means, roughly, that Stevens is asking if he should explicate the stanza's preceding "enigmatic and tantalizing" four lines about the red bird. She finds that the "uncrumpled" explication contained in the next five lines of the poem is unsatisfying: "[W]e are frustrated. The effect is to make the parable of the red bird more opaque, mysteriously significant, and mute when parable gives way to ineffectual paraphrase." This frustration, she says, is intentional and is created by Stevens in order "to convince us of the need for parabolic utterance, the dark conceits that mediate between the 'wordless world' and that articulateness that is the mark of consciousness."

Such differences in interpretations continue throughout Bloom's and MacCaffrey's analyses of the poem—one emphasizing erotic frustration revealed in the language, the other emphasizing the frustration of language in its attempt to speak the world of Eros. Because these interpretations are totally different and sometimes irreconcilable, it seems fruitful to consider the possibility that the poem may be "about" the kind of simultaneous interaction of opposing elements that is characteristic of Stevens' use of language, and that the "love" in the poem, as in the letter to Hi Simons

---

[61] This discussion follows MacCaffrey, "Ways of Truth," pp. 198-217.

CHAPTER FOUR

and several other poems that we mentioned earlier, may be an analogy or "illustration" of the poem's subject.

I find this possibility particularly convincing when we consider the tenth stanza of the poem and its critical "semblance":

> The fops of fancy in their poems leave
> Memorabilia of the mystic spouts,
> Spontaneously watering their gritty soils.
> I am a yeoman, as such fellows go.
> I know no magic trees, no balmy boughs,
> No silver-ruddy, gold-vermilion fruits.
> But, after all, I know a tree that bears
> A semblance to the thing I have in mind.
> It stand gigantic, with a certain tip
> To which all birds come sometime in their time.
> But when they go that tip still tips the tree.
>   (*CP*, 16-17)

Bloom tells us that the tree fails to fulfill "the desire for resemblances, giving only another emblem of solipsistic self-sufficiency, and one that borders on the grotesque by its phallic innuendo." (That grotesque innuendo is, I assume, the fact that the tree "stands gigantic, with a certain tip.") MacCaffrey, in contrast, concludes that the tree is a rather complicated image that "anticipates Yeats' great-rooted blossomer as an emblem for the life principle that is eterne in mutability," but, given the fact that Stevens' tree is nonmagical, the tree is ultimately "a careful analogy for 'a substance that prevails.'"

However, when we consider what we have learned from Stevens' use of similes throughout his poetic career, the word "semblance" in this stanza provides at least a threshold for understanding this poem. More than any other lines of his early poetry, the fourth and fifth lines of this stanza clearly state the complicated *relation* of language to itself, to the world, and to the mind. We are explicitly told that there is a tree—a tree that is initially taken to be a real object in the external world—that has a relationship to the "thing" he has "in mind." This relationship is carried and created by the word "semblance," and it is a relationship sustained and formed in language itself, specifically language that neither claims identity nor distinction, but similarity. The tree, of course, turns out not to be a real tree, for despite the claim that he knows no "magic trees," the tree figured here is mythical in its permanence. Thus, the tree is paradoxically permanent and non-existent, and whatever is explained by this tree is left unstated in the poem—except as the "semblance."

The subject of the poem, the "thing" he has "in mind" explained only as a "semblance," may well be the mysterious interaction of the unitive and disjunctive tendencies of language itself. The poem begins with a stated, even hyper-stated, anxiety about the fact that language divides. This anxiety is expressed in paradoxical negations of negations, as well as in the simile itself: "There is not nothing, no, no, never nothing, / Like the clashed edges of two words that kill" (*CP*, 13). It concludes with an affirmation of what division paradoxically brings together into being: "until now I never knew / That fluttering things have so distinct a shade" (*CP*, 18). Between the opening anxiety and concluding affirmation, Stevens wrestles with what seems to be an irresolvable contradiction, and in the image of sexuality he finds a figure that allows acceptance of that which both divides as it creates, fragments as it unites. We might expect, then, that the poem would be about simultaneous converging and dividing, and indeed Stevens tells us that "The honey of heaven may or may not come, / But that of earth both comes and goes at once" (*CP*, 15). The resolution that Stevens finds in this early poem, a resolution that is not naive, but sophisticated, is the "semblance."

The rest of Stevens' poetic career can be seen as the continued war between the "clashed edges" of "words that kill" and the "wished-for" seamless web of words *CP*, 17). As his poetry shows, the war came to be settled, although not statically so, by the exposure of language's being like a simile, in an actual use of similes so that we can say that similes are language's "Shapes / That are dissembled . . . / Yet still retain resemblances" (*OP*, 67).

In this respect, Coleridge again provides a useful and final point of comparison. In a passage in "On the Principles of Genial Criticism," Coleridge discusses resemblance, particularly the pleasure of resemblance:

> The BEAUTIFUL, contemplated in its essentials, that is, in *kind* and not in *degree*, is that in which the *many*, still seen as many, becomes one. Take a familiar instance, one of a thousand. The frost on a window-pane has by accident crystallized into a striking resemblance of a tree or sea-weed. With what pleasure we trace the parts, and their relations to each other, and to the whole![62]

In relation to Derrida's ideas—especially in terms of the word "trace"—we cannot ignore the suppressed irony of Coleridge's desire to "trace" the parts "to the whole." What is of interest to us, however, in relation to Stevens' poetry is not Coleridge's nostalgic desire for unity but rather his description of resemblance as something which is and which is pleasurable insofar as the "many," which "becomes one," is simultaneously "still seen as many." Thus for Coleridge, as for Stevens, "resemblance" satisfies the desires to unify and to distinguish—desires, as we have seen, that are themselves illustrations of the tendencies in language that Stevens' poetry explores. The simultaneity of Coleridge's "double vision" is of utmost importance here, as is the recognition that "resemblance," which holds both unity and distinctions, is the source of creative pleasure.

As Stevens says in "Notes toward a Supreme Fiction," "It Must Give Pleasure," and three times in "Three Academic

[62] Coleridge, "On the Principles of Genial Criticism," in Perkins, p. 443.

SIMILE

Pieces," Stevens draws attention to the pleasure of resemblance:

> So, when we think of arpeggios, we think of opening wings and the effect of the resemblance is pleasurable. (*NA*, 80)

> The proliferation of resemblances extends an object. The point at which this process begins, or rather at which this growth begins, is the point at which ambiguity has been reached. The ambiguity that is so favorable to the poetic mind is precisely the ambiguity favorable to resemblance. (*NA*, 78-79)

> The study of the activity of resemblance is an approach to the understanding of poetry. Poetry is a satisfying of the desire for resemblance. As the mere satisfying of a desire, it is pleasurable. (*NA*, 77)

Like the "interaction" that Stevens described to Simons as "a source of pleasure," this desire, called here the "desire for resemblance," is the pleasurable desire of poetry: it is not forced by the intellectual strain to replace belief or to resist the pressure of reality. It is pleasurable because it is a desire that manages to express the ambiguity latent in the act of language itself and, consequently, satisfies the desire for language to expose and express itself, the most pervasive desire in Stevens' poetry.

In simile, which has the same root as "semblance" or "resemblance," there is the "finding of a satisfaction" that Stevens demanded of "Modern Poetry." So, although Stevens may say that "Both in nature and in metaphor identity is the vanishing-point of resemblance," for Stevens such a condition does not point to the infinite abyss. He still insists that resemblance "binds together" (*NA*, 72), even if that binding resists being subsumed into identity. As Morton Zabel has said, Stevens' "work carried the radical stamp of a personality that was able, merely by the phraseology and figurative devices in which he dealt, to win half the battle of words and meaning."[63] With what we have learned of Stevens' use of simile, perhaps we can agree with Stevens that the "study of the activity of resemblance is an approach to the understanding of poetry"—and of language. Perhaps we can also better understand what Stevens means when he says that "in metaphor" "Resemblance . . . is an activity of the imagination" (NA, 73). Ultimately, the emphasis is on "resemblance," and in simile Stevens finds its most adequate form of expression.

[63] Morton Dauwen Zabel, "Wallace Stevens and the Image of Man," *The Harvard Advocate*, 127, 3 (Dec. 1940), 19-23; reprinted in Boroff, ed., *Collection*, p. 152.

CHAPTER FIVE

CONCLUSION

> He says no to no and yes to yes. He says yes
> To no; and in saying yes he says farewell.
> (*CP*, 414)

> The finally human.
> (*CP*, 504)

WITH THE INSIGHTS that we have gained from Stevens' use of similes, we are reminded of something that we have known all along and that Stevens seems to have recognized himself— that the meaning, the necessarily elusive center of Stevens' poetry, is described by and inscribed by the interaction of seemingly opposed elements. We should note with equal attention, therefore, the disjunctive possibilities that his disclaimers place upon poems characterized semantically by the desire for unity, and we should also seriously note the unitive possibilities that reclamations raise in poems ostensibly concerned with fragmentation; otherwise, we run the risk of over-reading (or under-reading) Stevens' poetry.

The implications of what we found in similes extends beyond the language of Stevens' poetry to language in general. Not only does simile satisfy the personal needs discussed in previous chapters, as well as satisfying the demands of opposing poetics, it also suggests that the necessary, simultaneous interplay of opposed tendencies seen in this form of language is the necessary condition and constraint for language in general. I should clarify at this point that I am not trying to isolate a particular occurrence in language as a

CHAPTER FIVE

function of simile alone. In other words, I am not trying to say that metaphor does one thing, while simile does another, or while another form of language does something else. Rather, I am suggesting that there are certain pervasive aspects of language that are captured and exposed in simile that we have seen instantiated in Stevens' use of similes. The corollary to this suggestion is that we should find that metaphors divide as well as unite and that fragmentation joins as well as severs. To some extent, this conclusion is precisely what was prescinded from Chapters Two and Three, and it is a conclusion that bears further elaboration here.

As mentioned in the first chapter of this study, I. A. Richards not only discusses the fact that the meaning of metaphor is the result of the interinanimation of tenor and vehicle, but he also says that "In general, there are very few metaphors in which disparities between tenor and vehicle are not as much operative as the similarities." Since Richards finds metaphor to be the "constitutive form" of language and its "omnipresent principle," his suggestion that metaphor has a somewhat dual nature can be applied to language as a whole.[1] Even more suggestively, given the recent deconstructive discussions of language, Richards says that "what a word means is the missing parts of the contexts from which it draws its delegate efficacy."[2] And we find an equally suggestive remark in Northrop Frye's most recent discussion of metaphor: "Metaphors of unity and integration take us only so far, because they are derived from the finiteness of the human mind. If we are to expand our vision into the genuinely infinite, that vision becomes decentralized."[3]

We find in other recent discussions of metaphor a similar awareness of the "disparity" inherent in metaphor: "Where

[1] Richards, pp. 127, 90.
[2] Ibid., p. 35.
[3] Northrop Frye, *The Great Code: The Bible and Literature* (New York: Harcourt Brace Jovanovich, 1982), p. 168.

179

CONCLUSION

there is metaphor, there is conflict. . . . Application of a term is metaphorical only if to some extent contra-indicated."[4] In a somewhat similar fashion, we find that "all metaphor involves a kind of twinning" and that the duality of metaphor "is necessary," even if that "duality is implicit, contained within an explicit unity and simplicity."[5]

The obvious extension of these various discussions of metaphor is that a statement made in the form of a metaphor implicity severs, fragments, or displaces. This extension unfolds again the complexity and delicacy of Stevens' considering metaphors, at times, as "Degeneration" (*CP*, 444), or as an "evasion" (*CP*, 373), or a "deviation" (*CP*, 471).

In a similar fashion, we have also seen that Derrida points out that "the passage from one structure to another" in language might be considered "negatively as catastrophe, or affirmatively as play," that he "agrees both that signs are indefinite . . . and that they mean." The consequence of these statements is that although it is possible to focus upon the displacement inherent in the sign and to conclude that "To mean . . . is automatically *not* to be,"[6] the possibility of meaning, and even of being, remains a necessary part of the structure of "differance." As Gayatri Spivak says in her introduction to *Of Grammatology*,

---

[4] Nelson Goodman, *Languages of Art: An Approach to a Theory of Symbols* (Indianapolis: Bobbs-Merrill, 1968), p. 69.

[5] Mackey, "Terms and Terminations," pp. 80-81. We find a similar dichotomy implied, although unintentionally, in *A Grammar of Metaphor* when Christine Brooke-Rose defines metaphor as a "replacement" or as an "identification" (p. 23). Her definition suggests that metaphor fragments as well as unites and points to the assumptions we have seen in the discussions of language as displacement and language as Adamic. In addition, see Monroe C. Beardsley, *Aesthetics* (New York: Harcourt Brace, 1958), pp. 152-55, 429-53; and Charles Feidelson, Jr., *Symbolism and American Literature* (Chicago: University of Chicago Press, 1953), pp. 44-76.

[6] Johnson, Introduction to *Dissemination*, p. ix.

> This possibility of Being must be granted (or rather is already of itself granted) for the human being to say "I am". . . . Even such negative concepts as "nothingness" or "nihilism" are held within this precomprehended question of Being which is asked and answered nonverbally, nonnominally, and without agency .[7]

Although he is not a deconstructionist, Kenneth Burke's discussion of the implicit duality of the "Negative" in *Language as Symbolic Action* has bearing here. Whereas Richards finds metaphor to be the constitutive form of language, Burke essentially finds the "Negative" to be the best model for understanding language and locates the "specific nature of language in the ability to use the Negative."[8] As he explains, however, the "negative is but a *principle*, an *idea*, not a name for a thing"; so, although the negative may be an obvious way of speaking that which "we do not speak," Burke insists that any "negative *idea* . . . also has about its edges the positive *image*" of what it negates.[9] Burke carries this insight further in his discussion of opposition:

> We should begin by noting that, considered simply as terms, the members of . . . pairs imply each other. . . . We can say with equal justice either that "order" implies "disorder" or that "disorder" implies "order"— and the same will be found true of "chaos" and "cosmos, insofar as they stand opposed.
> We would derive this state of affairs not from such *historical* "origins" or "firsts" as men's primitive battles with nature, wild beasts, and one another, but from the nature of that peculiarly linguistic marvel, the *negative*.[10]

---

[7] Spivak, Introduction to *Of Grammatology*, p. xiv.
[8] Burke, p. 419.
[9] Ibid., p. 10.
[10] Ibid., pp. 386-87.

CONCLUSION

More succinctly, Burke also says, "Insofar as negatives imply their opposites (as 'disorder' implies 'order'), the opposition between them is in effect 'timeless.' In themselves, as 'polar' terms, they have no progression or priority, but *merely imply each other*" (italics mine).[11]

Given the brief samplings of discussions of language cited above, we might conclude not only that metaphors and elements of fragmentation make "unheard" contradictions in the way that "as if's" and similes do, but also that language in general—or at least language which is self-conscious in the way that poetry is—works like similes, both positing and displacing at once. We might also conclude that any of the categories of language that we have examined (metaphor, fragmentation, simile) would suffice equally well as a model for understanding the particular aspects of language that we have been examining. In essence, I agree with this conclusion: as I have tried to show, the insights we gain from examining the action of language in simile are not especially radical, but indeed, "like a new account of everything old." However, in terms of Stevens' poetry, it was necessary to prescind from the earlier chapters what has been briefly elaborated here about metaphor and fragmentation in order to describe adequately the limits of language which his poetry seriously explores.

More important, by following this strategy, we were able to demonstrate the importance of Stevens' characteristic similes, how they provide a mode of expression that allows him to sustain the interplay of opposing tendencies of language, and subsequently to consider that simile provides a particularly useful model for understanding the necessary interaction in language. Simile has a certain advantage over both metaphor and fragmentation as a model for understanding certain aspects of language since it gives equal

---

[11] Ibid., p. 387. In addition, Christine Brooke-Rose briefly deals with "negative" or "denial" as "an implicit assertion" in *A Grammar of Metaphor*, pp. 116-17.

weight to both the converging and the diverging tendencies in language. For, despite the awareness of the inherent "disparities" in metaphor, most treatments of metaphor, in a kind of Romantic nostalgia for a belief in unity, tend to focus on the connections made in metaphor and to ignore the points of disconnection. Similarly, most deconstructive readings tend to emphasize the "abyss," the absence of meaning, and to de-emphasize the "capacity to mean." Simile, however, not only calls attention to both the joining and the dividing, but also exposes their inter-dependence. We should stress, however, that simile is only a model for understanding the latent tension in language: it is not that language is simile, but that it is like simile.

An extensive examination of the ramification of this suggestion is obviously beyond the realm of this study; it is, nevertheless, something which I think bears further thought. In relation to Stevens' poetry, however, we find that simile offers one final advantage: having seen how Stevens delicately sustains the opposing tendencies of language in his similes, we are encouraged to grant the possibility of a more complex movement in both his metaphors and his disjunctive elements than we might otherwise allow—to find in the poetry, and not just in the theory, that "The cry that contains its converse in itself" (*CP*, 471) is the principle of Stevens' poetry. By extension, we should find that, in addition to the obvious disclaimers of unity that Stevens weaves throughout his poetry, the metaphors themselves should bear their own points of fragmentation; similarly, in addition to the obvious reclamations, the disjunctive elements of Stevens' poetry should bear suggestions of unity. Although we could elaborate this at length, a couple of examples will suffice to show that this is true of Stevens' poetry and, I think, intentionally so.

We already know that at times Stevens conceives of metaphor as an "evasion" or "deviation": the fragmentation that is inherent in metaphor (but which metaphor tends to conceal) accounts for Stevens' ambivalent attitude toward metaphor. It also accounts for why, in a poem such as "World without Peculiarity," where a series of uniting metaphors culminate in a "single being, sure and true," we still feel something of a sense of loss and isolation.

As we have discussed in Chapter Two, the metaphors of this poem tend to bring the disparate elements—the "earth," the "fateful mother," the "thing upon his breast," the "hating woman," the "meaningless place," as well as the protagonist, who is both the "inhuman son" and the "human" of the poem—together into a "single being" and single, infused meaning. However, despite their movement toward unity, the metaphors of this poem ultimately fail to draw everything together into a single entity in which "difference disappears." For example, in the metaphoric statement that "the earth itself . . . is humanity," we are reminded, simultaneously, of the disparity between the earth and humanity and perhaps of the more painful fact that the "father," who is dead and presumably laid in the earth, is himself no longer a part of humanity. To a large degree, the attempt to bring the earth and humanity together in a metaphoric statement of identity makes the difference between them all the more painfully pronounced.

The other metaphors of this poem can be found to carry similar points of disparity, perhaps most obviously in the concluding lines:

> and, sometimes,
> He, too, is human and difference disappears
>
> And the povery of dirt, the thing upon his breast,
> The hating woman, the meaningless place,
> Become a single being, sure and true.

Despite the "single being, sure and true," we are reminded by the presence of the words themselves of the separate things of the poem, of the "poverty of dirt," the "thing upon his breast," the "hating woman," and the "meaningless place." Consequently, we are reminded all the more of what

CHAPTER FIVE

the protagonist of the poem wants to forget—essentially the isolation of the human condition. In the end, while asserting the possibility of a supreme unity, "World without Peculiarity" reminds us that it is, equally, a world of peculiarity. The poem, then, like many of Stevens' poems, ultimately examines the relation of things to each other; however, without the model that simile provides for understanding how Stevens deliberately makes contradictory statements *simultaneously*, I think it would be difficult to describe how (or why) Stevens is making such double statements in the metaphors of this poem.

In a similar fashion, with the perspective that simile provides for understanding the action of language in Stevens' poetry, we should examine the possibility that those elements of style that are usually considered disjunctive—the indefinite "it's," subjunctive verbs, conditional clauses, negations—also carry the possibility of being conjunctive, of working in the manner we earlier attributed to metaphor. We need, then, especially when reading the poetry of someone like Stevens, who was so clearly concerned with the nature of language, to note the "ember yes among its cindery noes" (*CP*, 529). As Stevens says elsewhere, "change composes, too, and chaos comes / To momentary calm" (*PM*, 123).

For example, we saw in Chapter Three that the fragmenting process of language in the excerpt from "Landscape with Boat" quickly leads to the "void" or abyss of the poem. However, in view of what we have seen in Stevens' use of similes and now even in his metaphors, we should temper this reading of the poem with the possibility that the very negations of the poem are forms of assertion, that they carry about their edges the positive images of that which is "denied." Thus, in the line, "It was not as if truth lay where he thought," not only does the "as if" posit the possibility that truth did lie where he thought and simultaneously negate that possibility, but the word "not" reiterates this dichotomy as well. Around the edges of the negative statement,

185

CONCLUSION

we hear the possibility that "It *was* as if truth lay where he thought." Similarly, the phrase "uncreated night" in the following line calls up the possibility of "created night."

Throughout this poem, the displacements made by the negative words and disjunctive elements continually evoke their positive possibilities. More interestingly, such a strategy appears to be an integral part of the poem's meaning. We find, for instance, in the concluding section of the poem, that Stevens deliberately reminds us of the possibility of union, of the sense of integration that the protagonist of the poem would have been able to feel, "Had he been better able to suppose":

> Had he been better able to suppose:
> He might sit on a sofa on a balcony
> ....
> And say, "The thing I hum appears to be
> The rhythm of this celestial pantomime."
> (*CP*, 243)

It is quite to the point that this conclusion evokes not only the connection between the human and the world but also the connection between language (in the form of " 'The thing I hum' ") and the world.

The protagonist, however, was "never" able to suppose such possible wholeness, as the lines preceding the conclusion tell us:

> He never supposed
> That he might be truth, himself, or part of it,
> That the things that he rejected might be part. . . .
> ....
> He never supposed divine
> Things might not look divine, nor that if nothing
> Was divine then all things were, the world itself,
> And that if nothing was the truth, then all
> Things were the truth, the world itself was the truth.
> (*CP*, 242)

CHAPTER FIVE

The effect of all the negations in the lines above is extremely complicated, but I think that they rather obviously are intended to remind us of what they negate—of what the protagonist might have supposed had he not been caught in the deepening "void" of his sense of isolation.

Again we find that this poem, like so many others, is concerned with the complex nature of the relation of things, and we also find that the divisive strategy of negation implicitly works in the fashion of simile, severing and joining at once. However, as in "World without Peculiarity," I think we would find it difficult to appreciate how Stevens makes these contradictory statements at once without the insights that his similes provide.

In the latest of his poems, Stevens is able to make the language of his poetry cry its "converse" without the convoluted and sometimes excessively self-conscious turnings of his earlier poetry. The later poems "became gentler; the surface of the poems was more discursive, in some ways, and less dazzling, yet neither so abstract nor so frequently embellished with the details that he had included for his own pleasure, as he once said it had been his habit to do."[12] Although I cannot prove the last point I wish to make here, I think that it was in similes that Stevens found precisely the simplicity and ease for speaking the complex interaction of language that he had desired all along and that also allowed him in other poems of *The Rock* to speak equally well the nature of language without the convolutions of some of his earlier poetry and even without the help of similes. Perhaps in their "plainness of speech" the complexity Stevens wishes to evoke is, paradoxically, heard all the more clearly.[13]

Not everyone agrees that the last poetry is the best. John Ciardi, for example, has said that the poems of *Auroras of Autumn* and *The Rock* are "still the work of the master, but of the master repeating himself and just a bit wearily. . . .

---

[12] Morse, *Poetry as Life*, p. 205.
[13] Ibid., p. 219.

CONCLUSION

[E]very poet past his first excitement is tempted to become talky and to borrow from himself, and of late Stevens seems to have succumbed to the temptation."[14] However, others have found that the grandeur of Stevens' latest poems is neither weary nor stale, even if the subject-matter of such poems as "Long and Sluggish Lines," "The Plain Sense of Things," and "An Old Man Asleep" (to mention only a few) does involve a growing weariness, a sense of lateness, winter, and impending death.[15]

As an example of what Stevens achieved in the poems at the end of his life, I would like to cite "Lebensweisheitspielerei" (which roughly means, "trifle of practical wisdom" or, idiomatically, "toy of thought"):

> Weaker and weaker, the sunlight falls
> In the afternoon. The proud and the strong
> Have departed.
>
> Those that are left are the unaccomplished,
> The finally human,
> Natives of a dwindled sphere.
>
> Their indigence is an indigence
> That is an indigence of the light,
> A stellar pallor that hangs on the threads.
>
> Little by little, the poverty
> Of autumnal space becomes
> A look, a few words spoken.
>
> Each person completely touches us
> With what he is and as he is,
> In the stale grandeur of annihilation.
> <div align="right">(<i>CP</i>, 504-5)</div>

---

[14] John Ciardi, "Wallace Stevens' 'Absolute Music,' " *The Nation*, 179 (16 October 1954), 347.

[15] Frank Kermode says that the last poems "are mostly poems of death, or of the achievement of a posture in which to meet it correctly" ("Dwelling Poetically in Connecticut," p. 256).

CHAPTER FIVE

Despite the falling, dwindling, and annihilation of this poem, the title is not simply ironic. As we have seen, throughout his career Stevens rejects the possibility of an eternal (and static) "paradise" in favor of the "imperfect" that "is our paradise." As he says so clearly in the early poem "Sunday Morning," "Death is the mother of beauty." The play, the joy, the movement of life necessarily includes the movement toward death; and without that fact, as Stevens is well aware, there would be no movement at all.

Stevens, however, is not merely repeating himself in this poem. In a certain simplicity that is perhaps all the more powerful, Stevens makes it painfully and beautifully clear that the complex, paradoxical human condition can indeed be defined by and as "a few words spoken"—or, to put it in other terms, that the complex action of language that Stevens has spent his career explaining in poetry is like the complex action of life itself. Between the limits of total being and total nothingness, both language and life find the space to move.

It is particularly appropriate, then, that the increasing nothingness in this poem, which is called up in almost every line, paradoxically begins to unite everything in its indigence, receiving its final figuration as "a few words spoken." And it is with this indigence as the background that it is possible for "Each person" to "completely" touch us "With what he is and as he is." The change from "what" to "as"— from identity to temporal seeming—summarizes the entire, complex movement of this poem that is expressed so simply, yet so well.

In poems such as this, as well as the many other poems from *The Rock* that have been examined in this study, I think that Stevens achieves the "finally human," the "acutest" human speech with which this study began. Samuel French Morse suggests that the human quality of the late poems has to do with the fact that " 'we' become[s] as important as 'I' or 'one.' "[16] And, although this is undoubtedly

---
[16] Morse, *Poetry as Life*, p. 213.

CONCLUSION

true, I think that the human quality of the last poems is a result of Stevens' ability to express the subtle relation between the paradoxical nature of language and that of the human condition. As Heidegger says,

> Man speaks. We speak when we are awake and we speak in our dreams. We are always speaking, even when we do not utter a single word aloud, but merely listen or read, and even when we are not particularly listening or speaking but are attending to some work or taking a rest. . . . Man is said to have language by nature. . . . It means to say that only speech enables man to be the living being he is as man. It is as one who speaks that man is—man.[17]

Heidegger also says something which I think applies particularly well to what Stevens attempts and achieves in his poetry: "To reflect on language means—to reach the speaking of language in such a way that this speaking takes place as that which grants an abode for the being of mortals."[18]

As Stevens says in a very late letter, "For a long time, I have thought of adding other sections to the NOTES and one in particular: *It Must Be Human*" (see L, 863-64). The last poems, I think, complete that section of the "Notes toward a Supreme Fiction" that Stevens felt he never wrote. Despite negative criticisms of his dandyism or abstractions, I think that Stevens' poetry speaks especially well to the paradoxical nature of the human condition. As he explores the limits of language, Stevens expresses human longing as well as human limitation.

It is part of his power as a poet that Stevens unfolds in language that which bears a relation to the paradoxical nature of life, which is enacted between birth and death, burdened with the knowledge that nothing can be fully known, yet which still asserts in words the only possible meaning. Ste-

[17] Heidegger, p. 189.
[18] Ibid., p. 192.

CHAPTER FIVE

vens' success is left in the poems themselves: they are, as he says of Ariel's poems, part of the "makings of the sun." Yet, however successful, he was a "man who needed what he had created" (*NA*, 51). The larger, more subtle success of his last poems lies in their note of acceptance—an acceptance achieved, at least in part, by the forms of language that he learned would express most clearly both what he wanted to say and could not say. As Stevens says, "the desire for literature is the desire for life" (*OP*, 227).

BIBLIOGRAPHY

Abrams, M. H. *Glossary of Literary Terms*. 4th ed. New York: Holt, Rinehart, 1981.

———. *The Mirror and the Lamp: Romantic Theory and the Critical Tradition*. New York: Oxford University Press, 1953; rpt. 1980.

Alan of Lille. *Anticlaudianus*. Tr. James J. Sheridan. Toronto: Pontifical Institute of Medieval Studies, 1973.

Altieri, Charles. "Wallace Stevens' Metaphors of Metaphor: Poetry as Theory." *American Poetry* 1 (1983): 27-48.

Aquinas, St. Thomas. *Compendium of Theology*. Tr. Cyril Vollert, S.J., S.T.D. St. Louis: B. Herder, 1947; rpt. 1958.

———. *On the Truth of the Catholic Faith: Summa Contra Gentiles*. Tr. Anton C. Pegis. Garden City, N.Y.: Doubleday, 1955.

Aristotle. *Poetics*. Tr. S. H. Butcher. *Aristotle's Theory of Poetry and Fine Art*. 4th ed., New York: Dover, 1955.

Augustine, St. *Confessions*. Tr. R. S. Pine-Coffin. Baltimore: Penguin, 1961.

Baird, James. *The Dome and the Rock: Structure in the Poetry of Wallace Stevens*. Baltimore: Johns Hopkins University Press, 1968.

Baker, Howard. "Wallace Stevens and Other Poets." *Southern Review* 1 (1935): 373-89.

Barfield, Owen. *Saving the Appearances: A Study in Idolatry*. New York: Harcourt, Brace, & World, n.d.

Barth, J. Robert. *The Symbolic Imagination: Coleridge and the Romantic Tradition*. Princeton: Princeton University Press, 1977.

Barth, Timotheus F. "Being, Univocity, and Analogy according to Duns Scotus." In *John Duns Scotus, 1265-1965*, pp. 210-62. Ed. John K. Ryan and Bernadine M. Bonansea. Vol. 3 of *Studies in Philosophy and the His-

tory of Philosophy. 3 vols. Washington, D.C.: Catholic University Press, 1965.

Beardsley, Monroe C. *Aesthetics*. New York: Harcourt Brace, 1958.

Benamou, Michel. *Wallace Stevens and the Symbolist Imagination*. Princeton: Princeton University Press, 1972.

Bentham, Jeremy. *Bentham's Theory of Fiction*. Ed. C. K. Ogden. London: Kegan Paul, Trench, Trubner, 1932.

Bernard de Clairvaux, St. *The Steps of Humility and Pride*. In *Treatises II*. Vol. 5 of *The Works of Bernard de Clairvaux*. Washington, D.C.: Cistercian Publications Consortium Press, 1974.

Blessing, Richard Allen. *Wallace Stevens' "Whole Harmonium."* Syracuse: Syracuse University Press, 1970.

Bloom, Harold. "*Notes Toward a Supreme Fiction*: A Commentary." In *Wallace Stevens: A Collection of Critical Essays*, pp. 76-95. Ed. Marie Borroff. Englewood Cliffs, N.J.: Prentice-Hall, 1963.

———. *Wallace Stevens: The Poems of Our Climate*. Ithaca: Cornell University Press, 1976.

Borroff, Marie, ed. *Wallace Stevens: A Collection of Critical Essays*. Englewood Cliffs, N.J.: Prentice-Hall, 1963.

Brazeau, Peter. *Parts of a World: Wallace Stevens Remembered*. New York: Random House, 1983.

Bréal, Michel. *Semantics: Studies in the Science of Meaning*. Tr. Mrs. Henry Cust. New York. Dover, 1964.

Brelet, Gisèle. "Music and Silence." *La Revue Musicale* 22 (1946): 169-81. Reprinted in *Reflections on Art: A Source Book of Writings by Artists, Critics, and Philosophers*, pp. 103-21. Ed. Susanne K. Langer. Baltimore: Johns Hopkins University Press.

Brogan, Jacqueline. "The 'Form / And Frame' of 'As If' in Wallace Stevens." *American Poetry* 3 (Spring 1986): 34-50.

———. "Stevens' 'Two Figures in Dense Violet Night.' " *American Notes & Queries* 23 (1984): 49-50.

———. "Wallace Stevens: 'The Sound of Right Joining.' " *TSLL* 28 (Spring 1986): 107-20.

———. "Wallace Stevens' 'Vacancy in the Park' and the Concept of Similitude." *Wallace Stevens Journal* 10 (1986): 9-17.

Brooke-Rose, Christine. *A Grammar of Metaphor*. London: Secker & Warburg, 1958.

Brooks, Cleanth, Jr. "Metaphor and the Function of Criticism." In *Spiritual Problems in Contemporary Literature*, pp. 127-37. Ed. Stanley R. Hopper. New York: Harper, 1952.

———. Statement in the Stevens issue of *The Harvard Advocate* 127, 3 (December 1940): 29-30.

Bruns, Gerald L. *Modern Poetry and the Idea of Language: A Critical and Historical Study*. New Haven: Yale University Press, 1974.

Burke, Kenneth. *Language as Symbolic Action*. Berkeley: University of California Press, 1966.

Carruth, Hayden. "Without the Inventions of Sorrow." *Poetry* 85 (1955): 288-93.

Cassirer, Ernst. *Language and Myth*. Tr. Susanne K. Langer. New York: 1946: rpt. New York: Dover, 1953.

Ciardi, John. "Wallace Stevens's 'Absolute Music.' " *The Nation* 179 (16 October 1954): 346-47.

Coleridge, Samuel Taylor. *Biographia Literaria*. Ed. George Watson. New York: E. P. Dutton, 1975.

———. *Lay Sermons*. Ed. R. J. White. Vol. 6 of *The Collected Works of Samuel Taylor Coleridge*. Ed. Kathleen Coburn. Bollingen Series, 75. Princeton: Princeton University Press, 1972.

———. Letter to John Thelwall. 14 October 1797. *English Romantic Writers*, p. 523. Ed. David Perkins. New York: Harcourt, Brace & World, 1967.

———. "On the Principles of Genial Criticism: Essay Third" [1814]. *English Romantic Writers*, pp. 441-48. Ed. David Perkins. New York: Harcourt, Brace & World, 1976.

BIBLIOGRAPHY

Conrad, Joseph. *Heart of Darkness* [1902]. Ed. Robert Kimbrough. 2nd ed. New York: W. W. Norton, 1971.

De Man, Paul. "Intentional Structure of the Romantic Image." In *Romanticism and Consciousness*, pp. 65-77. Ed. Harold Bloom. New York: W. W. Norton, 1970.

———. "The Rhetoric of Temporality." In *Interpretation: Theory and Practice*, pp. 173-209. Ed. Charles S. Singleton. Baltimore: Johns Hopkins University Press, 1969.

Derrida, Jacques. "Differance." *Bulletin de la Société française de philosophie* 62, 3 (July-September 1968): 73-101. Reprinted in *Speech and Phenomenon*, pp. 129-60. Tr. David Allison. Evanston: Northwestern University Press, 1973.

———. *Dissemination*. Tr. Barbara Johnson. Chicago: University of Chicago Press, 1981.

———. *Of Grammatology*. Tr. Gayatri Chakravorty Spivak. Baltimore: Johns Hopkins University Press, 1974, 1976.

———. "Structure, Sign, and Play in the Discourse of the Human Sciences." In *The Structuralist Controversy: The Languages of Criticism and the Sciences of Man*, pp. 247-72. Ed. Richard Macksey and Eugenio Donato. Baltimore: Johns Hopkins University Press, 1972.

———. "White Mythology: Metaphor in the Text of Philosophy." Tr. F.C.T. Moore. *New Literary History* 6 (1975): 5-74.

Dickie, George. *Aesthetics: An Introduction*. Indianapolis: Pegasus, 1971.

Doggett, Frank. *Wallace Stevens: The Making of the Poem*. Baltimore: Johns Hopkins University Press, 1980.

Doggett, Frank, and Robert Buttel, eds. *Wallace Stevens: A Celebration*. Princeton: Princeton University Press, 1980.

Emmet, Dorothy M. *The Nature of Metaphysical Thinking*. London: Macmillan, 1946.

BIBLIOGRAPHY

Empson, William. Review of *Selected Poems* by Wallace Stevens. *Listener* 48 (26 March 1953): 521.

Feidelson, Charles, Jr. *Symbolism and American Literature*. Chicago: University of Chicago Press, 1953.

Fitzgerald, Robert. "Thoughts Revolved." *Poetry* 51 (1937): 153-57.

Frye, Northrop. *Anatomy of Criticism: Four Essays*. Princeton: Princeton University Press, 1957; rpt. New York: Atheneum, 1967.

──── . *The Great Code: The Bible and Literature*. New York: Harcourt Brace Jovanovich, 1982.

──── . "The Realistic Oriole: A Study of Wallace Stevens." *Hudson Review* 10 (1957): 353-70. Reprinted in *Wallace Stevens: A Collection of Critical Essays*, pp. 161-76. Ed. Marie Borroff. Englewood Cliffs, N.J.: Prentice-Hall, 1963.

Goodman, Nelson. *Languages of Art: An Approach to a Theory of Symbols*. Indianapolis: Bobbs-Merrill, 1968.

Guetti, James. *The Limits of Metaphor: A Study of Melville, Conrad, and Faulkner*. Ithaca: Cornell University Press, 1967.

Hammond, Mac. "On the Grammar of Wallace Stevens." In *The Act of the Mind: Essays on the Poetry of Wallace Stevens*, pp. 179-84. Ed. Roy Harvey Pearce and J. Hillis Miller. Baltimore: Johns Hopkins University Press, 1965.

Hartman, Geoffrey. *Criticism in the Wilderness: The Study of Literature Today*. New Haven: Yale University Press, 1980.

──── . *Wordsworth's Poetry: 1787-1814*. New Haven: Yale University Press, 1964; rpt. 1971.

Hegel, G.W.F. *Reason in History*. Tr. Robert S. Hartman. Indianapolis: Bobbs-Merrill, 1953; rpt. 1978.

Heidegger, Martin. *Poetry, Language, Thought*. Tr. Albert Hofstadter. New York: Harper & Row, 1971; rpt. 1975.

Heringman, Bernard. "Wallace Stevens: The Use of Poetry." *ELH* 16 (1949): 325-36.

Hines, Thomas J. *The Later Poetry of Wallace Stevens: Phenomenological Parallels with Husserl and Heidegger.* Lewisburg: Bucknell University Press, 1976.

Holman, C. Hugh. *A Handbook to Literature.* 3rd. ed. New York: Odyssey Press, 1972.

James, William. *The Will to Believe: And Other Essays in Popular Philosophy.* New York: Longmans, Green, 1923.

Janson, H. W., and Joseph Kerman. *A History of Art and Music.* New York: Harry Abrams, n.d.

Jarrell, Randall. "Reflections on Wallace Stevens." *Partisan Review* 18 (1951): 335-44. Reprinted in *Poetry and the Age,* pp. 121-34. New York: Vintage Books, 1955.

Johnson, Barbara. "Translator's Introduction," pp. vii-xxxiii. Jacques Derrida. *Dissemination.* Tr. Barbara Johnson. Chicago: University of Chicago Press, 1981.

Juhasz, Suzanne. *Metaphor and the Poetry of Williams, Pound, and Stevens.* Lewisburg: Bucknell University Press, 1974.

Kaufmann, R. J. "Metaphorical Thinking and the Scope of Literature." *College English* 30 (1968): 31-47.

Kermode, Frank. "Dwelling Poetically in Connecticut." In *Wallace Stevens: A Celebration,* pp. 256-73. Ed. Frank Doggett and Robert Buttel. Princeton: Princeton University Press, 1980.

———. *The Sense of an Ending: Studies in the Theory of Fiction.* New York: Oxford University Press, 1966.

Kline, Morris. *Mathematics: The Loss of Certainty.* New York: Oxford University Press, 1980.

Klubertanz, George P., S.J. *St. Thomas Aquinas on Analogy: A Textual Analysis and Systematic Synthesis.* Chicago: Loyola University Press, 1960.

Kronick, Joseph G. 'The Metamorphic Stevens." *Wallace Stevens Journal* 6 (1982): 3-9.

Kunitz, Stanley. *A Kind of Order, A Kind of Folly.* Boston: Atlantic, Little, Brown, 1975.

Leach, Edmund. "Anthropological Aspects of Language:

Animal Categories and Verbal Abuse." In *New Directions in the Study of Language*, pp. 23-63. Ed. Eric H. Lenneberg. Cambridge, Mass.: MIT Press, 1964.

Lentricchia, Frank. *After the New Criticism.* Chicago: University of Chicago Press, 1980.

Levin, Harry. Statement in the Stevens issue of *The Harvard Advocate* 127, 3 (December 1940): 30.

Litz, A. Walton. *Introspective Voyager: The Poetic Development of Wallace Stevens.* New York: Oxford University Press, 1972.

―――. "Particles of Order: The Unpublished *Adagia.*" In *Wallace Stevens: A Celebration*, pp. 57-77. Ed. Frank Doggett and Robert Buttel. Princeton: Princeton University Press, 1980.

Lyttkens, Hampus. *The Analogy between God and the World.* Uppsala: Almquist and Wiksell, 1952.

MacCaffrey, Isabel. "A Point of Central Arrival: Stevens' *The Rock.*" *ELH* 40 (1974): 606-33.

―――. "The Ways of Truth in 'Le Monocle de Mon Oncle.' " In *Wallace Stevens: A Celebration*, pp. 196-218. Ed. Frank Doggett and Robert Buttel. Princeton: Princeton University Press, 1980.

MacCleod, Glen. *Wallace Stevens and Company: The* HARMONIUM *Years 1913-1923.* Ann Arbor: UMI Research Press, 1983.

McCall, Marsh H., Jr. *Ancient Rhetorical Theories of Simile and Comparison.* Cambridge, Mass.: Harvard University Press, 1969.

McCann, Janet P. "French Flowers: Baudelaire and Wallace Stevens." Ph.D. diss. University of Pittsburgh, 1974.

Mackey, Louis. "On Terms and Terminations: The Dissolution of the Medieval Metaphor." *Texas Quarterly* 21 (1978): 79-88.

―――. "Singular and Universal: A Franciscan Perspective." *Franciscan Studies* 39 (1979): 130-64.

Matthiessen, F. O. "Wallace Stevens at 67." *New York Times Book Review*, 20 April 1947, pp. 4, 26.
Metaphor. Special Issue of *Critical Inquiry* 5 (1978).
Miller, J. Hillis. "Stevens' Rock and Criticism as Cure." *Georgia Review* 30 (1976): 5-31.
―――. "Stevens' Rock and Criticism as Cure, II." *Georgia Review* 30 (1976): 330-48.
―――. "Theoretical and Atheoretical in Stevens." In *Wallace Stevens: A Celebration*, pp. 274-85. Ed. Frank Doggett and Robert Buttel. Princeton: Princeton University Press, 1980.
―――. "Wallace Stevens' Poetry of Being." *ELH* 31 (1964): 86-105.
Mills, Ralph J., Jr. "Wallace Stevens: The Image of the Rock." In *Wallace Stevens: A Collection of Critical Essays*, pp. 96-110. Ed. Marie Borroff. Englewood Cliffs, N.J.: Prentice-Hall, 1963.
Monroe, Harriet. "He Plays the Present." *Poetry* 47 (1935): 153-57.
Moore, Marianne. "There Is a War That Never Ends." *Kenyon Review* 5 (1943): 144-47.
―――. "Well Moused, Lion." *Dial* 76 (1924): 84-91.
Morris, Adelaide Kirby. *Wallace Stevens: Imagination and Faith*. Princeton: Princeton University Press, 1974.
Morse, Samuel French. "A Poet Who Speaks the Poem as It Is." *New York Times Book Review*, 3 October 1954, pp. 3, 21.
―――. *Wallace Stevens: Poetry as Life*. Indianapolis: Pegasus, 1970.
Munson, Gorham B. "The Dandyism of Wallace Stevens." *Dial* 79 (1925): 413-17.
Nemetz, Anthony. "The Meaning of Analogy." *Franciscan Studies* 15 (1955): 209-23.
O'Connor, Flannery. *The Habit of Being*. Ed. Sally Fitzgerald. New York: Farrar, Straus & Giroux, 1979.
Owen, Stephen, and Walter L. Reed. "A Motive for Metaphor." *Criticism* 21 (1979): 287-306.

Pearce, Roy Harvey. *The Continuity of American Poetry*. Princeton: Princeton University Press, 1961.
———. "Toward Decreation: Stevens and the 'Theory of Poetry.' " In *Wallace Stevens: A Celebration*, pp. 286-307. Ed. Frank Doggett and Robert Buttel. Princeton: Princeton University Press, 1980.
Pearce, Roy Harvey, and J. Hillis Miller, eds. *The Act of the Mind: Essays on the Poetry of Wallace Stevens*. Baltimore: Johns Hopkins University Press, 1965.
Phelan, Rev. Gerald B. *St. Thomas and Analogy: The Aquinas Lecture, 1941*. Milwaukee: Marquette University Press, 1941; rpt. 1948.
Plato. *The Republic*. Ed. Edith Hamilton and Huntington Cairns. Bollingen Series, 71. Princeton: Princeton University Press, 1961.
Poirier, Richard. *Robert Frost: The Work of Knowing*. New York: Oxford University Press, 1977; rpt. 1979.
Polanyi, Michael, and Harry Prosch. *Meaning*. Chicago: University of Chicago Press, 1975.
Porte, Joel. Letter to author. 4 February 1982.
Poulet, Georges. *The Interior Distance*. Tr. Elliott Coleman. Baltimore: Johns Hopkins University Press, 1959.
———. *The Metamorphosis of the Circle*. Tr. Carley Dawson and Elliott Coleman. Baltimore: Johns Hopkins University Press, 1966.
Ransom, John Crowe. "Poets Without Laurels." In *The World's Body*, pp. 55-75. New York: Charles Scribner's Sons, 1938.
Regeuiro, Helen. *The Limits of Imagination: Wordsworth, Yeats, Stevens*. Ithaca: Cornell University Press, 1976.
Richards, I. A. *The Philosophy of Rhetoric*. New York: Oxford University Press, 1936; rpt. 1976.
Riddel, Joseph N. *The Clairvoyant Eye: The Poetry and Poetics of Wallace Stevens*. Baton Rouge: Louisiana State University Press, 1965.

Riddel, Joseph N. "The Climate of Our Poems." *Wallace Stevens Journal* 7 (1983): 59-75.

———. "The Contours of Stevens Criticism." *ELH* 31 (1964): 106-38. Reprinted in *The Act of the Mind: Essays on the Poetry of Wallace Stevens*, pp. 243-76. Ed. Roy Harvey Pearce and J. Hillis Miller. Baltimore: Johns Hopkins University Press, 1965.

———. "Metaphoric Staging: Stevens' Beginning Again of the 'End of the Book.' " In *Wallace Stevens: A Celebration*, pp. 308-38. Princeton: Princeton University Press, 1980.

———. "Walt Whitman and Wallace Stevens: Functions of a 'Literatus.' " *South Atlantic Quarterly* 56 (1962): 506-20. Reprinted in *Wallace Stevens: A Collection of Critical Essays*, pp. 30-42. Ed. Marie Borroff. Englewood Cliffs, N.J.: Prentice-Hall, 1963.

Santayana, George. *Scepticism and Animal Faith*. New York: Charles Scribner's Sons, 1923; rpt. 1924.

Schwartz, Delmore. "The Ultimate Plato with Picasso's Guitar." *The Harvard Advocate* 127 (December 1940): 11-16.

Sheehan, Donald. "Stevens' Theory of Metaphor." In *Critics on Wallace Stevens*, pp. 31-39. Ed. Peter L. McNamara. Miami: University of Miami Press, 1972.

Shibles, Warren A. *Metaphor: An Annotated Bibliography*. Whitewater, Wis.: Language Press, 1971.

Simons, Hi. "The Genre of Wallace Stevens." *Sewanee Review* 53 (1945): 566-79. Reprinted in *Wallace Stevens: A Collection of Critical Essays*, pp. 43-53. Ed. Marie Borroff. Englewood Cliffs, N.J.: Prentice-Hall, 1963.

Spivak, Gayatri Chakravorty. "Translator's Preface," pp. ix-xc. Jacques Derrida. *Of Grammatology*. Tr. Gayatri Chakravorty Spivak. Baltimore: Johns Hopkins University Press, 1974; rpt. 1976.

Stevens, Holly. *Souvenirs and Prophecies: The Young Wallace Stevens*. New York: Knopf, 1977.

Stevens, Wallace. "The Noble Rider and the Sound of

Words." In *The Language of Poetry*, pp. 91-125. Ed. Alan Tate. Princeton: Princeton University Press, 1942.

Symons, Julian. "A Short View of Wallace Stevens." *Life and Letters Today* 26 (1940): 215-24.

Taylor, Wilson E. "Of a Remembered Time." In *Wallace Stevens: A Celebration*, pp. 91-104. Ed. Frank Doggett and Robert Buttel. Princeton: Princeton University Press, 1980.

Vaihinger, Hans. *The Philosophy of "As If": A System of the Theoretical, Practical and Religious Fictions of Mankind.* Tr. C. K. Ogden. London: Routledge & Kegan Paul, 1924; rpt. 1949.

Van Doren, Mark. "Poets and Wits." *The Nation* 117 (10 October 1923): 400-2.

Vendler, Helen. *On Extended Wings: Wallace Stevens' Longer Poems*. Cambridge, Mass.: Harvard University Press, 1969.

―――. "The Qualified Assertions of Wallace Stevens." In *The Act of the Mind: Essays on the Poetry of Wallace Stevens*, pp. 163-78. Ed. Roy Harvey Pearce and J. Hillis Miller. Baltimore: Johns Hopkins University Press, 1965.

―――. "Stevens and Keats' 'To Autumn.' " In *Wallace Stevens: A Celebration*, pp. 171-95. Ed. Frank Doggett and Robert Buttel. Princeton: Princeton University Press, 1980.

Walsh, Thomas F. *Concordance to the Poetry of Wallace Stevens*. University Park: Pennsylvania State University Press, 1963.

Ward, Wilfrid. "The Wish to Believe." *Witnesses to the Unseen*. Macmillan, 1893.

Wheelwright, Philip. *The Burning Fountain: A Study in the Language of Symbolism*. Rev. ed. Bloomington: Indiana University Press, 1968.

Williams, William Carlos. *Collected Poems: 1921-1931*. New York: Objectivist Press, 1934.

Williams, William Carlos. Review of *Man with the Blue Guitar and Other Poems*. *New Republic* 93 (17 November 1937): 50.
Wilson, Edmund. "Wallace Stevens and E. E. Cummings." *New Republic* 38 (19 March 1924): 102-3.
Winters, Yvor. "Wallace Stevens, or the Hedonist's Progress." *The Anatomy of Nonsense*, pp. 88-119. Norfolk, Conn.: New Directions, 1943.
Wordsworth, William. "Preface to the Second Edition of the *Lyrical Ballads*" [1800]. In *English Romantic Writers*, pp. 320-31. Ed. David Perkins. New York: Harcourt, Brace & World, 1967.
Zabel, Morton Dauwen. "Wallace Stevens and the Image of Man." *The Harvard Advocate* 127, 3 (1940): 19-23. Reprinted in *Wallace Stevens: A Collection of Critical Essays*, pp. 151-60. Ed. Marie Borroff. Englewood Cliffs, N.J.: Prentice-Hall, 1963.

INDEX

Abelard, 107
Abrams, M. H., 24, 73n
Adamic. *See* Language
Alan de Lille, 44, 59-60
Altieri, Charles: on metaphor and theory in Stevens, 170n
Analogy: Aquinas on, 167-69; Frye on, 169n; Aristotle on, 169n; compared to simile, 169
Aquinas, Saint Thomas, 167-69
Aristotle: on metaphor, 5; on simile vs. metaphor, 13; on analogy and catachresis, 169n; mentioned, 24
As if: rise of frequency in Stevens, 18-19; as double conjunction, 131-32, in Stevens, 132-38; relation to silence, 143-44
Atomic Age: Stevens' response to, 89-90
Augustine, Saint, 60, 83
Augustinian. *See* Language

Baird, James, 8n
Baker, Howard, 88n
Barfield, Owen: on consciousness, 97n
Barth, J. Robert, 58
Barth, Timotheus F., 168n
Beardsley, Monroe, 180n
Being, 52-55, 59, 154, 167-68, 180-81; *See also* Language; Metaphor.
Benamou, Michel: on modern consciousness in Stevens, 44; on Stevens' early poetry, 49n; on "as if" in Stevens, 133n; on Impressionist techniques in Stevens, 142; mentioned, 21n, 38n
Bentham, Jeremy, 129n
Bernard de Clairvaux, 108
Blessing, Richard Allen: on "Angel Surrounded by Paysans," 162
Bloom, Harold: on consciousness, 29; on Stevens' grammar, 67; on source of poetry, 70-80; on "Le Monocle de Mon Oncle," 171-73; mentioned, 17n, 90, 108n
Brazeau, Peter: on Stevens' religious conversion, 56n
Bréal, Michel: on metaphor, 5
Brelet, Gisèle: on silence and sonority, 141
Brooke-Rose, Christine: on disbelief in metaphor, 67; definition of metaphor, 180n; mentioned, 182n
Brooks, Cleanth, Jr.: on metaphor, 5; on critical response to Stevens, 7n
Bruns, Gerald L.: on poetic speech, 80-81; mentioned, 139n
Burke, Kenneth: on the principle of negativity in language, 101; on verbal realism, 114-15; on positive images in negatives, 181-82; mentioned, 145

INDEX

Carruth, Hayden: on social awareness in Stevens, 39-40; mentioned, 8n, 21n, 23n
Cassirer, Ernst: on identification in metaphor, 6
Catachresis, 169n
Church, Henry, 60, 107
Ciardi, John: on Stevens' late poetry, 187-88
Coleridge, Samuel Taylor: on imagination, 57-59; fictitious letter of, in *Biographia Literaria*, 115-16; on resemblance, 175; mentioned, 5, 50
Conrad, Joseph, 129n
Consciousness, 29, 97n, 98-99
Critical Inquiry (special issue on metaphor), 5

Dandyism: in Stevens, 7
Deconstruction, 8-11, 22, 23, 72-75, 80, 81, 82, 144
De Man, Paul: on common vs. poetic language, 27-29; on disjunction in language, 30, on dialectic, 49; on poetic intent, 64n; on relation of language and consciousness, 98-99; on irony and temporality, 109, 110n; mentioned, 51, 52, 76, 101n, 115
Derrida, Jacques: on deconstruction, 8-9; on metaphor vs. simile, 13; on *differance*, 16-17, 75; on signification, 22, 29, 73n; on infinite being, 26; on poetic language, 28; on metaphor, 31n, 64n; on signs, 109; mentioned, 10n, 23, 38, 60n, 69, 72, 79, 80, 81, 83, 84, 89, 95, 97n, 98, 110n, 111, 145-46, 175, 180
Dialectic, 49. *See also* Predication
Dickie, George: on metaphor, 4-5
Differance, 16, 17n, 69, 73, 74, 75, 95
Dif-ference, 143-44, 147, 169
Disclaimers: in Stevens, as resistance to *metaphor*, 67-71, 116
Disjunction. *See* Fragmentation; Language
Divisionism (Seurat), 142n
Doggett, Frank: on characteristic elements in Stevens, 12, on "Notes toward a Supreme Fiction," 18n; on Stevens' prose, 47; on contrary views in Stevens, 77; on Stevens' mode of composition, 90n; mentioned, 15n, 21
Duns Scotus, John, 60

Einstein, Albert: on the fiction of mathematics, 40-41; mentioned, 128
Emerson, Ralph Waldo, 17n
Emmet, Dorothy M., 168n
Empson, William, 87n
Enck, John J., 21n
Equivocation, 167

Fancy: vs. imagination, 57-58
Feidelson, Charles, Jr., 180n
Feo, José Rodríguez. *See* Rodríguez Feo, José
Fiction: belief in, 78
Fictionalism, 129-33

INDEX

Fitzgerald, Robert, 87n
Foss, Martin, 6
Fragmentation: rubric of, 23; as model for disjunctive poetics, 29; as opposed to metaphor, 74; positive aspects of, 106-9; negative aspects of, 109-11; as unitive, 179, 181-83, 185-87
Freud, Sigmund, 57
Frost, Robert, 165n
Frye, Northrop: on metaphor in Stevens, 8n, 36, 61-62; on simile, 12, 153; on simile as displaced metaphor, 14n; on radical form of metaphor, 37; on symbols, 41n; on anagogic level of poetry, 50-51n; on analogy of proportion, 169n; on metaphors of unity, 179; mentioned, 14

Giotto, 60
Goodman, Nelson: on conflict in metaphor, 179-80
Guetti, James, 30n

Hammond, Mac, 4
Hanley, Rev. Arthur, 56n
Hartman, Geoffrey: on Derrida, 22; on contemporary criticism, 23n; mentioned, 57, 110n
Hegel, G.W.F., 63, 107
Heidegger, Martin: on "dif-ference," 143-44; on language and man, 190; mentioned, 126, 145, 146, 169
Heringman, Bernard: on social relevance of poetry, 41-42; on "Notes toward a Supreme Fiction," 70; mentioned, 59, 91

Hermetic. *See* Language
Hines, Thomas J., 143n
Holman, C. Hugh, 14

Imagination: and reality, in Stevens, 3; in Coleridge, 57-59
Imagism: 26; Stevens' criticism of, 42n
Imagists: 42
Immediacy: as opposed to mediation, 54
Impressionism: in Stevens, 142
Interinanimation, 22, 50, 179
Irony, 50, 109, 110n. *See also* De Man; Fragmentation

James, William, 129n
Jarrell, Randall, 7n, 39n, 43, 87n
Johnson, Barbara, 72-73, 80, 82, 180
Juhasz, Suzanne: on metaphor in Stevens, 8

Kaufmann, R. J.: on copulatives as metaphors, 6
Kermode, Frank: on Stevens' fictionalism, 127n; on Stevens' late poems, 165, 188n; mentioned, 21n, 122, 130n, 143n
Kierkegaard, Søren, 63
Kline, Morris, 41
Klubertanz, George P., S.J., 168n
Kronick, Joseph G.: on resemblance in Stevens, 170n
Kunitz, Stanley, 93

Language: as unitive, 4-9; as disjunctive, 4, 9-11, 29, 30; poetic, 28-30; as logocentric in

207

INDEX

Language (*cont.*)
  Stevens, 34, 48, 56, 60-62; nostalgia in, 38; as Adamic, 46, 47, 80, 81; as incarnational, 49-50; as creation of *being* in Stevens, 51-54; relation to silence, 63-65; as Orphic, 80-81; as hermetic, 81; as Satanic, 81-82; as Augustinian, 82-84, 95, 111; as evasion, 94; as mediation, 105. *See also* Fragmentation; Metaphor; Simile
Leach, Edmund, 73-74
Lentricchia, Frank: on fictionalism, 127n, 130n
Levin, Harry, 8n
Litz, A. Walton: on "Le Monocle de Mon Oncle," 171; mentioned, 63
Logocentric. *See* Language

MacCaffrey, Isabel: on stylistic elements in Stevens, 11; on limits of language, 66; on "Le Monocle de Mon Oncle," 171-73; mentioned, 9, 108n, 140, 145n
McCall, Marsh H., 13
McCann, Janet: on Adamic vs. Satanic language in Stevens, 81-82
Mackey, Louis: on universals and singulars, 23-24n; on duality in metaphor, 180; mentioned, 38
MacLeod, Glen G., 26n
Mallarmé, Stephen: "comme si" in, compared to "as if" in Stevens, 133n; mentioned, 103n, 139n

Marx, Karl, 57
Matthiessen, F. O.: on Stevens' later work, 86n
Mediation: as opposed to immediacy in language, 54
Metaphor: as constitutive principle of language, 4-9, 179; as critical element in Stevens, 6-7; traditional preference for over similes, 12-14; rubric of, 23; as hypostatic union, 23; as model for unitive poetics, 29; as trinitarian interaction, 50-51; as creation of being in Stevens, 52-55; theological implications of, 55-65; as substitute in Stevens for imagination in Coleridge, 58-59; connection to *being*, 59; negative aspects of, 62-65; as disjunctive, 179-85
Metapoetry, 4
Michaelangelo, 142-43
Miller, J. Hillis: on imagination and reality in Stevens, 3; on competing theories of poetry, 4, 9, 24n; changing critical assessments of Stevens, 9-10; on *logos*, 44, 95n; on critical responses to Stevens, 74-75; on simultaneous extremes in Stevens, 77-78, 112; mentioned, 22, 81, 108n, 140
Mills, Ralph J., Jr.: on "Description without Place," 56
Moll, Elsie, 15
Monroe, Harriet, 87n
Moore, Marianne, 8n, 88n
Morris, Adalaide Kirby: on theological transvaluation in Stevens, 49-50n

208

INDEX

Morse, Samuel French: on critical reception of Stevens, 7n; on *Harmonium*, 90n; on "as if" in Stevens, 133n; on "Notes toward a Supreme Fiction," 157; on Stevens' late poems, 187, 189; mentioned, 123n, 166

Munson, Gorham, 8

Negative: as principle of language, 101; in Stevens, 101-4; as conveying positive image, 181-82

Nemetz, Anthony, 168n

Newmarch, Anthony, 141n

Nietzsche, Friedrich, 127n

Nominalism, 23, 23-24n, 115

Nominalists, 107

Nostalgia. *See* Language

O'Connor, Flannery, 108

Ogden, C. K., 129n

Ong, Walter, 38

Origination: in language, 27-28

Orphic. *See* Language

Owen, Stephen, 5n

Pearce, Roy Harvey: on "Notes toward a Supreme Fiction," 7, 157; on realism, 32-33; on problem of belief in Stevens, 44n; on Adamic language, 46n; on *The Rock*, 164-65; mentioned, 17n, 103, 113, 140

Phelan, Rev. Gerald B., 168n

Picasso, Pablo, 152

Plato, 24, 25, 106, 131

Poetics: unitive vs. disjunctive, 29, 95

Poetry: nature of, defined by Stevens, 3-4; conflicting theories of, 4; as sanction in Stevens, 38-39; as resistance in Stevens, 86-94

Poirier, Richard: on Frost, 165n

Polanyi, Michael: on simile and metaphor, 13

Porte, Joel: on Santayana and Stevens, 127

Poulet, Georges: on Mallarmé, 103n; on Coleridge, 116n; mentioned, 54, 95, 105

Pragmatism, 127n

Predication: dialectic vs. tripartite, 49, 100; in metaphor, 50

Presence/Presentation: in language. *See* Representation

Proportionality, 167-68. *See also* Analogy

Quinn, Sister M. Bernetta, 37, 91

Ransom, John Crowe, 39n

Realism, 23, 23-24n, 32-34, 59-60, 115

Realists, 107

Reality: and imagination in Stevens, 3; as violent in Stevens, 85

Reclamations: as resistance to *fragmentation* in Stevens, 111-12, 116

Reed, Walter, L., 5n

Regeuiro, Helen: on silencing of language in Stevens, 64; on similes in Stevens, 154, mentioned, 63, 108n, 140

Representation: problem of, in language, 161-64

209

INDEX

Resemblance: in Coleridge, 175; in Stevens, 150, 170n, 175-77

Richards, I. A.: on metaphor, 22, 27, 50, 125; on meaning, 54; on language and thought, 166-67n; on disparity in metaphor, 179; mentioned, 9n, 53, 57, 181

Riddel, Joseph N.: on critical reception of Stevens, 7n; changing interpretations of Stevens, 10; on unrepresented in Stevens, 11; on consistency in Stevens, 20-21; on Imagism in Stevens, 26n; on metaphors in Whitman and Stevens, 61; mentioned, 22n, 81, 108n, 166

Rodríguez Feo, José, 46, 93, 98, 104

Romantics, 57. *See also* Coleridge

Santayana, George: possible influence on Stevens, 127-28; in "To an Old Philosopher in Rome," 135-36

Satanic. *See* Language

Saussure, Ferdinand, 73n

Schiller, Friederich Van, 131

Schwartz, Delmore: on social relevance in Stevens, 87-88

Scotus, Duns: *See* Duns Scotus, John

Seurat, Georges, 141-42

Shakespeare, William, 23n

Sheehan, Donald: on subject and object in Stevens, 31; mentioned, 170

Shelley, Percy Bysshe, 17n

Shibles, Warren A., 5, 14

Signification. *See* Derrida; Fragmentation; Language

Silence: as extension of metaphor and fragmentation, 139 *passim*; in Stevens, 139-48; relation of to sonority, 141

Simile: in Stevens, 11-12, 18-22, 144-66; disparagement of, 12-14; increased frequency in Stevens, 18-19; as model for language, 25, 126-27, 178-79, 182-83; compared to "as if," 138; relation to temporality in Stevens, 146-47; relation to silence, 147; relation to presentation/representation, 151-52, 161-64, compared to analogy, 169; as irreducible dialectic, 169n; practical application of, in Stevens, 170-74

Simons, Hi: on metaphor in contemporary poetry, 12n; mentioned, 117, 119, 121, 122, 137, 141, 153, 154, 172, 176

Singulars, 23n

Spivak, Gayatri Chakravorty: on being, 180-81

Stevens, Elsie Moll, 15

Stevens, Holly, 18, 92-93

STEVENS, WALLACE: on the nature of poetry, 3; on metaphor, 6-7; early criticism of, 7-8n, 87-88; critical reevaluations of, 9-10; theological elements in, 33-35; poetry as sanction in, 38-39; criticism of, 39; response to "age of disbelief," 44-46, 78; religious conversion of, 56n; on imagination vs. fancy, 58-59; compared to Medievals, 59-60; re-

210

INDEX

sistance to unity in metaphor, 67-71, 116; poetry as redemption in, 84-85; resistance to the "pressure of reality," 84-94; response to war, 85-90; resistance to dogma, 92; contradiction in, 105; resistance to disjunctive language, 111-12; and the "will to believe," 128-29; similarities to Vaihinger, 129-32; defense of poetry, 131; on ambiguity in resemblance, 150; late criticism of, 187-88

letters written to: Elsie Moll (Stevens), 15n; Sister M. Bernetta Quinn, 37, 91-92; to José Rodríguez Feo, 46, 93, 98, 104; to Henry Church, 60, 107; to William Carlos Williams, 76-77; to Bernard Heringman, 91; to Hi Simons, 117, 119-20, 141

works (discussions are italicized):
"Adagia," 39
"Add This to Rhetoric," 81, *95-98*, 112, 155
"Anecdote of the Jar," 49
"Angel Surrounded by Paysans," *161-63*
"Artificial Populations," *138-39*
"As at a Theatre," *164*
"Asides on the Oboe," 47
"As You Leave the Room," 93, *113-14*
"Auroras of Autumn, The," 160
"Banjo Boomer," 69, 96, *105-6*
"Bed of Old John Zeller, The," *109*

"Certain Phenomena of Sound," *60-61*
"Chocorua to Its Neighbor," 44, *160*
"Clear Day and No Memories, A," 100-01
Collected Poems, 88n, 144, 161, 164, 165, 166
"Comedian as the Letter C, The," 30, 79
"Connoisseur of Chaos," 78, *119*, 155
"Contrary Theses, I & II," 106
"Course of a Particular, The," 125
"Creations of Sound, The," 160
"Credences of Summer," 160
"Death of a Soldier, The," 88
"Description without Place," 56, 88, *99-100*, *109-10*
"Desire & the Object," *122-23*
"Domination of Black," *20*, 154
"Emperor of Ice-Cream, The," *54*
"Esthétique du Mal," 82, 110, 160
"Examination of the Hero in a Time of War," *62-63*
"Extracts from Addresses to the Academy of Fine Ideas," 44, *88-89*, *113*
"Farewell to Florida," 75-77, 88, 99, 107
"Final Soliloguy of the Interior Paramour," *34-36*, 48, 165
"First Warmth," *113-14*
"Flyer's Fall," 92
"Glass of Water, The," 155

211

STEVENS, works *(cont.)*
"God Is Good. It Is a Beautiful Night," 54-55
Harmonium, 19, 47, 76, 77, 90n, 150, 151
"High-Toned Old Christian Woman, A," 92
"Idea of Order at Key West, The," *68-69*, 100, 151
Ideas of Order, 76
"Irrational Element in Poetry, The," 55, *86-87*
"Lack of Repose, The," 102
"Landscape with Boat," *102-4, 139, 155, 185-87*
"Latest Freed Man, The," 92
"Lebensweisheitspielerei," *188-89*
"Like Decorations in a Nigger Cemetery," 71, *151, 159*
"Load of Sugar-Cane, The," 11
"Looking Across the Fields and Watching the Birds Fly," 95
"Madame La Fleurie," *79-80*, 85
"Man and Bottle," *90*
Man with the Blue Guitar, The, 33-34, 154
"Man with the Blue Guitar, The," 36, 51, *94*, 105, *117-19*, 121, 125, *151-53*, 160, 161-62, 163
"Men That Are Falling, The," 33-34
"Metaphor as Degeneration," 180
"Monocle de Mon Oncle, Le," 138, 140, *170-74*
"Montrachet-le-Jardin," *40*

"Motive for Metaphor, The," *80*
"Mrs. Alfred Uruguay," 107
Necessary Angel, The, 40, 47, 58, 98
"Noble Rider and the Sound of Words, The," 3, *45-46*, 57-58, *84-85*, 153
"Notes toward a Supreme Fiction," 7, 60, *65*, 66, *70*, 81, 88, 89, *90-91, 107-8, 120-21, 137-38, 157-59*, 160, 163, 190
"Not Ideas about the Thing but the Thing Itself," *166*
"Of Bright & Blue Birds & the Gala Sun," *48, 155*
"Of Modern Poetry," *42-43*, 81, *155-56*, 164, 176
"Old Man Asleep, An," 188
"On the Road Home," *140-41*
Opus Posthumous, 62
"Ordinary Evening in New Haven, An," 32-33, *71-72*, 94, 133n, 159, *161*
Parts of a World, 76, 88n
"Plain Sense of Things, The," 188
"Planet on the Table, The," 45, 86, 165
"Plus Belles Pages, Les," 169n
"Poems from 'Lettre d'un Soldat,' " 88
"Poems of Our Climate, The," 26n, *69-70, 154-55*
"Poem That Took the Place of a Mountain, The," *66*, 81, 85, 165
"Primitive Like an Orb, A," *48-49, 68, 160-61*
"Prologues to What Is Possi-

INDEX

ble," 15-18, 32, 47, 111-12, 139, 147, 165
"Prose Statement on War," 88n
"Pure Good of Theory, The," 30-31, 160
"Repetitions of a Young Captain," 88
"Re-statement of Romance," 35
Rock, The, 5, 19, 164-66, 187-91
"Rock, The," 105, 140
"Sad Strains of a Gay Waltz," 39
"Sail of Ulysses, The," 32
"St. Armorer's Church from the Outside," 55, 165
"Sea Surface Full of Clouds," 150-51, 154
"Snow Man, The," 100, 100-101n, 113
"Someone Puts a Pineapple Together," 92, 160
"Somnambulisma," 95-96, 160
"Study of Images, I & II," 106
"Study of Images, II," 120
"Sunday Morning," 20, 64-65, 69, 91, 148-50, 154, 189
"Things of August," 63
"Thirteen Ways of Looking at a Blackbird," 106
"This as Including That," 122-25
"To an Old Philosopher in Rome," 64, 129, 133-36, 137, 139, 144, 148, 165
"To the One of Fictive Music," 99
"To the Roaring Wind," 47
Transport to Summer, 54

"Two Figures in Dense Violet Night," 136-37, 140-41
"Two Illustrations That the World Is What You Make of It," 106
"Two or Three Ideas," 43
"Two Versions of the Same Poem," 49n
"Vacancy in the Park," 11-12, 144-48, 165
"Well Dressed Man with a Beard, The," 62
"Woman Sings a Song for a Soldier Come Home, A," 88
"World as Meditation, The," 51, 165
"World without Peculiarity, The," 52-54, 184-85, 187
Style: disjunctive elements in Stevens, 10-11; qualifying elements in Stevens, 11, 19n, 67-68; characteristic elements in Stevens, 13, 145; development of in Stevens, 21
Symbol, 5, 41n
Symons, Julian, 39n, 87n

Tal Coat, Pierre, 163
Taylor, Wilson, E.: on religious feeling in Stevens, 56
Tel Quel School, 9, 25
Thelwall, John, 115n
Thomas Aquinas, Saint. See Aquinas, Saint Thomas

Universals, 23
Univocation, 167

Vaihinger, Hans: similarity to Stevens, 126-33, 138, 143
Van Doren, Mark, 7n, 39n

INDEX

Vendler, Helen: on disconnection in Stevens, 10; on stylistic elements in Stevens, 11; on "as if" in Stevens, 18n, 133; on qualifying elements in Stevens, 19n, 67-68; on critical treatment of Stevens, 92; on "Sunday Morning," 150; mentioned, 17n

Walsh, Thomas F., 51, 101
Ward, Wilfrid, 129n
Wheelwright, Philip: on identification in myth and metaphor, 9n; on metaphor vs. simile, 13; mentioned, 6
Whitman, Walt, 61
Williams, William Carlos, 26, 76-77, 87n
Wilson, Edmund, 7n
Wintors, Yvor, 7n, 39n
Wordsworth, William, 142

Yeats, W. B., 173

Zabel, Morton Dauwen, 176-77

Library of Congress Cataloging-in-Publication Data

Brogan, Jacqueline Vaught, 1952-
Stevens and simile.

Bibliography: p.   Includes index.
1. Stevens, Wallace, 1879-1955—Knowledge—Language
and languages.   2. Stevens, Wallace, 1879-1955—Style.
3. Simile.   4. Languages—Philosophy.   I. Title.
PS3537.T4753Z618   1986   811'.52   86-9468
ISBN 0-691-06689-2 (alk. paper)

GPSR Authorized Representative: Easy Access System Europe - Mustamäe tee 50, 10621 Tallinn, Estonia, gpsr.requests@easproject.com

www.ingramcontent.com/pod-product-compliance
Lightning Source LLC
Chambersburg PA
CBHW050632300426
44112CB00012B/1771